Praise for *Mahina Tiare: Pac*

" *Many sailing books talk of storms and survival, but few put you on deck in a hurricane, to let you feel the anguish and share the action as mountainous waves threaten to crash on the deck five-feet from you. This one does. It's an ocean odyssey not only for sailors who plan a long-distance Pacific passage, but for those who see themselves in such a saga only in their dreams.*"

John Macdonald, *The Seattle Times*

"*Not only cruisers take notice; anthropologists, botanists, zoologists, geologists or anyone with curiosity and a sense of adventure will appreciate a refreshing view by way of Pacific Passages.*"

Ruth Beebe Hill, *Author, Hanta Yo*

"*I would never have believed that an "adventure book" in an element so removed from me - the ocean - could captivate my attention as did Mahina Tiare. The style is fluid, direct, transparent and concentrated...I am powerfully impressed with how the inner journey transpired through the external adventures. Barbara and John's genius in establishing even short term human relationships radiating warmth and significance is most moving.*"

Hildegard Elsberg, *Poet*

" *...the reader's first reaction is a longing to follow in John and Barbara's wake. Eventually the realization dawns that the true message of this book is not how to enjoy an exotic location, but how to savor life in any location - to focus on the moment, open to learn whatever the people and place have to offer, sharing in return whatever it is you have to give.*"

Stephanie Williams, *Northwest Yachting*

An Exciting, Exotic and Enriching Adventure

Mahina Tiare, Pacific Passages is a story of adventure, discovery, sailing, written in two voices. John Neal provides the perspective of a veteran sailor; a man attuned to sea, weather and his sailboat. Barbara Marrett, artist and novice sailor, narrates sights, sounds and personalities.

Mahina Tiare transports Barbara and John 22,000 miles to the enchanted islands of the Galapagos, mysterious Easter Island, Pitcairn Island (home of Bounty mutineers), the Marquesas, Tahiti, Fiji, Vanuatu, New Zealand and finally Australia. A shipwrecked sailor, angry cargo cultists, descendants of Fletcher Christian and yuppies-turned-yachties are among the colorful characters encountered.

From Pacific Islanders, Barbara and John learned that gifts maintain their spirit when passed along. This book is written in that spirit of sharing.

Thank you for your interest in our books. To order additional copies, please complete order form below.

Mahina Tiare: Pacific Passages $19.95
Barbara Marrett & John Neal

Log of the Mahina $16.95
John Neal

Offshore Cruising Companion $50.00
John Neal

North to Alaska Video $19.95
Barbara Marrett & John Neal

Sailing to Cape Horn Video $29.95
John Neal & Amanda Swan

Sailing to Antarctica Video $29.95
John Neal & Amanda Swan

Washington State residents add 7.5% sales tax .... _____

Shipping (1st item $3.00, add'l items $1.50 each) .... _____

Total $_____

Shipping Information:

Name _____

Postal Mailing Address _____

City _____ St._____ Zip_____

Please send check or money order to:

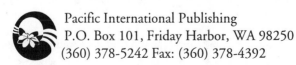
Pacific International Publishing
P.O. Box 101, Friday Harbor, WA 98250
(360) 378-5242 Fax: (360) 378-4392

MAHINA TIARE

Pacific Passages

By John Neal

Log of the Mahina

By John Neal and Barbara Marrett

Offshore Cruising Handbook

MAHINA

TIARE

Pacific Passages

Barbara Marrett
John Neal

Pacific International Publishing
Friday Harbor, Washington

Grateful acknowledgment is made for permission to reproduce the following material: Excerpt from *Blue Highways* by William Least Heat Moon. Copyright © 1982 William Least Heat Moon. Reprinted by permission of Little Brown and Company. Excerpt from *Tracks* by Robyn Davidson Copyright © 1980 by Robyn Davidson. Reprinted by permission of Pantheon Books, a division of Random House, Inc. Excerpts from *The Songlines* by Bruce Chatwin. Copyright © 1987 by Bruce Chatwin used by permission of Viking Penguin a division of Penguin Books USA Inc. Excerpts from *West with the Night*, copyright © 1942, 1983 by Beryl Markham. Published by North Point Press and reprinted by permission of Farrar, Straus & Giroux, Inc.

Pacific International Publishing
Post Office Box 101, Friday Harbor, WA 98250

Copyright ©1993 by Barbara Marrett

Library of Congress Catalog Card Number 92-91094

ISBN 0-918074-04-5 Softcover Edition
ISBN 0-918074-05-3 Hardcover Edition

Third Edition, Revised 1997
3 4 5 6 7 8 9 10

Design: Barbara Marrett
Photography: John Neal, Barbara Marrett
Cover Design: Mitzi Johnson
Maps and computer graphics: Bruce Conway

The text of this book is set in Adobe Garamond.
This book is printed on acid-free recycled paper.

Printed in the United States of America

For
Joseph Edward Marrett
and
Rose Mary Neal

Contents

Preface XI

Prologue XIII

CONTENTS

MAPS

Preface

Barbara Marrett and John Neal share in the writing of their cruise journal. They have distinctly different voices but to keep the reader on course have indicated points where the pen changes hands. John provides the perspective of a veteran sailor, a man attuned to sea, weather and his sailboat. Barbara, artist and novice sailor, narrates sights, sounds and personalities. Her insights are attuned to the inner voyage.

Mahina Tiare, the couple's 31-foot fiberglass sloop is also a character in the book. Tiare means flower in Polynesian and Mahina means moon. Hina, the goddess associated with the moon, presides over death and rebirth in Polynesian myths.

Prologue

Barbara: I first learned about John from an article in our small town newspaper, *The Friday Harbor Journal*. Intrigued by this handsome adventurer who wore an earring and a white cap, I thought: he's probably one of those strange people who lives on a boat — and likes it. Ours paths soon crossed and I was invited aboard *Mahina Tiare* for dinner.

Agreeing to sail to Easter Island with John on our first date was an easy response; I had no idea where it was. I had grown up in rural New York, the only offshore experience I had known was with my parents aboard the cruise ship, *Queen Elizabeth II*.

When it came time for John and me to leave, I sold my graphic design business, moved out of the cottage I loved, said good-bye to friends and clients. The separation was agonizing. I had taken everything in my life for granted until it came time to let go.

This story really begins with John's love of the South Pacific and his desire to share it with me. Although I love the ocean and possess a healthy dose of wanderlust, I had never imagined myself sailing long distances. I didn't realize people did this for pleasure until I jumped on *Mahina Tiare*, John's magic carpet, and was whisked away.

John : At age 20, I read Robin Lee Graham's *Dove*. Graham had circumnavigated the world in a 24' sailboat, experiencing exciting adventures en route. I put down the book, sold my motorcycle, bought a little 20' Vivacity sailboat and learned to sail on the waters of Puget Sound and the San Juan Islands in Washington State. While on a backpacking trip to Hawaii one Christmas, I admired the sailboats anchored offshore on Kauai. What better way to explore tropical places, I asked myself, than sailing into exotic ports?

Within days of returning from Hawaii, I quit my job and put my sailboat up for sale. She sold quickly, and I was just able to afford a 27' Swedish-built Vega sailboat which I named *Mahina*. A new job aboard a 50' sailboat gave me the chance to learn more about sailboats in a short amount of time.

On July 14, 1974, just six months after returning from Hawaii, I sailed from Seattle. The passage to Hawaii was a deceptively easy one, and soon after arrival I met a young couple who had just returned from a magical six-month cruise of the Marquesas Islands (French Polynesia). Viewing their snapshots of friendly Polynesians living in near-deserted valleys surrounded by giant stone carvings and waterfalls, severely altered my Protestant work ethic. In a week I had found a woman who would sail with me. We provisioned *Mahina* and set sail for the South Seas. It was nearly a year-and-a-half later that I returned to Seattle. The articles I had sent back during my cruise had created enough of a following to bring requests for a book. *Log of the Mahina, A Tale of the South Pacific* became a bestseller, was picked up by Book-of-the-Month Club and launched me on a West Coast lecture circuit.

Later, in 1978, I sold the cabin I had built on San Juan Island to buy a larger boat, *Mahina Tiare*, a 31-foot Hallberg Rassy fiberglass sloop built in Sweden, 1976. Over three years, I sailed her to New Zealand and back to the Northwest, picking up crew along the way.

Drawing on my sailing experiences, I started giving weekend seminars to help other sailors prepare for the big leap to offshore cruising. Four years and 25 seminars later, I began thinking about those least-visited South Pacific islands, places I had missed on earlier cruises. I had collected information on the Galapagos, Easter and Pitcairn Islands for several years. During my twice-yearly visits to Tahiti to conduct cruising seminars I asked questions around the harbor, eager to find anyone who had recently sailed from these isolated islands. Aside from a few boats that had briefly visited the Galapagos, the only people I talked with about Easter and Pitcairn had visited there three years earlier. All the cruisers said the same things: Easter and Pitcairn were very distant and difficult to sail to and, if you actually made it to the islands, the anchorages were unsafe. The *U.S. Sailing Directions* warn: *"The weather is never good for more than a few days at a time at Easter Island. Ships anchoring off the island should be ready to sail on short notice. There are abrupt and violent wind changes."*

On my first date with Barbara, I showed her a picture book of Easter Island and asked if she'd like to sail there. Six months later we were married, less than one year later I had sold Mahina Cruising Services. And we were more or less ready for a sailing adventure of a lifetime.

VOYAGE ONE

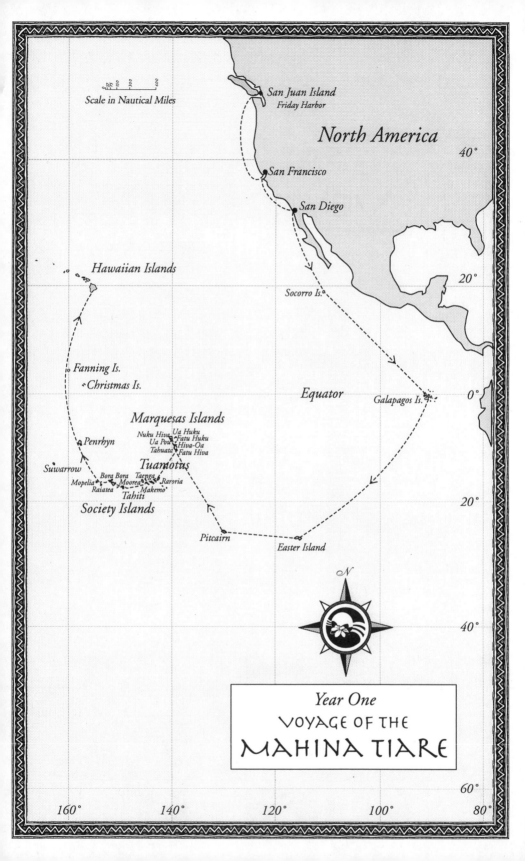

Scale in Nautical Miles

San Juan Island
Friday Harbor

North America

40°

San Francisco

San Diego

20°

Hawaiian Islands

Socorro Is.

Equator

Galapagos Is.

0°

Fanning Is.
Christmas Is.

Marquesas Islands

Nuku Hiva *Ua Huku*
Ua Pou *Fatu Huku*
Tahuata *Hiva-Oa*
Fatu Hiva

Penrhyn

Tuamotus

Suwarrow

Bora Bora Taenga
Mopelia   Moorea Raroria
Raiatea Makemo
Tahiti

Society Islands

20°

Pitcairn

Easter Island

N

40°

Year One
VOYAGE OF THE
MAHINA TIARE

60°

160°   140°   120°   100°   80°

Chapter 1

ALONE WITH
THE SKY AND SEA

July 7, 1986, Barbara: Today, I gave away the last key on my key ring. I feel I have broken the ties to my old life and am already gone from Friday Harbor. Walking into my former office, I don't have to concern myself with customers, deadlines, or temperamental equipment. I have an incredible sense of freedom and feel like a new person, light and childlike.

We invite most of the town to our bon voyage party on the docks at the Port of Friday Harbor. When we finally leave one friend remains to cast off our lines. Some neighbors on a Vega 27 give a long blast on their air horn as we ease out of the slip.

Our departure to Port Townsend, Washington is delayed by so many last minute errands that we hit Cattle Pass (at the south end of San Juan Island) at the worst possible time: a max flood of over 2 knots, and a fresh southerly, both against us and making for very rough seas.

The weather is cold and nasty. Progressively adding more clothes and feeling queasy. I ask John, "Are we having fun yet?" The fuse has blown on the autopilot and the wind vane isn't set up yet. We are steering by hand, and it is all I can manage to keep the boat on course.

July 8: After long hot showers at Point Hudson Marina, we walk up to Port Townsend Sails to pick up our re-cut drifter sail. What a wonderful, light sail loft; high ceilings, huge windows, varnished wooden floors. The air is filled with music and the walls covered with sailing posters and photos. The all-woman crew is intent on their work.

We motorsail easily to Port Angeles, the tide helping us along instead of bashing *Mahina Tiare* into the short, steep seas for which the Straits are famous. After arriving at Port Angeles Boat Haven, we walk

3

to the nearest store with a list of food items we have forgotten or haven't had time to buy — even more things to organize and stow. When will it end?

In the marina, we meet Bobbi and Bertram Levi, a physical therapist and her urologist husband. Their boat *Able,* is a handsome, traditional Lyle Hess-designed 24-foot wooden cutter that Bertram had built over the past five years in Port Townsend. They, too, are doing last minute stowing and plan to leave in the morning for Hawaii.

Below decks on *Able* is a salty blend of shiny brass, gleaming varnish on custom woodwork, deck prisms and a stainless steel bucket for a head. *Mahina Tiare* seems like a plastic tub in comparison, but I wouldn't trade boats. Twenty-four feet is just too small for a 6-foot-2 and 5-foot-8 crew, and — let's face it — it is hard to read magazines while sitting on a bucket. It is reassuring to talk with other people crazy enough to leave safe surroundings and head across an ocean.

July 9: We leave Port Angeles at 5:30 a.m. to catch the tide. I sleep in until 9:00 a.m., luxuriating in the fact that I really don't have to get up for any reason, knowing that when I do get up, the seas are so rolly that I will feel seasick anyway.

Lying in bed while John manages the boat, I feel the need for some focus of my own. I plan to capture the fleeting events and impressions of the trip by writing and sketching events in this log. I do not view this trip as a vacation, but a drastic change from the way I've been living. A chance to learn to relax and see what fills up the blank page I have created with my life.

This afternoon we motorsail with the ebb current, fog obscuring the peaks of Vancouver Island (Canada) on the right, the Olympic Peninsula on the left. The sky is streaked with gray clouds — layer upon layer. The seas even out into long gentle swells in anticipation of the ocean.

We arrive at Neah Bay several hours earlier than planned, fueling up at the Bay Fish Co. between fish boats unloading salmon and taking on ice. The seawater here is salmon-colored, and has a pungent odor. The two cannery buildings are on high pilings — old and rambling, with peeling blue paint. I sense a sadness to Neah Bay. Stuck out on the tip of the Olympic Peninsula, the old growth fir trees seem to hold a permanent low gray fog, timeless and enduring like the Makah

Indians who have lived here for centuries.

I call John Patz who is working with the Indians as a physician's assistant while he studies to become an M.D. Tall and gentle with dark complexion and features that hint of his Indian blood, I used to accompany him to Neah Bay on weekends when he and I were dating three years ago.

He drives us to Hobuck beach, a deserted stretch of white sand along the Pacific where he and I once collected sand dollars. As we walk along the wild, remote shore, all of the separations I have made, all of the choices that bring me to Neah Bay — the last protected water before we hit the turbulent ocean — seem full of pain. Why am I restless? What is the constant call to do something daring and unknown, while at the same time I am shy and scared of changes and crave finding a place where I will feel at home? I feel totally vulnerable; I have kicked out from under myself all my support systems except for John Neal.

July 10: A rainy day in Neah Bay — I spent the morning organizing and stowing provisions that were in boxes under the salon table and stashed in the forepeak. There must be nothing loose to fly around the boat when we hit rough weather.

There is only one store in Neah Bay: Washburn's. The totem poles that used to greet visitors to the store are gone, but the store is better stocked and better organized than when I last saw it. Baby clothes, logging and fishing supplies, and groceries reflect local interests.

July 13: This is the day. The sun shines and the gloom of Neah Bay disappears with the fog. The winds have shifted to the north.

Leaving the Big Salmon Marina is a relief. The fishermen from the trailerable fishing boats around us clean the fish on the dock and throw the remains into the water. Stripped and bloated carcasses float by the docks everywhere; the stench is nauseating. Greedy gulls, frenzied by the fresh kill, reel overhead. The filth in the water — not only fish guts, but oil spills and garbage — upsets me.

We pull out of Neah Bay at 2:12 p.m. and average 6 knots with fresh northwesterlies. At 6:20 we pass a huge freighter anchored several miles offshore, and at 10:00 p.m. a Princess Cruise liner passes us, lit up like a stadium during a night baseball game.

July 14: I came on watch at 2:00 a.m. and found John totally exhausted from hours of dodging fishing boats. Not only is sailing at night a completely new experience for me, but it is my first ocean passage. The seas appear confused, a choppiness left over from four or five days of southerlies whipped up by 25 knots of wind.

The lights of other ships show up like halos on the horizon. I am drawn to them but realize they are to be avoided like the false navigation lamps lit by pirates to lure unsuspecting ships to their doom. I feel queasy, every smell exaggerated and sickening. Crackers and cold, cold water are my panacea.

July 15: Getting ready for a watch is a major undertaking. First I must locate my mound of clothing, then proceed to dress in an orderly fashion: two pairs of socks, two pairs of pants, flannel shirt, wool sweater and jacket, waterproof jumpsuit, safety harness, flotation vest, hat, mittens, and boots.

Waking up at night at sea, a little tossed and tumbled; glowing kerosene lamps and mahogany paneling around me is like waking up in another century. I envision the ghosts of past sea voyagers sitting around the settee, silent witness to an old tradition. I feel close to the boat, as if I have cut all ties with the mainland. Taking watch, my safety harness seems an umbilical cord attaching me to the boat. The boat is a womb, my security in a floating world. The watch seems to last forever. I force myself to think of things that will keep me from falling asleep. I scan the horizon continually from inside our enclosed dodger. Then every ten minutes unzip the back of the dodger and step into the cockpit, looking around thoroughly for ships. I jog in place to get some blood circulating.

John's care and consideration make the passage tolerable. He makes sure I eat and drink whether I feel like it or not, and lets me sleep over my three hour watch.

John: Had bacon and eggs for breakfast, our first really hearty meal. I am finally starting to get over my queasiness. I never get seasick, but at the start of each passage, and especially when I haven't made any long trips in several years, I am tired and uneasy for several days. I wonder why in the world I'm doing this to myself.

Add to this the stress of navigating in rough weather (I finally got a good fix today), and concern about Barbara (what if she says "No More!" when we arrive in San Francisco?). Also, there are a dozen little projects that need to be done on the boat. But things are starting to fit in the groove and I feel better about everything. I am sure glad that we haven't had headwinds or headseas so far!

Barbara, 3:00 p.m. I feel bored and uneasy. I don't know if I will survive the next couple of days. I feel like I have lost my will to live. These days at sea go on forever. I plan to accomplish many things during this passage, i.e., practicing celestial navigation, doing weather plotting, learning the intricacies of the wind vane but since we are under way, I feel so blah that the smallest task becomes insurmountable. It is all I can do to stay awake and watch for ships. I begin to question my sanity for wanting to sail.

In the distance I see dolphins, then closer and closer until they are speeding alongside us, darting in and out from bow to stern. What sleek and playful creatures they are. When I let out a cry of delight, John wakes up concerned, but then joins me in the cockpit to enjoy their show. I whistle back at them, and they come very near the bow where I am leaning almost close enough to touch them. They flip on their sides. We see each other eye to eye, their white sides parallel to the water surface, the color of the water turning the white a cobalt blue as they swim deeper. Two types swim near, Pacific White Sided dolphins and Dall's porpoises. John says they are a good omen. It seems they came to entertain and cheer me.

At dusk the setting sun lights up the sky in a silver-apricot hue, silhouetting the huge cumulus clouds which hem the western horizon, then billow up in fantastic shapes into the dome of the sky. The clouds resemble giant theatrical characters — seemingly alive as they keep changing and evolving into new figures: geisha girls, a cowboy wearing a Stetson, praying hands, Victorian ladies in fancy hats. It is an engaging display to take my mind off the impending darkness.

July 16, 2:00 a.m.: The stars are making a splendid showing, the Milky Way a luminous pool with shooting stars falling in the foreground. I listen to *The Larry King Show*, a call-in radio program with a rude host in New York. So this is how nocturnal Americans spend the wee hours of the morning.

I spot my first ship since Neah Bay. I reflect on how crowded parts of our nation are, while out here, only 60 miles from the coast, there isn't a vessel in sight for days. It is reassuring, not lonely to be on watch with only the company of sea and sky.

7:00 p.m.: Today was great. The seas evened out, the sun shone, the winds decreased. John let me sleep in an extra hour. Felt listless, so exercised for 20 minutes and then washed my hair in our tiny stainless steel galley sink. This is the first day I am actually a little cheerful. Before I took off on this trip I heard horror stories of mates abandoning ship at their first port of call and how miserable life at sea can get. I was prepared for the worst, so at my worst I knew that what I was experiencing was normal. I was not prepared, however, for the joyous events, like dolphins and sunsets that brighten the monotony of the days like colorful blooms on a monochromatic desert landscape.

July 17: The sounds of rushing water, snapping sails, and the boat's creaking and popping are constant companions. The following winds and seas push and rock us along downwind. I am struck by the sheer power of the wind and water, and am amazed at the strength of our boat. I understand now how dangerous sailing can be, one false move and one of us could be over the side.

July 18, 1:30 a.m.: Often I am in the midst of a vivid dream and am convinced there are other people aboard when John tries to shake me out of a heavy slumber to stand watch. This morning I woke up thinking, "Why do I have to steer? What about the other couple, how come they never steer?" Of course, there is no one else aboard but perhaps my subconscious is craving company.

John heats up some noodles, offering something to help me wake up and keep me occupied for awhile. The stars are my companions, the Big Dipper to our stern, the Seven Sisters and Cassiopeia to port. It is damp and chilly.

7:30 a.m.: My watch again, it is easy to get up; John has the cabin warm with our kerosene heater. For the first time since Neah Bay, no heavy seas, just gentle swells and a soft fog.

John, 5:50 p.m.: Five days after our departure, we sail under the Golden Gate Bridge into San Francisco Bay. Afternoon rush hour is going full tilt above us, and the setting sun is illuminating the bridge. Windsurfers with bright sails dash back and forth under the bridge; they pass us in blazing bursts of speed.

Friends who had visited us in Friday Harbor had suggested we tie up next to them at their parent's dock in Tiburon, but I have lost the

Moorish houseboat, San Francisco Bay

scrap of paper with directions. I remember that Dean's parents' house is at Paradise Cay — which I found on the chart — so we decide to see if we can locate them. As it turns out, their dock is the second one inside the breakwater, and Dean and Kopi Carmine are aboard *Martha Rose*. They help us tie up and soon we are swapping stories about our trips down the coast. I first met the Carmines in Lahaina in 1974, following their return from six months in the Marquesas. It was they who convinced me to extend my trip to include the Marquesas.

After dinner, we relax in the hot tub with a glass of chilled wine. What a drastic change: at sea one night and the next, tied to a friend's dock and sitting in the hot tub looking down at the boats. We have arrived in California.

July 19, Barbara: John is in the thick of several projects, including work on the engine and trolling generator, installing a solar panel, SatNav (satellite navigator) new ham radio and alternator.

Dean buys us three small bottles of wine (for celebrating each quarter of the passage finished) and a bottle of champagne to celebrate our arrival in the Galapagos, our first landfall. Kopi and I share thoughts and recipes on her boat. Her words prepare me for the unknowns of the long passage ahead, and give me encouragement.

I am thrilled about not knowing what is ahead. Maybe I should be fearful but I'm not, just worried about being uncomfortable or running out of money. To me the trip is like hitchhiking, which always involves an element of surprise and trust. At the time I was hitchiking (early 70's), each trip brought me in contact with generous and fascinating characters.

Aug. 5, 11:20 a.m.: We leave the fuel dock in Clipper Harbor, Sausalito, passing a strange and fantastic floating menagerie in the bay, everything from a Taj Mahal houseboat and a tropical island on a barge houseboat, to the town dump afloat.

Fog shrouds the Golden Gate Bridge as we sail out into the Bay, and the fog horns calling back and forth to each other sound like some huge animal's mating call. John is below, navigating, intent on keeping us out of the shipping lanes and off the rocks.

Aug. 6: Thus far the trip to San Diego is much gentler than the trip to San Francisco. The weather is lukewarm and mildly overcast, the swells small and the winds light. We motor the entire way, only turning off the engine to replace the water pump seals. I am grateful for this small bit of silence.

I began reading Isak Dinesen's *Out of Africa* yesterday and continued to be absorbed today. Having no distractions other than checking our course and the autopilot during my watches, I feel suspended, floating in time, out of touch with day-to-day reality. Isak Dinesen's words are my waking and dreaming reality. Her words paint shimmering African landscapes and portraits of natives so striking that I dream about them as old friends, familiar with the creases in their faces and their manner of speech. At this moment, her world is much more real than my reality on board.

Aug. 7: Finished *Out of Africa*. Isak Dinesen's magical stories have prepared my senses for my own adventurous journey.

While in the cockpit, absorbed in a book, I hear a whoosh. I look up to catch a glimpse of the graceful tail of a humpback whale as it silently slips back into the sea, only 50 feet astern of us. Their tails are wonderfully rubbery, curving up as the whale surfaces, then down as it descends, water streaming off the smooth black surface in strings of droplets like pearls. Their hugeness makes the surrounding ocean surface seem to well up as if from some strange seismic disturbance. They inspire awe and an ancient fear, such as early men must have felt toward the mastodon. I feel minute and defenseless; I hope that the whale will come close enough so I can get a better view, but not so close as to endanger our boat.

7:00 p.m.: The sun sets in hazy shades of rose and apricot as we near the friendly, rounded but barren-looking Channel Islands, their mountains partially obscured by cloud tufts. The light breeze, warm and dry, carries the delicious sweet scent of earth. Gazing around 360 degrees makes one feel at the center of the universe. It seems obvious that the earth is round when you are at sea. It's not surprising that seafarers were willing to accept this notion while their landbound counterparts still believed the earth was flat.

John, 9:00 p.m.: There are three oil exploration ships and two stationary platforms around Point Conception. I change course to avoid a two-mile floating cable towed by the closest boat, and marked by a strobe light on the end. There is a light fog, and in the darkness navigating and avoiding them is a challenge. We are also very close to the main shipping lanes and several freighters pass by. There is a Navy firing range on and around two of the islands we will be passing, but I am unable to raise anyone on the radio to ask if shooting is going on.

Aug. 8: We motor through the Channel Islands without getting bombarded by the Navy, and then, on a whim, decide to stop at Avalon Harbor on Santa Catalina Island.

Being a sunny mid-summer Friday night, the moorings inside the breakwater are totally packed, boats rafted together like sardines. The only other option, if we choose to stop, is to anchor off, outside the breakwater in 90 to 120 feet of water amidst a crowd of pleasure and fishing boats, all rolling heavily in the swells.

We decide to give it a try and anchor off the casino. Instead of pumping up our dinghy, we catch the shore boat. It is an unexpected bonus to be off the boat earlier than planned.

Barbara: Small tourist shops and a curious but successful mixture of Spanish red-tiled-roof architecture and New England-style clap-board structures line the winding streets. Tall, narrow houses are wedged together on steep streets with pocket gardens and tile terraces. The centerpiece of Avalon is the 1929-vintage Art Deco casino and theater built by the Wrigley family, former owners of the island. Surrounded by tall, thin palms the circular structure looks like it was built by the Moors. In fact the entire town when viewed from the water looks like a Mediterranean village perched and terraced up the slopes of a valley.

John: After a couple of hours hiking and exploring, we caught a ride back to *Mahina Tiare*. An unattended 18-foot speedboat had dragged anchor and was too close for comfort. That, plus the uncomfortable rolling, helps us decide that a night at sea would be more advantageous, so we hoisted anchor and headed for San Diego.

After a calm and windless warm night with very little traffic, we arrive at the entrance to Mission Bay, San Diego at 9:15 a.m.

This is the first passage I have made with a SatNav aboard, and I am fascinated by how accurately the system works, virtually leading us in through the breakwater!

I choose to stop in Mission Bay instead of San Diego Harbor because I'd been told by cruising friends of a 72-hour free and legal anchorage which just happened to be near their house.

The friends are Bruce and Kathleen Decker whom I met in 1980 in Tonga, and who offered us showers and laundry when they heard we might stop in San Diego. After anchoring in the protected, small Bonita Cove, we head ashore to find their house.

The next five days pass quickly. Bruce came to the beach to pick us up in a white, custom two-seater Cadillac convertible. We met their daughter Christy, born in Australia. The last time I had seen the Deckers was in Tonga where they were frugal cruisers, sailing toward Fiji and Australia in their Mariner 31 ketch.

Now, clad in pinstripes, Bruce works in an office with an expansive view of the harbor. They are saving up for their next boat and cruise.

August 14: After uneventful passages from Neah Bay to San Francisco and then to San Diego, it seems that we might be tempting fate to leave San Diego for the Galapagos in the middle of the Mexican hurricane season. And on a Friday. One superstition I've always ignored; it's bad luck to start a voyage on a Friday. I weigh the odds. We could enjoy a mellow anchorage in San Diego for a few months until the hurricane season has passed. But every time we go to a grocery or marine store, several $50 travelers checks disappear, the money going for items we *really* need. So, if we wait, we will end up basically broke, and will arrive at Pitcairn and Easter Island in poorer weather.

I decide to tempt fate and try to make it past the 600-mile stretch

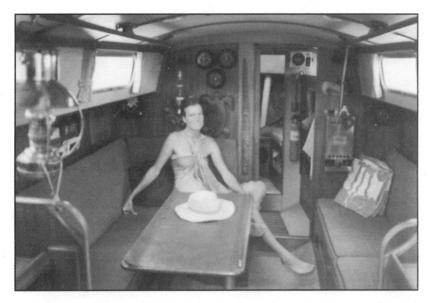

Mahina Tiare's mahogany interior, looking forward using a wide angle lens. The saloon table lowers to form a double berth which we use at anchor. At sea we sleep on the narrow settee berths with lee cloths to keep us from rolling out. The head and hanging locker are forward. Beyond them is the forepeak with two berths. Our kerosene heater is mounted on the main bulkhead. We have a two burner kerosene stove and two kerosene lamps. Twelve-volt lights, which run off the ship's battery, are our primary source of light. Handrails along the overhead give us something to hang on to in rough weather.

of Mexican coast, where our sailing course will be right through the top of the northwest-bound hurricanes as they scream up the coast, before turning out to the west toward Hawaii. This will be Barbara's first long ocean passage and, by the look of the Pilot Charts, probably the most difficult in the 60,000 miles of sailing I've done on the Pacific. If we make it past the hurricanes unscathed, we'll then have light headwinds to contend with for over 1,000 miles, a high percentage of calms and, finally, strong contrary currents just before the Galapagos.

Originally I had planned a non-stop passage from San Diego to Easter Island, 3,500 miles of difficult sailing, a real endurance test of both a new sailor and a new marriage. After studying the pilot charts in more detail, I discovered that a stopover in the Galapagos would shorten the longest passage to 2,600 miles and give us a better angle on the wind for Easter Island. Though we will be sailing exactly on the track of the hurricanes, I am counting on sailing through this area as quickly as possible (about five and one-half days) and hope to miss the predicted one hurricane per month.

August 15, Barbara: Our final day in San Diego. I buy a few last minute items as John gets things stowed on the boat and made ready for sea. Provisioning for this trip is much different than if we were simply heading to Tahiti. If all goes according to plan, it will be seven months before we arrive in Tahiti, the first stop where major reprovisioning is possible. We stock up on soups and small cans of tuna, chicken, salmon, clams and ham. One of these cans per day, per person, is more than enough protein for our lunch and dinner meals. Counting up the main course items is an easy way of judging if we have enough food on board. We fill up the remaining space with canned cheese and butter; powdered milk; canned, freeze-dried, fresh vegetables and fruits; freeze-dried dinners (which are our lightweight emergency foods); pastas; grains; flour; beans, and condiments. Long lasting provisions include three cabbages, 20 pounds of carrots, 30 pounds of onions and 30 more of potatoes, a few acorn and winter squash, two dozen hard green apples, a half-dozen limes, oranges and grapefruits, wrapped in aluminum foil to preserve them. We coat six dozen eggs in Vaseline which will preserve them over a month unrefrigerated.

I realize that I should have been living aboard *Mahina Tiare* for several months before leaving port to get accustomed to boat living. Moving out of a cottage I loved and coming aboard at the last minute was difficult. I am still adjusting to the small space of a 31-foot boat. John can stand upright only under the hatch in the main cabin of *Mahina Tiare*, which is raised a few inches from the rest of the cabin top. Theoretically, the boat sleeps six: two in the forepeak and two in a double berth which is created by lowering the settee table and adding cushions. The quarterberth and other settee each sleep one. In reality, the boat is so full now that we can only use the two berths in the main saloon.

John plans to support us partially by sewing canvas sun awnings and repairing sails for other boats, so the forepeak area is filled with bolts of fabric, sewing supplies, a sewing machine and two folding bicycles. I hope to supplement our income by painting signs, so my box of sign-painting supplies is in the quarterberth, which is solidly packed from bunk to ceiling with food and spare parts. Each one of *Mahina Tiare's* lockers is filled in an efficient way — so efficient that it is a major inconvenience getting anything. Like a jigsaw puzzle, I have to remember exactly how I removed a piece or I will not be able to replace it. Getting at storage underneath the berths might take an hour of shifting gear.

This compulsive packing is the hardest part of living on the boat. I am slowly learning patience and to do without the hard-to-get items. Still, I have fits trying to extricate some things. Usually, John comes along and patiently gets them for me.

Mahina Tiare has a small ice box, but the places we will be traveling the first part of our trip will not have ice. Counter space consists of a 2 x 2-foot square. We have a two-burner kerosene stove, but no oven. I have two frying pans, a sauce pan and a four-quart pressure cooker. My meals are very simple — another new freedom.

John: At 4:30 p.m. we motor to the fuel dock in Quivira Basin, top up fuel and water and enjoy the last cool cockpit showers with unlimited water. Before we leave the dock, an 80-foot gleaming white motoryacht pulls up to the other side of the fuel dock, her skipper announcing to the attendant that they would need several thousand gallons of fuel. When I ask the owner his destination, he says Hawaii will be the first stop on their around-the-world cruise. He mentions that years ago he had circumnavigated the world on a 32-foot Tahiti ketch but now he wanted a little more comfort and speed, with 30 more feet of boat and twin diesels. When I mention that the Galapagos will be our next port, he says: "Aren't you a few months too early?"

After clearing the Mission Bay breakwater, we have lumpy seas and 15 to 20 knots of wind, so we both feel queasy. Dinner is a quick affair, soup and toast. As the sun sets we get a good bearing on the Coronado Islands, six miles inside the Mexican border. Looking at the coast from seaward, we observed a solid blaze of lights as far north along the California coast as we can see, but no lights visible on the Mexican side of the border.

Chapter 2
SURVIVING
HURRICANE JAVIER

Aug. 17, Barbara: Alone again with the elements. For me, it is the changing faces of nature that add the variety to our passages. Instead of a static, controlled home environment, we are constantly challenged to find ways to keep the boat moving, stay cool or warm, keep the batteries charged and the water tanks filled. It seems as if everything from the stove to sails requires attention, but we have the time to spend on these chores. And the chores directly concern our survival. On the boat, ties to the past and future are cut off; we exist in the present.

Aug. 18, John: Hurricane Howard, which has been moving up the coast south of us, was downgraded to a tropical storm. Today is the first really warm day of the passage. We shower and shampoo in the cockpit and end up feeling a lot better. I remove, clean, and re-bed a leaky genoa track that has been dripping into a bookshelf, staining and swelling our paperbacks.

Aug. 19, Barbara: Sitting alone in the cockpit at night with the moon as my companion, surrounded by a gentle vast rolling sea, I feel as though the sea could reach in and grab me. I would simply be gone — I am a tiny speck on such hugeness. Later, when clouds cover the moon it becomes a strange white night, a hazy, dusk-like atmosphere; the horizon obscured. There is no point of reference. It is like floating in infinity.

Aug. 20: Very hot today, no cloud cover to dissipate the sun's intensity. All day I looked longingly at the purple depths surrounding us. I wanted to forget my fears, jump in and feel the cool liquid around my body. At 6 p.m. John takes the plunge, and after he is back aboard I jump in. Ah, delicious water, cool enough to soothe but not to chill.

Grabbing onto the trailing line, the boat looks high and inaccessible from the water's surface. I wonder whether some huge marine predator might seize this naked, squirming, white body trailing from a rope like bait on a line. What courage a salmon must have to leave its stream and swim out into this vastness.

We have a 500-mile celebration with wine tonight, a good time to visit and share feelings. Somehow being in such close proximity with another person and no set work pattern tends to make me introspective. It's good to plan social events to break the routine of the passage. John and I go through most days in silence, but attuned to the rhythm of each other and the sea.

I read over John's log entries and realize how differently we perceive things. He is concerned with the practicality of running *Mahina Tiare*, with what we have eaten or done during the day. He is solid and present, while my mind takes me on journeys within. Together we form a balance.

Tonight is the kind of night which makes me feel this is what sailing is all about — warm gentle winds, full moon, stars and slight swells quietly undulating and making only whispering sounds against the hull. The air is heavy enough to caress, but not stifle — it gives the sense of moving through a substance as surely as the boat is moving through the water.

Aug. 23, John: A great day. We've averaged 4 knots under sail most of the day. The winds have been very light for many days and we haven't been able to cover our goal of 100 miles per day. The rumor I heard about the fuel from Mission Bay containing a lot of water wasn't a rumor. I have drained the water separator on the fuel filter six times, and worried that I would run out of fuel filter elements long before Tahiti at this rate. I spent several hours re-wiring my seven year old trolling generator, and it actually works again, producing 4 amps at 5 knots.

The forecast for our area of the ocean which we received from the National Weather Service transmission from San Francisco today told of two separate hurricanes. Hurricane Javier is 420 miles south of us and is forecast to move west, toward Hawaii, at 14 knots. Javier is packing winds of 100 knots. Also in the picture, but not threatening us, is Hurricane Isis, 240 miles west and heading to Hawaii at 14 knots.

17

Aug. 24: Hurricane Javier is now located 210 miles south and reported to be moving *northward*— directly towards us — at 8 knots with 110-knot winds in the center. Gale force winds within 110 miles of center.

Hurricanes in this area are newly-formed storms, slow-moving, powerful, very concentric, their hurricane-force winds covering a relatively small area. According to the Pilot Charts, they usually head west toward Hawaii this time of year, not coming so far north. As they move west they grow in size (radius of hurricane-force winds) but diminish in peak wind velocity. But the gale force winds cover a larger area, and the speed of movement of the entire storm system picks up. Hurricanes or tropical depressions can move as fast as 35 knots.

We prepare for the hurricane by reducing sail to a storm jib and deeply reefed mainsail. We tighten the hatch closures and replace the dorade vents on the cabin top with deck plates. Our boat speed is down to 3 1/2 knots with the storm jib and triple-reefed main, so at 8:50 this evening we replace the storm jib with a 100 percent working jib. This brings our speed up to 4 1/2 knots. We tack onto a new course of 105 degrees, (roughly east), toward Mexico and away from Javier's track. We are now 200 miles southwest of Cabo San Lucas, the southern tip of Baja California and about 420 miles west of Manzanillo, Mexico, 60 miles from the uninhabited, 100-foot-high Roca Partida, which we must avoid.

Please God, help us to get through Javier safely and quickly. Thank you for taking care of Barbara and me.

August 25, Barbara, Midnight: Tonight is dark and moonless, impossible to see even the bow. The seas are building, waves crashing violently as we beat to windward. Each wave sounds like a battering ram against our hull, capable of shattering the bulkheads into splinters.

The cabin, all vents and hatches fastened tight, is like a sauna. Still, the frothing seawater finds its way into the cabin through leaky ports and spray from the cockpit. The bow is often buried and decks are deluged in green water. The seas are coming from three directions as if we are inside a gigantic washing machine.

The fatigue and violent motion make it difficult to concentrate, to decide on a course of action. Reading Bowditch's *American Practical Navigator Volume I*, on tropical hurricanes in the dimly lighted, airless cabin, John and I have different interpretations of how to determine the "dangerous semicircle" of the storm.

I quote from the book: *"It is customary to divide the circular area of the storm into two parts. In the Northern Hemisphere, that part to the right of the storm track (facing in the direction toward which the storm is moving) is called the dangerous semicircle. It is considered dangerous because (1) the actual wind speed is greater ... (2) the direction of the wind and sea is such to carry a vessel into the path of the storm (in the forward part of the semicircle). The part to the left of the storm track is called the navigable semicircle."*

We are in the dangerous semicircle. Our best hope for getting out is to keep the boat moving to windward as fast as can be done, and pray that the storm veers off westward. We are still steering due east toward Manzanillo. The critical weather reports from the National Weather Service come only every six hours — not frequently enough to keep an accurate position on a fast-moving storm. The hourly report on WWVH seems inaccurate — it gives a position of the storm's center that we figure is wrong by nearly 60 miles. As we listen, fighting off sleepiness and nausea, each report and each satellite fix places us dangerously closer to Javier and the tiny Isla Roca Partida. One report put the hurricane's center 55 miles southwest of us, winds steady at 110 knots and gusts to 135 knots!

On this inky black morning, John changes down to the storm jib and puts another reef in the main. I worry about him on deck alone. The sail's head is now well below the spreaders. We change course, heading NNE, to avoid running into Isla Partida. The SatNav is proving invaluable. Too overcast to take any sun shots with the sextant, we are unsure of what the hurricane is doing to the currents.

At 6:00 a.m., overcome with exhaustion, I collapse onto the settee. A very tired John remains on watch. An explosive sound awakens me. Has *Mahina Tiare* come apart under the stress? Glancing around the cabin I discover that one of John's tool drawers has jumped out of its track and bounced against the galley drawer on the opposite side of the boat. Tools and splintered wood litter the cabin.

Our Monitor wind vane steers flawlessly through these horrendous conditions. To steer by hand for any length of time is impossible, the need for constant pressure on the tiller causing fatigue.

Sunrise is welcome, even though it reveals the towering green walls of water surrounding us. We are drenched in sweat and salt spray.

9:54 a.m. John: We receive a satellite fix which puts us at 19° 52' N, 111° 26' W, or 103 miles north of Hurricane Javier, the storm still packing 105-knot winds in the center and gale force winds for a radius of 110 miles. If Javier doesn't change course again, it will move further away from us every hour. Our winds should drop from the 60 knots we now experience. We have tried heaving-to, essentially slowing the boat speed to 1 or 2 knots. In the confused seas this is less comfortable than carrying on close-hauled on a course that will get us out of the hurricane's dangerous semicircle.

9:00 p.m.: The center of Javier is now 140 miles from us and moving northwest at 8 knots. The maximum forecast winds are down to 90 knots, and the radius of gale force winds, now 95 miles. Our wind has been steadier, no more violent gusts, the wind speed perhaps down to 45 knots since sunset. It is nearly impossible to judge the height of the seas; they are uneven, and still coming from two directions. I do think that they have subsided slightly. I just wish I could sleep. I am so tired now that twice I have fallen asleep while trying to hang on at the chart table long enough to plot the hurricane's and our positions. I awaken with a start when my head bonks the chart table. I have given up trying to look for ships. I can't even see the bow of the boat in the darkness and spray. There isn't a hint of light on deck — no stars, no moon, no phosphorescence in the waves, just total darkness. But we no longer have to worry about being driven onto the lee shore of Roca Partida. Our tactic of heading away from the hurricane track and Islas de Revillagigedo has paid off; we are now 68 miles north of the nearest island. If we hadn't altered course, we would have been very near Roca Partida when Javier passed within 40 miles of it.

I feared that this hurricane on our first long ocean passage would convince Barbara that sailing long distances was a stupid thing to do but, in reality, I think she has weathered this storm better than I. She is able to fall asleep in less than a minute, no matter how rough it is and earlier, at the height of the hurricane, she even said, "This is exhilarating. I am awed by the forces around us."

Coming this close to a hurricane is a new experience, and one I do not want to repeat. It is just plain scary! I have experienced more wind in a springtime gale off the Oregon Coast, seas over 30 feet but from one direction. That made it easy to set the boat up to run under bare poles towing warp, downwind. The seas today were incredible! One minute they were towering 30 feet above, then crashing down on top of us. The next minute we were sailing off the top of a wave and plummeting 20 feet down in a violent and uneven trough. I rejoiced *Mahina Tiare* was fairly light and very strongly built.

Barbara, 10:00 p.m.: I wake up, but getting up is difficult. When I'm asleep I'm oblivious to everything. I dread waking up sweaty, with a bitter, nauseating taste in my mouth, and eyeballs that feel like lead sinkers.

A brown booby bird with a silly grinning beak and sleek lines came gliding by the boat today, then settled on the water. It bobbed up and down on the steep waves like a cork, as if saying, "Take heart, you will weather this storm as effortlessly as I do".

Aug. 26, John : Javier is now 230 miles away and moving west at 14 knots, maximum winds only 85 knots. As long as it doesn't recurve, we're in the clear!

At 1:30 a.m. we changed course back to the south. We replaced the storm sail with the working jib and shook out one of the three reefs in the mainsail. The only damage to the boat is the broken tool drawer. I can epoxy it back together when things settle down.

Barbara: A muggy, lethargic morning. The wind is down, but the seas are sullen. Around noon a thick band of opaque clouds appears, its dark edge parallel to the water. The wind and waves stir as it quickly approaches. Soon the clouds pour a cool staccato rain and we dance to the drumbeat, shouting and revelling in the relief from heat and grime. We frantically lather our crusted bodies, trying to wash off the soap before the rain stops. Rain continues to pour down, so we stop up the deck scuppers and rinse all our salty clothes and towels. Shivering and excited, we act like miners who have just struck gold. Greedily, we gather 20 gallons of sweet rainwater. Every quart translates in my mind to clean hair and clothes and sweet water in our tanks. We work furiously, and when the rains ease we feel rich indeed.

We are now only 50 miles from Socorro Island, and would like to anchor there briefly to rest. Two days ago John spoke with Les Whitely on Moorea via ham radio. Les mentioned having stopped at Socorro seven years earlier on his way to the Marquesas. At that time there was a small Mexican naval base on the island. Fresh water, he told us, was available from a spring near the anchorage. We have no charts of the island and Socorro is just a quarter-inch dot on the overall chart, but we decide to look for a safe anchorage.

Aug. 27: Socorro Island, 250 miles south of Cabo San Lucas, is in sight as the sun rises over mellow seas. Birds cluster white on dark cliffs off the rocky islets of Socorro's north shore. The island looks friendly and inviting with a chartreuse covering. Worn peaks and valleys end abruptly at the shoreline where sheer rock cliffs drop perpendicular to the ocean. It's as if the soft greenness was sliced sheer by a jagged blade, causing an angular scar facing the breaking seas. We contact the commander of the base via VHF radio. He encourages us to moor overnight in a small semi-protected bay. Ashore, he checks our passports and boat numbers then graciously gives us fuel and water. Hurricane Javier had also struck and damaged Socorro's small settlement. Doors and windows were ripped from the hinges of cement block buildings. But the hundred enlisted men, their wives and children are accustomed to hurricanes, accustomed to living on this sparsely vegetated remote island.

Aug. 31, 8:00 p.m.: It is a week after the hurricane. Gentle water surrounds us, making it difficult to believe that the savage sea we had experienced could be so calm. A warm and light breeze caresses us, dulling our sense of those screaming winds that had torn at the sails.

Today is hot, almost windless. We motor much of the day and accomplish a lot. John changed the engine oil, patched a tear in the dodger and cleaned out the lazarette. I vacuumed, cut John's hair, put new insulation in the drawers that hold silverware, pots and pans. I made pizza and green pea salad for dinner, then did exercises. We celebrate the half-way point between San Diego and Galapagos with a bottle of Korbel champagne, a bon voyage gift.

Sept. 1, 1:00 a.m.: I hear dolphins, and hurry to the bow. I see them as glowing streaks shooting through the water, zig-zagging like sparkles from a magician's wand, so quick as almost not to be here. Occasionally an indistinct shape, surfacing for air, makes a swishing sound. I want to repay the dolphins for putting on their show, but I know they sense my delight. Dolphins are believed to have powerful bio-radios easily receiving human brain waves.

We enter the doldrums or Inter-Tropical-Convergence-Zone (ITCZ), a name with an ominous ring. The air here, like the air before the hurricane, has a disquieting, charged feeling, heavy and foreboding. Dense black clouds obscure much of the sky, obliterating the stars. John calls these dry squalls. Silent, round flashes of lightning appear at random on the horizon like dynamite blasts. I feel that I might suddenly find myself in the midst of a conflagration.

Sept. 2, John: For almost an hour this morning a red-footed booby circled the boat, occasionally landing on the water ahead of us, checking us out as we sailed by. When he decided to try landing, his first target was the outboard motor on the stern pulpit, something too slippery to hang onto. Finally, he landed on one of the stern pulpit rails. At first he had trouble balancing and kept falling over backward, but he eventually got the hang of it. He settled down to six hours of preening and drying his feathers. Shortly after he landed I went below to get our cameras, but before I got back on deck we were in the middle of a real rip-snorter of a squall. Unfortunately our largest jib, a lightweight drifter, was extended with the whisker pole, and we were at once overpowered. I set the Monitor wind vane to steer us dead downwind, trying to blanket the drifter as much as possible behind the mainsail.

We still were screaming along at over 8 knots and the drifter was flogging, so I went forward and dropped the pole. But I neglected to tell Barbara to sheet the drifter in the minute the pole was off. The drifter wrapped itself many times around the forestay, wildly flogging in the increasing wind and rain.

All this time the bird stayed perched on the stern pulpit, just two feet from where I was at the tiller, wings flapping to maintain balance. Barbara was scurrying around, trying to block the scuppers, shampoo, and catch some rain before the squall passed. Even though the air temperature registered 90-degrees, the force of the wind had me shivering. After an hour, I wondered whether we hadn't stumbled into the tropical disturbance reported south of us. After three hours the squall passed, the sun came out, I hoisted more sail, Barbara went below for a nap, and the booby bird went back to preening its feathers. Now four more birds circle the boat, eyeing our hitchhiker enviously, and checking out landing spots. Perhaps these are Galapagos birds hitching a ride home.

Sept. 7: We aren't out of the convergence zone yet, and light, squally headwinds, punctuated by many hours without wind, have been the routine for the past week. We have done a fair amount of motoring, and this afternoon the main diesel tank ran dry. I added 10 of the 20 gallons of fuel we have in jerry jugs. Those squally headwinds frustrate me; I have never done as many changes on any passage.

I read *Blue Highways* by William Least Heat Moon today, a great story about a man who takes off in his van after his wife leaves him and he loses his job. He travels around the country, staying on back roads (the ones colored blue on highway maps) and visiting small towns. His book gave me the idea of buying a van after our cruise and driving down the West Coast on Highways 1 and 101, stopping to see friends and relatives, then across to New Mexico and Colorado, to the Carolinas, then up to New York and maybe as far north as Maine before heading back to the Pacific Northwest. It's rather pleasant to think about something different and distant on such a day at sea.

Sept. 8: A mellow morning, only small squalls. After the wind died, we motored much of the day. I am really enjoying Barbara's company. She is turning out to be a good friend indeed. At noon today, we have only 479 miles to go to the first island in the Galapagos.

Sept. 10: Yesterday was rough and we spent all day sailing with the main reefed and a working jib. A seam opened up in the lapper and I had to take it down. It took two hours to dig the sewing machine out of the quarterberth and repair the stitching. Today is mellower, but we're still going to weather and are not able to lay a course for the Galapagos.

Sept. 11: Earlier today the container ship *C.G.M. Gauguin* passed us, headed from Tahiti to Panama, Norfolk Virginia, Spain and France. I'd seen the ship many times in Tahiti, and the captain answered my call on the VHF and asked if they could give us any supplies or assistance. After thanking him I assured him that despite our close encounter with hurricane Javier everything aboard seemed shipshape.

Chapter 3

GALAPAGOS:

MEETING DARWIN'S BEASTS

Sept. 12, Barbara: For the last few days I have been reading books on the Galapagos, my favorite is: *Galapagos, Islands Lost in Time* by Tui De Roy Moore, a young Galapagos writer and photographer.

I learn that the Galapagos were probably first visited by Incas. Inca legends tell of a King's visit to "Islands of Fire;" where he witnessed the eruption of one of the Galapagos archipelago's volcanoes. Pre-Spanish pottery shards point to the presence of these early Indian visitors.

Pirates and whalers called these islands "Enchanted Islands," and found food, water and safe anchorages after many months at sea. The Spanish called them "Galapagos," after the then-abundant giant tortoises.

"Uninviting" was the description by the Bishop of Panama, whose ship, blown 500 miles off course in 1535, made him the first European to visit the islands.

Isolation and the harsh environment have fostered development of unique species of flora and fauna. Charles Darwin's theory of evolution — *The Origin of Species* — resulted directly from his scientific observations of these species. Darwin, a young English naturalist, was aboard *HMS Beagle*, when it cruised the Galapagos on its circumnavigation in 1835.

The Galapagos Islands were formed by the eruption of underwater volcanoes and the upheaval of submerged lava flows beginning ten million years ago. Approximately five million years ago the first islands pierced the ocean's surface. Their slow formation continues today; steaming fumaroles mark the active volcanoes whose periodic eruptions add new lava layers to their imposing slopes.

The convergence of three tectonic plates influences the intense underwater volcanic activity. The Nazca plate carries the archipelago three inches toward South America each year. As the plate moves eastward, the older islands to the east are carried away from the areas of most volcanic activity. Seven active volcanoes continue to form the most western islands, Isabela and Fernandina.

Ecuador claimed the Galapagos in 1832, and created a prison colony. Population fluctuated from 25 persons in the entire group in 1849, to several hundred at the start of World War II. From 1924 to 1935, German and Norwegian settlers arrived. Those who stayed are now community leaders.

During World War II the United States had a military base and airfield on Baltra Island. In 1959, a century after the publishing of *The Origin of Species*, plans were initiated for the construction of the Charles Darwin Research Station at Academy Bay. The station is very active today with more than 50 scientists and students from various countries researching everything from the volcanoes to lava lizards.

Sept. 13, John, 6:00 a.m.: The wind died at 1:30 a.m. this morning and we are motoring again. We expect to run out of fuel at any time and that will be it for the engine, except for the two gallons I put aside for getting into Academy Bay, one of the ports of entry for the Galapagos. I sighted Pinta Island at sunrise, only 16 miles away.

Barbara: We'd hoped to anchor at Pinta but rough seas sent us on, a big disappointment for me. I have yet to learn that you can't be in a hurry or count on anything at sea. The weather is involved in everything from anchoring to cooking. One minute it's so hot you can't breathe and the next you are shivering in a squall.

Marchena Island, predominantly dark volcanic rock with a few roundish grey-green areas, juts up ahead of us. The volcanic flow from the crater to the ocean looks like someone has poured chocolate syrup over it.

A minor crisis — our water supply tastes foul. One of the small pleasures of an unbearably hot day is drinking decent water. We added some chlorine and hope this will help.

John, 3:20 p.m.: We made it! The last few miles were slow — motorsailing into headwinds and choppy seas. The 2 knot contrary current shown on the chart was flowing at least that strong. We decided to stop at Marchena rather than try and beat up the channels against wind and current in the dark with very little fuel reserve.

We found an anchorage at Caleta Black, a somewhat protected indentation in the coast. A friend had stopped here 15 years earlier and marked it on our chart. We anchored in 30 feet of water with a clear black sand bottom. I let out a sigh of relief; we had completed our longest and, hopefully, most difficult passage. And had arrived safely. All I can think of now is a few quiet days in one place, resting and repairing *Mahina Tiare*.

Sept. 14, Barbara: Rowing into shore in our inflatable dinghy gives me the impression that we might be landing on the moon. Everything is a drab brownish-black, from the sandy beach to the lava rocks which form arches and fantastic shapes jutting into the sky. One can almost hear the hiss of molten lava as it cooled in the seawater to form the sculpted shapes around us.

The armored primitive bodies of marine iguanas are heaped in piles, discernible from the rocks only by their droopy tails with spiny crests. These cold-blooded creatures are unique to the Galapagos, the only species of lizard in the world totally dependent on the sea for sustenance.

The first bits of color we encounter on approaching shore are the bright scarlet Sally Lightfoot crabs, named after an exotic dancer of years ago. They are clambering over rocks and dining on lush green seaweed.

Landing the Avon on warm sand, we see strange tracks: large, closely-spaced prints straddling what appear to be a bicycle tire track. Really, the fat tail of a marine iguana dragging in the sand, and his four big-toed feet. As soon as he sees us he freezes, his excellent camouflage his best means of defense.

A pair of oystercatchers trot up the beach on long, pink legs. Their red eyes, rimmed in orange, peer out at us suspiciously as they make a racket. Then calming down, they search for dinner, probing the sand with their long, thin, red bills.

Gray lava gulls — one of two species unique to the Galapagos — land near shore and commence a strange crackling laugh, but the oystercatchers chase them away.

I think the oystercatchers want to chase us away, too. I feel out of place on the Galapagos, as if I am a hostile stranger. Animals blend in, adapted to this harsh environment. It is man who has brought destruction to many of the fragile ecosystems here, introducing destructive insects, goats, pigs, cattle, black rats, cats, horses, donkeys. In many places these creatures have damaged the flora and fauna by overgrazing scarce vegetation or by preying on indigenous forms of life.

Hundreds of thousands of the Galapagos tortoises were decimated, first by English pirate ships, then by whalers and sealers in the 18th and 19th centuries. Providing an excellent source of fresh meat for hungry sailors, tortoises could live for a year or more without food or water in a ship's hold.

(We learned on arrival in Academy Bay that Marchena is strictly off limits to everyone, our going ashore did pose a threat to the ecosystem. We regret having gone ashore.)

Sept. 15: A comfortable day at anchor, dry, cool and breezy. All the accumulated dampness and mold quickly disappeared as we brought cushions and clothes into the sun to air. Our spirits, dampened by a difficult and wet passage, revived.

Tonight we went for a sunset row and saw blue-footed boobies perched on a brown volcanic arch. Silhouetted against the sunset sky with a pale moon in the background, they made a spectacular sight. A pelican, on his white, guano-streaked perch, eyed us without much interest while above a frigate bird soared – a black angular shape against the orange sky.

Sept. 16: Snorkeling in the cold water, our wetsuits bright against the clear green depths, I hold onto John's hand feeling like a child seeing an undersea garden for the first time. He points out a rainbow-colored parrot fish, a stealthy moray eel, and a multitude of other wonders.

We swim with the dinghy to our black sand beach where I spend hours sketching the enigmatic marine iguanas, getting acquainted with their habits and habitat. The adults are very cooperative models, but one rambunctious juvenile keeps climbing all over the piles of adults. Finally he can contain his curiosity no longer and crawls up to me. I shy away, my movement discouraging any further pursuit. They are harmless, but still I don't have the urge to pet them or have one crawl up my leg. They inspire a primeval fear, yet I find myself

Juvenile sea lions, always looking for a good time

developing an affection for these spiny, loose-skinned creatures.

A Darwin's finch makes himself at home among the iguanas who seem oblivious to him as he picks ticks from their skin. Movement is constant as iguanas, with their long clawed dragon-like feet, walk all over each other,

Sept. 17: We weighed anchor and traveled two miles east to a tan sandy beach anchorage, with low banks and a strange silver-gray dwarf forest above. Anxious to stretch our legs and intrigued by our first glimpse of vegetation, we don wetsuits and swim, towing the dinghy toward shore.

An immature hawk, orange and tan with black markings, watches us beach the dinghy. Then, as we are about to photograph her, she flies down and lands on a rock much closer to us. Cocking her head in every direction she seems intent on a good view of these strange two-legged visitors. We walk to within a couple of feet of her and she patiently and curiously waits as we photograph her from every direction.

Creeping up the rock behind the hawk I am startled by a loud, human-sounding groan. Looking over the ledge, I spot three beautiful golden sea lions in the sand below me. We startled each other! But I snap a quick photo before they squirm down the sand through graceful lava arches that lead to the sea.

I feel sorry for the sea lions on land; they seem at such a disadvantage dragging their heavy bodies across sand and rocks and lifting themselves with the stumps of their flippers. In the water it's a different matter; they are delightful acrobats, tumbling and playing in the surf, sleek and swift as torpedoes.

Sept. 18: Packing the dinghy with camera and snorkeling gear, lunch and drinking water, we started off in the early morning. We rowed along the shoreline to the east, passing cliffs and lava flows full of blow holes, caves and arches.

When we reached a forested headland with flat rocks at the water's edge, we pulled the dinghy ashore and took off walking over the smooth black lava, stopping to marvel at the bright creatures in the tide pools. Climbing the sandy bluff above the coastal lava plain, we hiked along the edge of the forest. Stands of broad oval-padded Opuntia cactus trees surrounded us. The forest had a pungent, licorice smell. The trees had few leaves, but bright clumps of green and orange lichen clung to the trunks and branches. Fat Galapagos doves rattled around in the dry grass. Darwin finches flitted about, criss-crossing our paths at shoulder height, and brazen black and white mockingbirds trailed on the ground. Tiny birds, large-billed flycatchers, followed us. It was like exploring an enchanted forest; if we had stood still the birds would have landed on us.

After an hour we headed back toward the dinghy, passing a grey hunched heron feasting on delicacies trapped in a tide pool. He resembled an old man intent on something in front of him. We made friends with a sea lion, who moved his head coyly at John's words and bellowed when we walked away. An attentive lava lizard, about three inches in length, watched as we returned to the dinghy.

Rowing back to *Mahina Tiare*, three juvenile sea lions spotted us and came zooming out to play. They snorted and cavorted, coming closer and closer to the dinghy. As if on a dare from his companions, one bold sea lion nudged the back of the dinghy as he shot past, then decided to join us. He effortlessly lifted himself up on the side of the Avon, his wet whiskered face inches from my lap. I let out a scream and, startled by my voice, he quickly slipped back into the sea. Perhaps we were the stangest animals he had ever seen.

The dusk sky silhouetted a wooden fishing trawler in the distance, a dozen frigate birds wheeling and diving around it. The *Reina Isabela* motored by slowly. Four men worked under a blue tarp filleting fish, salting them and storing them in 40-gallon wooden barrels. They gave us five gallons of diesel and a fresh fish after we told them about our long journey and need for fuel. We gave them cans of food.

Sept. 20, John: Woke up at 6:30 a.m., hoisted the dinghy aboard, deflated and folded it up. The bottom was covered with small barnacles after only one week in these nutrient-rich waters. We set sail at 7:30 a.m. for Santiago Island, 30 miles to the south.

At first we were able to make 4 knots to windward into the light headwinds and choppy seas, but the farther into the channel we got, the stronger the current set against us. Our speed made good over the bottom fell to less than 2 knots. As reluctant as I was to use any of the precious fuel we had been given, it became apparent that the only way we would reach Santiago before dark was to motorsail.

We crossed the equator at 1:10 p.m. I reminded Barbara of the tradition of initiating new sailors into becoming shellbacks when they cross the equator under sail for the first time. So when we toasted crossing the line, I poured my glass of wine over her head. I'd say that she got off pretty easy, compared to sailors that have had their heads shaved and thrown into the water.

Barbara: At 3:30 p.m. we arrived at Buccaneer Cove, a blue bite out of rust colored sand. The land, parched and barren against clear azure sky, hints of the American Southwest. To the right rises a 500' domed hill, its face dancing with waving horizontal striations of brown stone. Arched caves and grottoes at its base echo the barks and groans of the sea lions. On the left, 100' spires of fiery red, guano-streaked, rock and cactus covered islets form the foreground to angular cliffs behind.

The cold, blue-green water is alive with fish and punctuated by white splashes as the spiralling frigate, boobies and pelicans dive bomb for dinner.

Awed by the bioluminescent sparkles as we dipped our oars into black water during a moonlight row, we momentarily turned on the outboard. A green triangle of biological brilliance, a natural tail-light, instantly trailed our stern.

Sept. 21, John: I awoke long before daylight to fix the stove which was squeaking in its gimbals as *Mahina Tiare* rolled in this open anchorage. I thought I heard voices, but since the sea lions on shore had kept up a constant territorial barking I wasn't sure.

But when I looked out the companionway, I saw a fishing boat anchored about 50 yards away, between us and the beach. It hadn't been there at midnight when I went on deck to check the anchor, and in the light of the full moon it looked like the crew were headed ashore in a skiff. Fine, I thought, just some fisherman stopping for the night. I went back to bed.

Hideous, bloodcurdling shrieks awakened me a half hour later. I heard roars and the screams of sea lions. And then the sound of very excited and possibly drunk men. What the hell was going on? I looked toward the beach with binoculars, but couldn't make out any more detail than men moving around in the moonlight about a quarter of a mile away. As the bloodcurdling screams increased, all I could figure was that these men must be poachers, catching and clubbing to death the playful sea lions. My mind raced; it was dark, the island uninhabited, and no one knew we were there. If these people were bold enough to illegally slaughter helpless sea lions, what would they do to two yachties who just happened to observe the whole debacle? I hoped they would ignore us and leave after they had their sea lions. But just in case, I dug out our flare gun, loaded it, and set it and our 200,000 candlepower spotlight on the cockpit sole. I went back to bed but not to sleep.

The next time I got up to check with the binoculars, a hint of dawn made it possible to see the men on the beach more clearly. Four or five came out to the fishing boat in the skiff, raised anchor and reanchored nearly in the surf line. Great, I thought, now they must be getting ready to load the dead sea lions aboard. As the sky lightened I saw what they were taking aboard was a fishing net filled with hundreds of pounds of squirming fish. The other end of the net was attached to a stake on the beach. The seals and sea lions were not dead, but were cavorting and bellowing with delight as they feasted on all of the fish that spilled out as the net was pulled aboard the boat.

Within half an hour the sun rose and the nameless boat hoisted anchor and motored quietly out of the bay. I feel foolish for letting my imagination carry me away, but there was a full moon and this was Buccaneer Cove!

32

Barbara: I rolled out of bed groggy this morning, but John was bright-eyed and ready to go exploring ashore, so we landed through the surf before 6:30.

John walked to the caves and crevasses on the beach to photograph nursing baby sea lions, their fat mothers dozing on the sand while their offspring suckled.

Absorbed in his task, John didn't see the large shiny sphere appearing intermittently along the surf line, swimming closer to where he stood. Finally a huge bull seal lion with whiskered head and gaping red mouth emerged from the water and let out a series of very loud, sharp barks and growls. A bit startled, John kept shooting photos. Suddenly, with alarming speed, the 500 pound bull hauled himself onto the beach and started toward John. Not wanting a confrontation with a jealous husband, John retreated from the bull's harem at a run. We were later told that if you approach the female sea lions by land or sea, the territorial bulls may charge you. However, if you stay clear of the harem, the curious adolescent sea lions delight in cavorting with you underwater.

John: Around dusk, a tourist boat nosed into the bay and anchored. We rowed alongside and asked to buy some diesel. We simply don't have enough to make it to Academy Bay if the currents and wind don't improve. The captain said, "No problem," and was disappointed that we had brought only one five gallon jug for them to fill. They insisted that we come aboard and visit. Shortly we were chatting with Carlos Valle, a slight, neatly-groomed Ecuadorian guide who spoke excellent English. Also aboard, an Englishmen, four Ecuadorian tourists and three crew members — all spending a week on one 40-foot boat.

The captain offered us cold sodas, and when he learned of our recent 30-day passage, he said, "Here, you must take this fruit and fish." Twelve years earlier he and two companions were fishing among the islands when their engine broke down. For two months they drifted in the hot equatorial sun living only on fish and scarce rainwater. Eventually the currents carried them to Costa Rica. Here was someone who could appreciate our lust for fresh fruit!

Sept. 22: At last we headed for the port of entry, called Academy Bay by visiting yachts, Port Ayora by locals. At first we had good winds and made 5 1/2 knots on our course for Santa Cruz Island, 40 miles south. But the winds lightened and became headwinds. The current increased as we sailed away from the shoreline of Santiago Island, so we ended up motorsailing again. Just before we reached tiny Jervis Island three different species of dolphin descended on us from all directions.

After about ten minutes a loud THUD shook the boat. The dolphins immediately disappeared. We figured one of them must have mistimed his pass and slammed into the hull instead of shooting past it. Later, when snorkeling around the boat, we checked for any clues like scuff marks on the bottom paint, but found none.

Sept. 25: We spent two days anchored at Bahia Conway, Santa Cruz Island, waiting for more favorable sailing conditions before heading for Academy Bay. Beset again by light headwinds and a 2 knot contrary current, we resorted to motorsailing. Rounding the west coast of Santa Cruz Island and heading east, the coast became greener and greener. But we had yet to see any human habitation on any of the islands.

As we entered Academy Bay, palm trees, mangroves and cactus trees lined the harbor, and we could see the green hills in the distance behind the town. The water was a bright aqua color, and the west side of the bay was filled with perhaps 40 of the oddest assortment of charter and fishing boats I had ever seen. Later we learned that the local tradition is to build rough fishing boats but now, with tourists wanting to see the outer islands, the boat builders start with a wooden fishing boat hull, then build the largest deckhouse-cabin they can to accommodate the maximum number of passengers. A few large classic schooners and ketches also served as charter boats, but several had their topsides modified for more accommodations. The results looked bizarre.

Only one other cruising boat swung at anchor in the entire bay. But what a boat! A hundred feet overall, 75 feet on deck, complete with varnished topsides and square sail. It was built in Norway in 1889. *Svanhild* had originally been a sailing freighter only recently converted to a yacht, a truly impressive yacht. Anchored right on top of *Svanhild* was the *Santa Cruz*, a 230-foot mini-cruise ship built in Spain specifically for service in the Galapagos. She nearly always carried her maximum of 90 passengers and five naturalist guides on her seven-day cruises of the islands.

On the waterfront, the Captain de Puerto's office was well marked. Carefully negotiating the narrow, rocky entrance to a shallow harbor, we tied the dinghy up to the bunker-style cement port building.

Barbara: The captain, Theodore, a smooth, fair-skinned man with watery green eyes, explained to us in English that our permission from the Ecuadorian Navy to cruise the islands with a guide on board had not yet arrived. Therefore we are limited by law to a maximum stay of 72 hours and only in Academy Bay. Without a word from us, he continued, "I am a generous man, and since you have made a 30-day passage, you need more than three days to rest, reprovision and refuel, so I will allow you a week. During this time your boat must remain in Academy Bay, and if you want to visit other islands it is necessary to hire two guards from me to watch your boat while you go exploring on one of the local charter boats."

He invited us to tie our dinghy in his private little harbor whenever we were in town, and eagerly offered to change our U.S. dollars into Ecuadorian Sucre at a better rate than the local bank. His parting advice: "Never drink the local water without boiling it." He suggested that we see if the Hotel Galapagos would sell us rainwater. Our search for water is very serious; we last filled our tanks six weeks ago in San Diego, and we are down to less than a couple of gallons.

A ten-minute walk along the dusty waterfront road brought us to Hotel Galapagos. Here we met Forest Nelson, an American, who had married a local woman and built the hotel twenty years ago. Now in his seventies, he was a solid presence, with sun spotted skin and snow white hair. Impatiently he stated, "I no longer sell water and don't know where you can purchase any." His manager confided that Forest had grown tired of people asking him for water and had dug out the storage tanks and sold them.

Sept. 26: Now desperate for water, we approached a rusty freighter which was anchored in the entrance to the bay and was in the slow process of unloading cargo with lighters and speedboats. After tying the Avon alongside, we scrambled up a Jacob's ladder and were given permission from the crew to fill our jerry jugs. Three hours later we had 70 gallons of water. The water from the ship came from Guayaquil and was at least as bad as the Galapagos water, just not as salty. But

Svanhild – a Norweigian communal boat in Port Ayora, Galapagos

guaranteed if untreated to give you amoebic dysentery. We take for granted something as simple as clean, safe drinking water, but in Ecuador it is a political issue.

Getting fuel was easier. We loaded our four jerry jugs in the dinghy, motored into the Port Captain's mini-harbor and helped his assistant empty a 55 gallon fuel drum into our jugs along with a large plastic container on loan from them. Still, getting fuel and water is an all day affair.

Sept. 27: By prior arrangement, Carlos Valle, looking trim in his khaki guide shirt and shorts, met us at the Darwin Research Station at Academy Bay. Sundays the station is closed to visitors but Carlos showed us the breeding house for the endangered sub-species of Galapagos tortoises anyway. The tortoises in the pens were about four inches across. Outside they were full-grown. If you've ever had pet green turtles — the kind that fit in your hand — seeing a two-hundred pound turtle will make you feel like Alice in Wonderland. The muscular neck of an adult tortoise is the width of an adult human's thigh and is covered with a scaly gray skin which looks rough. Actually it feels smooth as snake skin when you stroke it, something the tortoise enjoys immensely.

The next set of wooden gates Carlos unlocked was strictly off limits to tourists. Behind them were breeding pens for land iguanas, seriously endangered by introduced mammals. Thought to have evolved from a green lizard, (the same mainland lizard the marine iguana evolved from) the land iguanas are much more flamboyant. Bright ochre colored heads and rust colored bodies camouflage them in their land-based habitat.

That evening we had dinner of oatmeal mash aboard the Norwegian cruising boat, *Svanhild*. Several of the crew were ill (stomach problems), so we didn't get to visit with all 16 of them. Those we met were experts at cruising and scamming. Scamming is what long distance cruisers do to continue voyaging without running out of food or money.

Each of the *Svanhild* crew had assignments. One crew member was recording interviews with other crew members and local people, then selling the tapes to a Norwegian radio station. Two were teachers for the five children aboard. They took the kids ashore on excursions when serious work needed to be accomplished on the boat. Another was writing articles for a Norwegian newspaper, his pieces accompanied by numerous sketches of their adventures. The first mate had been writing a series of articles for a sailing magazine; these stories eventually turned into a book. One chap was videotaping their trip; he planned to sell the film to a television station. The ship's steward was responsible for knowing where the tons of food was stored, and for timing major purchases in countries that would be the least expensive. Everyone's separate earnings and income went into a communal "pot" from which the food and boat expenses were paid. Originally Obben and Berit (the captain and his wife) had planned to finish off a Colin Archer designed 40-foot ketch and sail around the world with their son, but then decided it might be boring just the three of them. That was when they rounded up 16 friends to be co-owners. Somehow they persuaded their local bank in Floro, Norway, to grant them a four-year interest-free loan, enough time to purchase and refit *Svanhild* and circumnavigate the world. On returning to Norway they have it worked out to sell half interest in the boat to a historical museum (paying off their loan) and still get to sail the boat six months a year.

The crew knew how to economize. With compromising palates

Wild tortoises are shy, retracting their heads when approached

Land iguana, Darwin Research Center

they kept costs down by eating lizards, boa constrictors, wild goats or whatever was free or cheap in the country they were visiting. Today they loaded up free avocados from the highlands of Santa Cruz and were busy stocking the walk-in freezer with inexpensive beef and goat meat purchased in Puerto Ayora. We also watched the men bob through town hauling hundred pound bags of rice, flour, and oats on their backs. Except for the captain and his wife, each of the crew were aboard for one-year stints. The crew people we met had careers, ranging from a sophisticated fashion designer to a biologist to a down-to-earth woman cabinet maker.

During dinner I started shivering and felt very cold despite the 80-degree temperature. Although we had carefully boiled the water from our tanks we had eaten ashore today and I probably picked up amoebic dysentery from unwashed lettuce.

Oct 1, John: A great day of adventure. Barbara was feeling stronger, so we met Carlos to catch a bus to the highlands. The buses were a challenge. The seats were made for kids and covered in cracked brown plastic. The dirt roads were badly rutted, the shocks had long since gone, and we were sandwiched in like sardines. Getting off, away from the dust and fumes, was the best part of the trip.

Leaving the bus we discovered terrain far different from what we had seen in the Galapagos so far, rolling hills covered with umbrella-like tree ferns and Scalesia trees whose limbs were softly wrapped in lichen.

Carlos, an ornithologist, had come to guide us and to photograph birds for an upcoming lecture tour in the United States. The most spectacular he pointed out, a vermillion flycatcher, was a blood red dot of feathers, perched on a barbed wire fence.

Next Carlos showed us tortoise paths that suggested mini-bull dozers had been running through the tall grass. Without a place to hide on our approach, the tortoises retracted their heads into their cara-paces, this movement accompanied by a hissing sound as the air was partially forced out of their lungs.

Oct 3: While we were ashore filling up jugs with brackish green water for showers, we ran into the Port Captain to whom we confided our trouble with intestinal afflictions. Barbara and I each spent two days in bed with fever and chills. We had cleared out the previous day so he was surprised to see us again. He understood our predicament but couldn't help laughing as we communicated mostly in pantomime.

Later that afternoon a local resident in a speed boat stopped by the *Mahina Tiare* and, after looking at our homeport on the transom, asked: "What part of Friday Harbor are you from?" We explained that being such a small town (1,500 people), it didn't really have too many different parts. He then wanted to know if we'd ever met his ex-wife, Jane. Barbara told him she had rented office space to her. Franklin Angermeyer responded with a broad smile, then invited us to his after hours cabaret where he conveyed the story of an escape from Nazi Germany by three close relatives.

Disgusted with what they saw as the dangerous rise to power of a mad Bavarian, the Angermeyer brothers sold everything in 1935 and, saying good-bye to their family in Germany, bought a small sailboat. The boat was full of dry rot, but somehow made it to England where they bought a better boat. Sailing across the Atlantic, through the Panama Canal to the Galapagos, they arrived as the war was heating up.

The three brothers married local women and started a new life. Franklin's father, one of those brothers and now seventy-something, dresses in bright Indian clothes and wears his white hair long. His little stone house, on a sea wall near the dinghy landing, sits on the west side of Academy Bay. He enjoys meeting visiting cruisers.

Oct. 4: We tidied the boat for sea, then set sail for Fernandina Island. Around midnight we sailed past the lights of Villamil on the western point of Isabela Island.

Several of the guides had encouraged us to stop at Fernandina and Isabela islands. Stay on the tourist trails and don't disturb any plants or wildlife, they advised, and your visit wouldn't have a negative impact. Arriving at Tagus Cove (Isabela Island) on a broad reach just before dark, we were so tired that all we could manage was a dinner of freeze dried chicken stew, then make the bed and fall in.

Oct. 5, Barbara: I started this morning off in tears for no apparent reason. Maybe the amoebas from the dysentery have affected my brain. The little yellow squares of freeze-dried scrambled eggs tasted like sea water and had the consistency of foam rubber. Our tank water is tasting weird again. We have to boil all our water and soak all vegetables in iodine for half an hour.

After breakfast we rowed the Avon toward the concrete landing made for the launch from the charter boats. Tagus Cove is world-famous for all of the ships and yachts names that have been carved into or painted on the rocks around the bay. We recognized several, including *Dove*, (Robin Lee Graham, the youngest circumnavigation), *Yankee* (Irving Johnson's schooner), *Svaap* (William Robinson of Tahiti), and *Migrant* (old friends). The oldest we saw was carved in 1847, probably from a whaling ship out of New England. The area is now part of the national park, so we didn't add *Mahina Tiare* to the lists. And we stuck to the marked trail. Our trail led up past stands of aromatic silver-barked palo santo trees to the rim of an azure crater lake. Further up the trail we came to a ridge with an expansive view of "Caleta Black" Bay, and acres of lava fields from Darwin Crater, one of Isabela's active volcanoes.

After returning to *Mahina Tiare*, a swift four-mile reach brought us to Punta Espinosa on Fernandina Island. We landed the dinghy at a designated tourist area, on a beach littered with sea lions. Two newborn pups played while their mother dozed. About two feet long, amber colored, their flippers had fur on the outside and a soft looking black leather on the inside. It tickled when they sniffed at my hands.

Flightless cormorants, wings extended, looked like a fringe of tattered laundry hung out to dry at the water's edge. They are an endemic species whose survival is not dependent on the ability to fly away from predators or to their food source, thus their wings have atrophied.

John: Several years ago in New Zealand waters I saw blue penguins. Ever since I have dreamed of seeing penguins again in their natural environment. I even considered sailing to Antarctica. Naturalists had told us that Punta Espinoza contained the majority of the Islands' scarce penguin population, so we spent hours in the dinghy exploring every inch of shoreline. At dusk we spotted some white specks against the black lava in a tidal lagoon. Penguins, sure enough. They were tiny, around 14 inches, and were hopping about on the rocks on webbed feet. When they noticed us they plopped into the water and — presto — turned into ducks. With necks erect, heads parallel to the water and bodies floating on the surface, they looked and swam like ducks. These birds are shy and scarce since the warm waters of El Nino in '82 and

'83 diminished their food supply.

What are penguins doing on top of the equator? Frigid waters flow up the coast of South America from the southern tip of the continent. These nutrient rich waters support abundant sea life which in turn supports the seabird, penguin and sea lion populations. Any changes in currents — several converge at the Galapagos — cause major climatic changes that drastically affect plants and animals.

Oct. 8, Barbara: We are still feeling a little sick from our bout with the local water-borne bug and haven't been putting much energy into cooking. Tonight I thought I'd remedy this — no canned or freeze-dried for dinner; instead, fresh fish. Some funny fish have hung out under the boat the entire time we've been anchored in the Galapagos. They are scaleless, up to a foot long, have boxy heads with beetle brows and raised suction cup mouths. Extremely curious, they devour anything from bits of sponge to kitchen scraps.

The *Svanhild* crew said these fish had eaten the grass around their water line, were easy to catch and good to eat. They followed John around like puppies as he scrubbed the bottom, occasionally nibbling on his diving mask. He had to shoo them away from his head when they got too friendly. I grabbed a pail, threw in some carrot scraps as bait and dropped it over the side. The fish came right to the surface for my bait, but weren't so obliging as to swim into the pail. Then John grabbed the gaff hook and nabbed one easily on the first swipe. The fish, making horrible gasping sounds, immediately blew up like a rubber ball. The next five swipes with the gaff netted two more fish. That was enough for me; our agreement was, if John caught and killed, I'd clean. He had done his best to kill them, but when I reached in for the first fish they all still squirmed. John said they might keep flopping for hours. Great. I picked up one fish but it wriggled and squirted out of my hands. I finally cornered it in the scuppers. Pinning him down to the cutting board with a knife, I apologized for what I was about to do, then proceeded to filet my first fish. To my dismay the further down his body I went with the knife, the more he flopped. The next fish was larger and easier, but there wasn't much meat on him either. I threw back the third fish.

The fish, sauteed in butter with onions, lemon and garlic, tasted great, but it was hardly worth the trouble of catching and cleaning. I liked them better as pets.

While reading through a cruising medicine book the following day, I came across a passage which made me glad our fish harvest was so small. I learned that puffer fish have the remarkable ability to inflate themselves like balloons by swallowing large quantities of water or air. They lack ordinary scales. Some puffer fish have spines, thorns, or naked skin and are encased in a bony boxlike covering. *"Never eat a fish that blows itself up like a balloon. Puffer fish poisoning is a violent biotoxin, the most toxic parts of the fish are the skin, liver, ovary and intestines,"* (none of which we ate). We didn't get sick and decided not to take chances with strange fish in the future, regardless of what the Norwegians said.

Oct. 9: John and I took the dinghy to the nearest white sand beach this morning, observing green turtles returning to the sea after laying their eggs on shore. When we arrived back at *Mahina Tiare* the wind had shifted, causing the anchor chain to wrap around sharp submerged lava boulders. Incoming swells were jerking the chain taut, finally snapping the rope bridle that went from a deck cleat to the chain with a loud BANG! Breakers of several feet in height now hemmed us in on both sides, and what had been a sheltered, calm anchorage an hour earlier was now a dangerous lee shore.

Preparing for a quick departure if necessary, we hoisted the Avon on deck, deflated it, removed the floorboards and stacked them forward of the mast. As the boat heeled to a sudden gust of wind the floorboards slipped off the cabin toward the toe rail and sea. I reached for them, getting a tenuous grasp as I was flung backward against the rigging. I ended up sprawled on the deck with my legs pointing skyward. But the floorboards were saved and I was none the worse for my aerobatics.

Oct. 11: All last night we pitched and rolled, so I was grateful when we weighed anchor this morning bound for Easter Island and what John assured me would be a much easier passage than the one to the Galapagos. But we were leaving on a Friday again; after our last Friday departure we had met up with Hurricane Javier.

Looking back on the barren, mist-shrouded volcanic islands as we sailed away, our thoughts were of the inquisitive animals. Every day we spent exploring seemed highlighted by one particular species; one day it was marine iguanas, the next day hawks, followed by turtles, tortoises, land iguanas, lava and swallowtail gulls, and penguins. Man is a relative newcomer to the Galapagos Islands, and except for a few settlements his influence is not readily seen.

By contrast, the 1,900-mile journey ahead will take us to Rapa Nui or Easter Island. Also volcanic in origin and more remote and less visited than the Galapagos, Easter Island's fascination lies in her past civilization — a civilization that vanished as quickly as it appeared, taking with it the secret of its thousand huge stone statues and hieroglyphic writings.

Chapter 4

NARROW ESCAPE FROM THE NAVEL

John: Under way by 7:45 a.m., we had to motorsail a few hours to get clear of the lee of Fernandina Island. The seas were choppy due to the strong currents and waves refracting off Isabela and Fernandina. Not able to steer a course of 205° directly for Easter Island; the best we could hold was between 250° and 260°. The night turned pretty bumpy. Around 2:00 a.m. the wind dropped, the seas mellowed out. By morning the wind had shifted, allowing us to steer 225°. I wish the wind would back to the southeast as it's shown on the Pilot Charts. That would allow a direct and shorter course.

I cleaned and greased the outboard motor, then succeeded in dropping a socket overboard and snapping off the tension screw on the motor mount. Barbara partially compensated with a great dinner of fresh hot corn bread, soup and cole slaw.

Oct. 12, Barbara: I spent the day reading *Merck Manual,* trying to glean information on the amoebas and *Dr. Cohen's Healthy Sailor Book* to try and find the best way to treat our suspect drinking water. I ended up being horrified by the numerous parasites the human body can play host to, many of which can be picked up in the places we have been, and will be, visiting.

Dr. Cohen's book presented an array of ingeniously venomous marine plants and animals, everything from stonefish and stingrays, which hide in sandy shallows, to lethal cone shells, poison snakes and sharks. The Doc takes some of the fun out of swimming, shell collecting, or even wading.

Cohen's chapter on sailing psychology was both amusing and informative. John and I can relate to the sense that other people are on board when actually it's only the two of us. My favorite account of this phenomenon is from Vito Dumas who once thought he overheard conversation coming from the forward locker of his boat while singlehanding from France to South America. *"Listen,"* began a voice *with a strange Spanish accent, "I'm going to look for something to eat."*

"Shut up, he'll hear you!" replied the second voice.

"No, he won't!" Although there was no way two men could fit in his forward locker, Dumas, when able to leave his position at the tiller, checked the locker. Still convinced he had heard the two men talking, Dumas concluded they must have swum away.

This is my second long ocean passage and contrary to what I thought, each passage takes on its own character. The color and temperature of the water, wave patterns and steepness of the swells seem to vary infinitely. True, this is the same boat on which we sailed down the North American coast, but now we are making the passage from the Galapagos to Easter Island. The fabled trade winds fill our sails on a beam reach — steady, constant, reliable, and yes, it is different in both subtle and obvious ways. It takes a bad passage to make a good one appreciated.

Oct. 14, John: The wind keeps shifting, forcing us to sail closer to the wind. The seas are confused and reefing the mainsail helps steady things out a bit.

Oct. 15, Barbara: I was overly optimistic about the good weather. We've had squalls much of today, and the trip is becoming more difficult by the day. Increasingly I hear the sound of water rushing by the hull. I listen to banshee-like screams as the wind vibrates in the rigging. Then THUD, a wave strikes our port bow. Spray flies over the deck and hits the windshield and dodger. *Mahina Tiare* heaves and twists in response, as if reeling from a powerful slap in the face. I feel guilty about wanting time to pass, about doing nothing constructive with myself. I look forward to sleep. I think of the *Tao Te Ching*, which states, *"A good traveler has no fixed plans and is not intent on arriving."* I am not being a good traveler.

At 5:00 a.m. a thick mass of black clouds caps the sky except for a little patch where the setting moon lights the horizon. The swift black

46

Fixing the windvane's control line while the electric autopilot steers

waves show their silhouettes against it.

A weld broke on the self-steering vane this morning, where one of the control lines fastens to its rudder. We immediately rounded up into the wind, and John set the electric auto-pilot on. By leaning way out over the transom while I held onto his legs, John managed to tie the line around the vane's rudder shaft. It is working well now. I try not to think about what it would be like to hand steer down here without a vane.

Oct. 16, John: The wind continued to increase today, reaching 25 to 35 knots, with 12 to 14-foot seas. We hit 7.2 knots of boat speed during an early morning squall. This is supposed to be a light-air passage. Wow!

Barbara: I cried today, wanting the noise and motion of the boat to stop and give my tired senses a rest. The waves were large and frightening when they hit us the wrong way. It seemed the sea was doing its best to dampen our spirits by throwing buckets of water at us, spraying the cockpit, causing everything below to levitate. While making dinner, a big wave sent a two-gallon tin of freeze-dried peas flying. The plastic top of the can popped off, showering the cabin with thousands of dry green pellets. I couldn't help laughing and the sound of my laughter surprised me. I'd not laughed in three days. I wasn't sure if it was because the thousands of peas cascading around the cabin was funny or it was out of frustration. Whichever, I've been finding dried peas everywhere since.

Oct. 17: I've been reading *Blue Highways* by William Least Heat Moon: "*Sitting full in the moment, I practiced on the god-awful difficulty of just paying attention. It's a contention of Heat Moon's — believing as he does any traveler who misses the journey misses about all he is going to get — that a man becomes his attentions. His observations and curiosities, they make and remake him.*"

This sentiment is why I felt guilty wishing away an uncomfortable passage. How can I assign value to some time and not to other time? It is all part of the journey.

At sunset we changed from a small working jib to storm jib and John rolled the third reef into the mainsail, the same sail combination we had used during the hurricane. We had been reducing sail for three days as the squalls chased us southwest. Tonight the elements have proved the most dramatic of this passage. The dark blue walls of water on our beam seemed from far away, incessant as if rolled off an assembly line at a cosmic wave factory. They showed frothy crests and white patches on their steep sides.

Squall clouds, whose fuzzy forms look like gray ghosts rushing at us, obliterate the cheerful lemon moon. The boat rolls violently from side to side. I am tired. I have given up expecting conditions to get better; it has been going on too long to get upset.

Oct. 18: I woke up from an afternoon nap to find John smiling at me from the opposite settee; sun, blue skies; calmer seas prevailed. I feel ashamed that I wished the passage time to pass faster.

Oct. 19: The sunshine and calm seas of yesterday were short-lived. We spent this day threading our way through a line of squalls. In the afternoon a rogue wave smacked us on the beam so hard that the eight-quart stainless steel pressure cooker locked on the gimballed kerosene stove, flew off, hit my ankle, then bounced up and smashed my knee. Sometimes I feel I'm participating in a slap-stick routine.

Oct. 20, John: The winds are finally easing. At 3:00 a.m. our speed was down to three knots, so for the first time in several days I am able to lower the storm jib and hoist the small working jib; also knock out two of the three reefs which means bringing our speed up to 41/2 knots. I didn't want to hoist too much sail since the sky still looked unsettled, more squalls possible. I'd rather sail a little slower and not worry about getting out of bed in the middle of the night (when I'm off watch) to make sail changes.

Oct. 21: Finally, good sailing conditions and we averaged 5 knots all day. I was able to roll out the last reef in the main. After vacuuming and putting the cushions in the sun to air, we spent much of the day reading. In the evening we talked via ham radio with Seattle friends, Paul and Karen on *Nutra*. They left the West Coast a year ahead of us and are now nearing Rarotonga in the Cook Islands. Karen's pregnancy is making her seasick much of the time. She plans to fly to New Zealand from Rarotonga and Paul hopes to pick up crew before sailing on to join her.

Oct. 25, Barbara: I finished Thor Heyerdahl's *AKU-AKU* today and now am anxious to see the mysterious stone statues and underground caves of Easter Island which he describes in the book. The seas are calm, the evening sky studded with stars. I experience a strong feeling of anticipation, and no longer feel like we live in the middle of nowhere, going nowhere. I will spend my three hour night watch designing and cutting out the fabric for a Chilean courtesy flag to fly from the shrouds, a requirement for all foreign yachts.

Oct. 26: At 10:20 a.m. the gently sloping volcanic hills of Easter Island appeared on the horizon, beautiful and alluring from the distance. At sunset we approached the sleepy looking village of Hangaroa. Its few houses and palms were conspicuous against the barren slopes. Smoke billowed from a fiery orange patch on a ridge of Rano Kao volcano at the southern tip of the island. We wondered whether the volcano remained active. As night fell the orange line of fire extended, glowing bright against the black starry sky. Using binoculars we discovered that it was only a brush fire, not a lava flow. The anchorage off the village was only slightly rolly, and the thought of an uninterrupted quiet night of sleep together seemed a luxurious reward after our long and difficult passage.

John: After anchoring, we sit in the cockpit savoring a glass of wine and enjoying the last streaks of the sunset enhanced by the exotic sights and smells of land. I am filled with happiness and anticipation. Happiness because we have made it to the island that was the focus of our cruise — the place to which I had proposed sailing with Barbara on our first date — and full of anticipation at exploring this remote place and meeting its people. On the one hand, I feel like putting the dinghy together and rushing in to explore the village tonight; on the other hand I am tired, and am content to enjoy the moment. I think of our first date and the book on Easter Island I had shown Barbara in Friday Harbor. Now we are together here. Indeed, things are very right with my world.

Oct. 27 : Te-Pito-te-Henua, meaning the navel-of-the-earth, is what Easter Islanders have traditionally called their triangular island, 13 miles at its longest point and ten miles at its widest. Having sailed here as the first islanders did, we feel the name is appropriate. Situated at 27° south and 109° west, approximately 2,500 miles west of Chile and 900 miles east of tiny Pitcairn Island, it is often referred to as one of the most isolated islands in the world.

It's not a hospitable place. Easter Island has a well-deserved reputation for dangerous anchorages and has long been dreaded by navigators for its shifty and often violent winds. Until the construction of an airport in 1966, the island was visited only once or twice a year by a government supply ship from Valapariso, Chile. Now, in addition to the infrequent ship's visits, there are one to two flights a week by Lan-Chile 707s, bringing food, supplies and a few passengers.

Barbara: Early this morning the Hangaroa Port Captain (a Chilean naval officer) with a five-person entourage approached us over the lumpy seas in a weathered wooden fishing launch.

I ran to the head to get dressed but saw a face at deck level, outside the head window. John was yelling for me to come on deck and help fend them off but it was too late. I heard a heart-stopping crash. An 18-inch piece of our teak toe rail was split off as the bow of the launch caught under the rail and the surge lifted it sharply. The Port Captain's assistant continued to try and hold their bow too close to us. He gave me a weak smile through the head window in response to my dismayed expression.

We managed to help the five officials aboard without further mishap, even though both boats were rolling heavily in the unprotected anchorage. They were all polite and, between our Spanish and their English, we were able to satisfy all of their questions. We were never able to figure out (however) what official capacities were assigned

50

to three of the men.

After they left, we inflated our Avon sportboat and motored through the chop around the corner and between several sets of rocks and breakers into the relatively calm and tiny man-made Hanga Piko harbor. We measured the water's depth inside the harbor, hoping that we could squeeze in with our 4'7" draft. We tied the Avon alongside a handsome old 20-foot open fishing skiff. Its owner, a jovial Chilean fisherman named Ricardo, spoke some English and quickly introduced us to the harbormaster. They carried on an intense conversation in Spanish, the upshot being they thought *Mahina Tiare* might squeak into the harbor. They said it would be safer than staying anchored in the open ocean, unless the wind backed around to the west and blew straight into the harbor. When I asked the harbormaster if he would mind coming out to *Mahina Tiare* to lead us in, he jumped into the Avon at once.

John: The trip in the dinghy back to *Mahina Tiare* was a wet one, straight into the wind and chop, and slow; we simply couldn't plane with three people and our 7 1/2 hp motor. Once aboard, the harbormaster offered to help and I showed him how to operate the manual anchor windlass. He soon tired of its modest speed and pulled up our 200 feet of chain and 35-pound CQR anchor hand over hand, as if they were toys.

The harbormaster had pointed out the shallowest spots as we came out in the dinghy, and I was grateful to have him in the cockpit as we attempted the narrow entrance. I tried to enter the harbor as slowly as possible, but the following seas pushed us in faster than I would have liked. We hit bottom once, at the entrance, with a solid thud!

Once inside, there wasn't enough depth to motor a 180 degrees to get the bow headed out toward the entrance. So I jumped in the Avon and slowly pushed the stern around while Barbara and several people who had gathered on the wharf tried to keep our bow pulpit from getting crunched against the rough concrete wall. Once we had *Mahina Tiare* turned around, we started rigging mooring lines, eleven in all and totaling over a thousand feet. They crisscrossed the harbor like a spider web and would keep us from grinding against the concrete wall or from being swept onto rocks only two boat lengths astern of us.

Barbara: While we secured the mooring lines and dinghy, a middle-aged woman with the generous mouth and soft features of a Polynesian, appeared from the burgeoning crowd. She was waving and yelling, "Hey, I'm an American — come have a beer!"

The lines secured, the woman — her name was Monica — lined up someone to guard the boat. She explained, "Easter Island people, they steal. You have to have a guard." She told us that the battery had been stolen from her truck, parked right in front of her house, that morning. Apparently this is not a new problem — drawings from La Perouse's visit in 1789 depict islanders snatching the unattended hats of French naval officers.

Monica introduced us to Mario, a thin, handsome 75-year-old man who already had been hired to guard the generator within 50 feet of where we had tied up. Mario said he would gladly watch our boat any time, and that we need not pay him.

An ancient red Chevy pickup that Ricardo had borrowed waited for us. We drove a half-mile, on an unpaved red dirt road, into the middle of Hangaroa town. Stopping at the only restaurant, the Iorana Korua, Monica and Ricardo insisted on buying us drinks.

Monica then took us to her three-room plywood cabin so that we could make a collect phone call to the States. Two months had passed since we had checked our bank balance or received any mail. She was one of the fifty residents to have a telephone. Instead of a phone book, they simply had a sheet with the names and numbers of all the people on the island with phones. For as long as we were on Easter Island, Monica offered to be our guide. We were Americans and she, married to an American and having lived in Virginia for fifteen years, considered herself an American also.

Monica pointed to several faded color photos. "These are my children, five from four different men." She explained that when life became hectic due to too many suitors, she accepted the marriage proposal of an American satellite technician. She moved to Virginia, leaving the care of four of her children to their fathers and aunts. She was from the Pakarati family, her father and uncles were mentioned in Thor Heyerdahl's book, *AKU-AKU*, as knowledgeable about former crafts, fishing techniques and farming on the island. "I was thirteen when Heyerdahl first came to Pascua," Monica told us. "Me and my family helped him find the statues. I think my people came from South

America."

The question of where Easter Island's inhabitants came from is one of the mysteries that have intrigued archaeologists, anthropologists and ethnologists for years. Based on linguistic and cultural characteristics, as well as legends and studies of stone adzes and other tools, most scientists believe the people came from Eastern Polynesia, probably arriving in two migrations, one from the Marquesas and one from Mangareva.

Heyerdahl, citing certain plants found on Easter Island which are

Monica Pakarati

indigenous to South America, and stone block work and sculptures similar to those found in the Andes, theorizes that South American Natives drifted or sailed to Easter Island on balsa wood rafts. To substantiate this theory of east-west migration, Heyerdahl built the raft *Kon-Tiki* in Peru in the 1950's and sailed it from South America to the Tuamotu Islands. The voyage of *Kon-Tiki* is documented in his book by the same name.

Oct. 28: Monica and Ricardo decided this was the day for us to tour the island. We contributed the money for gas, they enlisted their Chilean friend, Fernando as driver and his '69 Red Chevy pickup as conveyance. The doors wouldn't quite shut, the glove box fell open at regular intervals, and the transmission frequently popped out of gear as we bumped our way along the primitive roads. John bounced around in the back, getting covered with fine, red volcanic dust. The rest of us squeezed in the front seat, laughed a lot, sort of a nervous reaction. Other than Monica, we didn't understand all of what each other was saying, or whether the car and road had anything in common.

Ricardo, a Chilean, had been living in Brazil for seven years where he worked as a Fiat and Volkswagen car salesman. He also owned a sportfishing charter boat. He was on Easter Island for an extended vacation, and was making a little money by fishing in an outboard-powered launch he'd purchased and selling his catch to the stores in Hangaroa. He'd visited Miami and Disney World and proudly told us about his '67 Mercury stored at a friend's house in Florida.

Fernando was fair skinned, stocky and a wheeler-dealer. He never told anyone what he did back in Santiago, but he had arrived by plane with several hundred pounds of frozen beef and was trying to make money by selling the meat to the locals. Few people had money for beef and the two hotels on the island were empty. He either gave it away to friends or traded for meals and beer.

Once we left town we saw no trees, just grassy slopes studded with volcanic boulders which had tumbled down from their peaks to end up in piles along the rugged shoreline.

Monica explained that, despite the rich volcanic soil, the rock-strewn terrain combined with the constant wind prevents much other than grass from growing. The soil is porous, and water from the frequent violent rain squalls does not stay on the surface but collects in underground caves, lava tubes and grottoes, or runs underground into the sea. In the past islanders had collected their drinking water at the base of seaside cliffs, which gave rise to the belief by early European visitors that the islanders drank seawater.

We stopped along the coast where four giant statues, (moai) had been pushed over and lay face-down in a rubble of small stones. Their topknots, huge stones carved from red volcanic rock, were strewn before them. Each of the moai had previously rested on a stone platform called an "ahu". This ahu had a small compartment in the

middle, which had probably been covered by one of the toppled moai. The bleached skull and bones nestled in the compartment seemed to jump out of the gray rock surroundings. Monica said, "It's a joke. Someone put those bones there. They aren't old." We knew that some of the ahu were for burial, so we weren't sure what the joke was.

Moai buried up to their necks on the slopes of Rano Raraku

The island's ahu are constructed of large hewn stone blocks, terminating at each end with stone ramps. The largest on the island is 435 feet long and 12 feet high. Some are built with a specific orientation to the sun. Although ahu are of several different designs, all are stylistically similar to maraes, religious platforms found in Polynesia. Archaeologists estimate that the first of these religious platforms was built on Easter Island before 800 A.D. At least three hundred ahu can be found on the island, something that suggests many small, separate population groups scattered along the coastline. Often the remains of stone-lined earth ovens, (umus) and round stone hen houses, (hara moas), are located nearby.

The stone foundations of narrow houses, 60 to 150 feet long, perhaps communal houses, are often found in front of the ahu. Early Europeans described these reed houses as resembling overturned canoes. It is believed that the ahu were in existence long before the moai were erected, and that the sculpting of the moai took place between 1100 and 1689 A.D. The many existing ahu provided a convenient base for the carvers' moai. Varying in appearance, the moai are thought to represent revered persons. The majority represent males; only two smaller female moai have been found. Looking at the ruins today, it is difficult to imagine anyone existing in these arid, barren places. Hangaroa village, with its few trees and gardens, is presently the only inhabited place on the island.

Monica hurried us along to Rano Rararku, birthplace of the moai. A long extinct volcano, Rano Raraku's steep cliffs are alive with moai in various stages of carved completion. The longer we looked at the mountain, the more moai we saw, their long telltale noses and rounded stomachs jutting out from the rock face. Over three hundred moai still lay in this immense workshop. The largest, if it were completed, would be 60 feet tall.

Several completed statues patiently wait at the base of the volcano, the grassy slopes covering all but their heads. Some lay face down, arms pinned to their sides, while others are on their backs, staring up at the sky. Often it is not the size or shape of the moai which captures the imagination but the unlikely positions in which they are found.

Many mysteries surround the moai. How were statues weighing up to 100 tons transported over rocky terrain to rest on 15 foot high ahus as far as eight miles away? How were they lowered from the rim of the volcano, hundreds of feet down to its base? Why was their workshop so suddenly abandoned, tools scattered around partially completed figures? These and many other questions concerning the fairly high level of technology achieved by this Stone Age culture still confront scientists whose task is made more difficult by the kidnapping and murder of all Easter Island noblemen and chiefs in the mid-19th century. Over half the population were carried off by force to work as

Restored moai atop an ahu, Anakena

slaves in Peruvian guano mines under abysmal conditions. Those who were returned, after intervention by the Catholic Bishop of Tahiti, brought back smallpox which decimated all but 175 of the residents in 1871. These events account for the lack of local knowledge of relatively recent Easter Island history.

As we climbed the slopes of Rano Raraku, Monica theorized that boredom caused her ancestors to create the moai, "Here they were stuck on this island. So someone said, let's get to work and build something." When we asked her how they were transported, she replied, "They walked."

From the rim of the volcano we could see the deep blue crater lake below surrounded by beige-colored bluffs — a colorful scene despite the gray, drizzly sky.

Bumping across from Rano Raraku on the south side of the island to the north coast, we stopped at the Riviera of Easter Island, Anakena. The water in the bay was a transparent green; a white sand beach was bordered by palm trees under which picnic tables had been placed. Anakena is an official park but we were the only visitors. King Hotu-Matua, the legendary Polynesian discoverer of Easter Island, landed his fleet of canoes here. Five restored moai sitting atop their ahu stare inland from the edge of the beach. A solitary moai, restored by Thor Heyerdahl to its vertical position using local hand labor, stands off to one side.

We hurried to the truck as a squall struck and made it back to Fernando's house in Hangaroa just as the radiator boiled over.

Dinner was waiting for us, a mound of thin gray beefsteaks Fernando had flown in. We ate on "borrowed" plates, our silverware and plastic cups also borrowed from the Lan-Chile airplane. After dinner Fernando gave me two cowrie shell necklaces which had been the only decorations hanging on the bare aqua walls of his rented home. Our party continued later at the expensive, but empty, Hanga Roa Hotel where we were treated to drinks paid for with more of Fernando's beef and where we watched a bit of video-taped Chilean television.

At sunset we left the hotel in a happy state of exhaustion and walked the half-mile to *Mahina Tiare*, the boat patiently waiting for us in Hanga Piko Harbor.

Oct. 29.: Hard to get out of bed in a cold cabin with the drumming of a torrential downpour. Firing up the kerosene heater for the first time in months, we tried to dry the boat and our damp clothes. Dressed in foul weather gear, we headed for town carrying empty jerry jugs for fuel and knapsacks for vegetables. As soon as we entered the large shed that served as a market, a slim, attractive woman approached us and introduced herself as Marianna. Her coloring and features appeared more Spanish than Polynesian, and she explained that her ancestors were from the ariki, or noble class of Easter Island.

The moai are thought to have been effigies of members of the ariki who, according to island legend, had long, aquiline noses and fairer skin and hair than the commoners who were forced to sculpt the statues. There is conjecture, but no evidence, that the ariki were of South American descent while the commoners were Polynesians.

Marianna prepared a jicama, a white crunchy vegetable, topped with a squeeze of lime and a pinch of salt, for us to sample. It tasted like a cross between a radish and a cucumber. She was a great saleswoman and we were eager customers, the vegetables were far fresher and more varied than those we'd purchased in the Galapagos.

Marianna led us around the corner to the tourist area where several island women stood dressed in winter coats of the '50s and '60s. They stood among tables of wood and stone carvings, shell necklaces and faded postcards. The women wanted to trade our spare clothing and shoes for up to half the price of their curios. We were the only tourists in the market – and probably on the island.

We met Marianna's tall and silent teenage son, Marco, who stood in the shadows looking mysterious in a long dark wool cape. He, like his mother, was a wood and stone carver.

After buying 50 postcards from Marianna, she gave us a rongo-rongo, a small wooden board covered with carved pictograph motifs, somewhat similar to Egyptian hieroglyphics. It had taken her two days to carve the board with a shark's tooth. The rongo-rongo is a replica of the boards used by priests in the past, the true meaning of which is now a mystery. Most likely it is a mnemonic device for chanting. She also gave John a 14-inch stone replica of a moai that Marco had carved. Thus began the long saga of gift exchange between Marianna and the crew of the *Mahina Tiare.*

Leaving the market, our bags laden with vegetables and carvings, we stopped at a small store to buy eggs and bread. Marianna followed us in, whispering that the food prices were cheaper at the co-op down the street. Town consisted of a bakery, a few small food stores and curio shops.

We stopped by the Port Captain's office on the way back to the boat to look through his log book. Only seven boats had stopped at Easter Island that year — two supply ships, two cruise ships, two French and one Australian sailboat. We were the first American boat in two years, and the average length of stay of the other boats was two days. The last boat to visit had been an Australian ketch, a father and his two teenage sons aboard. The boys had befriended a 17-year-old local boy who sailed with them to Tahiti, then flew back. The last yacht before the Aussies was a 28-foot plywood sloop from Tahiti that was now "on the hard" near where we were moored in Hanga Piko. The port captain told us that the skipper, while anchored off Hangaroa, had been having a wild time at the disco the night before. He didn't wake up when the wind shifted the next morning. His anchor had dragged, smashing his boat on the lava boulders on the beach. The harbormaster had tried to warn the Frenchman on the VHF but, without a boat, was powerless to do anything else. Several local fishermen in their out-board-powered skiffs managed to pull the boat out of the breakers when the sea subsided, then drag it over into Hanga Piko, sans keel, where the skipper sold it for salvage.

Arriving back at *Mahina Tiare,* we found seven persons standing near admiring her. One man had brought us a large sack of kumera (Polynesian sweet potatoes) and squash. After 45 minutes of answering questions and explaining that we didn't have room to take passengers to Tahiti, we went aboard for a quick dinner, then fell asleep exhausted by the day's adventures.

Oct. 31: Besides growing vegetables and carving, Marianna had several horses to rent out. This morning she and Marco showed up trailing an extra horse and a bridle. I rode with Marco; John and Marianna had their own horses. We had planned on renting just the horses, but we got two guides thrown in with the deal.

Our first stop, about a mile from town, was a series of underground caves whose entrances were from a sunken pit. Protected from the constant winds, a thick clump of bushes and banana trees grew in the depression. Water was slowly dripping from the ceiling of the cave. The hollow sound echoed from the smooth lava rock, the cave smelled of ferns and damp earth. The cool water tasted sweet. Marianna said: "This is a drinking cave. There are also sleeping caves, refuge caves, and bleaching caves."

Today sleeping caves are still used. Marianna often rents horses by the week to Tahitian travelers who tour the island on horseback and each night sleep in a different cave. In the past, young girls spent months in the bleaching caves to lighten their skin and during times of civil war, the islanders used underground caves and lava tubes as hideouts.

Our day in the hard, unpadded wooden saddles ended after we had seen several restored archaeological sites. We slid down from our horses to hobble back to *Mahina Tiare.*

Nov. 2: Late this afternoon we decided to visit the Rano Kau volcanic crater and the historical site of Orongo village. We hitched a ride to the crater rim and stared down at the green mat of reeds on the surface of the crater lake. Circles of blue water dotted the reed coverings. It is in this moist protected crater that some of the plants used for food and clothing in the past still grow today.

The Orongo village site, perched on the narrow rim of the crater, is a sacred site on Easter Island. In the setting sun the stylized carvings of birdmen, spirits, and fertility symbols were strikingly shadowed and seemed to dance. Hundreds of these deeply etched, finely finished petroglyphs are incised into the reddish basaltic rock. We explored the network of small houses built with stacked flat stones and sod roofs. Near the cliff's edge was a semi-circle formed by carved boulders and the wall of one of the stone dwellings. The series of small square entrances facing seaward intrigued me. I was eager to explore the interior rooms — they appeared dry and relatively light inside. As I crouched down to enter I felt a strong, almost tangible energy radiating from the opening. Reluctant to violate that energy, I stayed outside and peered in. Could this energy be the mana (power) of the birdman?

Legend tells of the yearly celebration of the cult of the birdmen in the village of Orongo until the mid-1880's, (when the islanders were kidnapped). Priests responsible for the ceremony that chose the birdmen lived at Orongo year round. In July, the general population gathered on the slopes that led to Orongo. Feasts, dancing and sacrifices took place while they anxiously awaited the selection of the year's birdman. Representing their masters, servants of the island's chiefs would risk their lives climbing down the 1,000-foot cliffs to the sea, then swim out through the heavy surf and shark-infested waters to one of three small islets a half-mile offshore. Swimming over the reefs and through the breakers, the servants would settle in grottoes on the islet to await the return of the migratory black terns. The object was to get the first egg laid on the island before anyone else. This accomplished, the sacred egg was tied to the lucky man's head with strips of leather after which, surrounded by his competitors, he swam back to Easter Island. He climbed the steep cliffs and presented the egg to his master who then became birdman for the year. As birdman, he was considered the embodiment of the supreme creator spirit, *make-make*. He personified fertility and would ensure the return of the terns and the laying of eggs. The birdman, due to his sacred position, had to spend a year alone in a small stone hut surrounded by severe taboos.

It was dark by the time we started the two hour hike down the mountain. Moonlight made the road easy to follow. We made it back to *Mahina Tiare* but, charged with the excitement of exploring this sacred site, it took us awhile to fall asleep.

Nov. 3, John: Knowing that our luck with good weather at notoriously stormy Easter Island wouldn't hold forever, we started preparing mentally and physically for a quick departure. I hoisted myself aloft in our bosun's chair and was reassured to find no cracks or problems with our new rigging. Most critical to our staying inside Hanga Piko Harbor was checking the weather daily, and being prepared to leave quickly once westerly winds were forecast, winds that would make the harbor dangerously untenable. So our first stop in town was at the airport weather office where a Chilean meteorologist, Julio, interpreted the latest weatherfax chart and showed us a depression south of Tahiti that was slowly moving toward Easter Island. It would probably produce weather rough enough to force us out of Hanga Piko.

Downtown we admired an intricately carved miro-wood birdman sculpture in the shop of Hugo and Cecilia. It was over our budget, but the carvers said that they would trade with us for part of the price; we entered into negotiations. After two hours of intense bargaining we had traded two Tahitian pareus (sarongs), one radio-cassette player, one Tahitian music tape, Monoi scented oil from Tahiti, a gold male leaf necklace, a bottle of French perfume, a bed sheet and $40 U.S. cash for the carving. It was an exhausting process. Afterward Hugo invited us over to his house, in back of his workshop, for coffee and homemade cakes. He seemed very happy but slightly embarrassed by his wife's hard bargaining.

Marianna and Marco arrived on horseback around sunset, bringing the vegetables we had ordered earlier in the day. Marco, like every other teenage boy on the island, wanted to sail with us to Tahiti. When we told the boys we weren't sailing straight for Tahiti, instead spending four months sailing through the Islands of Eastern Polynesia, they thought that was even better. Easter Island has a long tradition of young men trying to get to Tahiti in small skiffs or rowboats, totally unprepared for the 2,500 mile long journey. Those who make it are heroes; the others are never heard from again.

Nov. 4: We spent part of the morning filling water tanks, filling our five gallon jugs from a hose in a crumbling old guard house, then carrying them 400 yards, tying on a line, and lowering them eight feet down from the wharf to *Mahina Tiare*.

I made my daily stop at the airport weather office and, after checking the location of the slow-moving depression, invited the weatherman, Julio Duarte, and his family over for dinner that evening.

They arrived as the wind and swells switched from NE to NNW. The swells rolling into Hanga Piko harbor caused Julio's lovely Chilean wife and daughter to turn several shades of green. They made it into the dinghy and back to shore without dinner, of course.

Nov. 5: Getting ready for our next passage, we pulled the 200 feet of primary anchor chain up on deck, then carefully restowed it just forward of the mast step. We dove into the 67-degree murky water and scrubbed the luxuriant growth off *Mahina Tiare's* bottom. I spent some time shifting rocks around under our keel and was able to make more depth by simply rolling the rocks to either side of the keel.

Nov. 6, Barbara: We had become friends with Mario, the man watching the generator and our boat when we were gone. He had fair skin, clear blue eyes and long white hair. A few tobacco-stained teeth made up his smile. He wore a frayed straw hat and long black wool cape with the collar turned up (despite the mild weather, he was always cold). We brought him hot drinks every morning and would talk. One day he said to John, "I don't have much money, but I have the beautiful sky to look at and my freedom." He pointed a long, bony finger at the sky and his eyes sparkled as he smiled. Quitting a well-paying civil service job in Santiago when he was 40 to live the life of a skier and traveler, he eventually ended up on Easter Island as a wood carver. He told us about his brother, a professor at Columbia University in New York, and about sailing off the coast of Chile in a 36-foot sloop in 1950.

The five dollars a day he received as a guard was not enough to keep him supplied with cigarettes, but the other islanders watched out for him.

Monica and Ricardo came by this morning, worried that we might have left without saying good-bye. Monica had made elaborate cowrie shell necklaces and bracelets for us and insisted we come for lunch.

After our farewell feast we stopped next door to Monica's brother house. We had hired Nicholas to carve salad tongs with moai on them. He seemed forlorn and older than his 50 years. He coughed a lot; many of the people have hacking coughs from the damp climate and years of smoking strong, roll-your-own tobacco.

John: At the airport weather office the latest weatherfax chart indicated the depression coming from the west would arrive by noon the next day. It's 20-25 knot NW winds would make our moorage in Hanga Piko untenable.

When we arrived back in the harbor, we saw that the wind had already backed from NE to north, and the conditions in the harbor were getting rougher. We spent an hour in the wind and driving rain, adjusting our dock lines and adding still more chafing gear. We made plans to leave as soon as we could get our clearance papers in the morning.

Nov. 7, 1 a.m.: We were awakened by the loud report of two of our four 5/8-inch nylon bow lines snapping. On deck, a nightmare scene. It was totally black, blowing 25 to 35 knots with driving rain. To rig new bowlines was slow and difficult work. Since all of our anchor and dock lines were in use, I had to tie the chafed lines together. The tide was extremely high, no doubt caused by the water being forced into the tiny harbor by winds that had switched to west and were blowing directly in the entrance. Huge breakers rolled through the narrow harbor entrance to crash in a cascade of spray on the concrete bulkhead 50 feet astern of *Mahina Tiare*. As our bow lifted in the breakers, then crashed down in the troughs, the loading on the dock lines and cleats was incredible. Even with nine lines, *Mahina Tiare* surged drunkenly in all directions.

I tried to get a little sleep while on anchor watch under the dodger, but at 2 a.m. the night guard said that we should leave at once if we didn't want to lose our boat. But that was impossible in the dark. I spent the next hour on deck adjusting the mooring lines and chafing gear. When particularly large breakers rolled through the harbor, they would plunge our bow under and send a wave of solid green water sweeping aft over the decks.

By 3 a.m. the situation had worsened. The tide was dropping and now in the troughs between the breakers we would hit the solid rock harbor bottom with a **thunk** that shook the entire boat, mast and rigging. I doubted that we would survive the night. If our dock lines broke again at the same time, the breakers would smash us into the concrete wall astern, and there was absolutely nothing we could do about it. Trying to motor out through the breakers in zero visibility while the keel smashed on the bottom in every trough would have been suicidal. That night, for the first time in my life, I called for help.

The Port Captain had told me that they maintained a 24-hour radio watch on Channel 16 among other marine distress frequencies. I knew from an earlier radio check that he could monitor our transmissions in his office, but that night there was no response to my calls. At 3:30 a.m. the local fishermen in their 20-foot wooden outboard fishing skiffs started struggling back into the harbor, bailing furiously to keep their open boats afloat. Ricardo's boat was the last to make it into the harbor, and he got his prop caught in our mooring line. I hung from the pulpit to help him lift our bow line clear and fend his boat off. I apologized for our line being in the way, but he said, "Don't worry about that, it looks like you need some help here!" He was soaked, exhausted and shivering. We handed him a thermos of coffee. He tied up his partially flooded boat on the shallow, semi-protected side of the harbor then drove up to the village to wake up Monica — it was 4 a.m. — so that she, too, could come down and help.

At 5 a.m. I was able to raise the Assistant Port Captain on the radio and, using my limited Spanish, requested our clearance papers and our passports stamped so that we could leave as soon as possible.

By 8 a.m. the Port Captain, his assistant, the Hanga Piko Harbor Captain, Ricardo, Monica, Mario and several fishermen were all assembled, ready to cast off our lines. Ricardo and friends had built a bonfire nearby and stayed up in case we needed help. The green uniformed Chilean Chief of Police came by and stamped our passports at the last minute; we could now legally leave. Barbara, jumping ashore to hug all our friends, saw the tears in old Mario's eyes when she said good-bye. A bottle of Gato Negro red and white Chilean wine were his parting gifts to us.

The solid Harbor Captain who had piloted us into the harbor came aboard to guide us out. We positioned friends on each of our nine mooring lines to untie them one at a time, starting with spring lines and stern lines. Meanwhile I took up some of the load by putting the engine cautiously in gear, careful not to catch any of the lines in the prop before Barbara and the Harbor Captain could get them aboard. I motored slowly, paralleling the wharf, through the breakers. Just as we reached the end of the wharf, the engine started to die and we smacked solidly on the rocky harbor bottom. (I later discovered a leak in the fuel line caused by a worn O-ring.) I increased the throttle to the maximum and the engine picked up RPMs as we smashed out through the breakers. Our friends cheered.

Ricardo had been standing by in his fishing boat in case we got stuck on the rocks. Now he followed us out until we were a quarter of a mile offshore, then came alongside to take our pilot back ashore. He came alongside too fast and from quite an angle. He smashed into us at the shrouds. We saw a chunk of wood go flying off into the water and assumed it was more of our teak toe rail. Barbara ran forward and hung out from the shrouds, fending them off and searching for the wood.

Ricardo spotted the wood and yelled to us that it was from his boat. With that he waved good-bye. The deck was a tangle of chafed and gritty dock lines, muddy footprints and a thick layer of volcanic soil that had blown off the wharf. But we had survived. We sailed into the vicious storm front with only our storm jib and deeply reefed mainsail up, crashing along at 6 knots toward tiny Pitcairn Island. Another Friday departure.

Despite Monica's warnings, we had nothing stolen from us during our visit on Easter Island; instead we had exchanged many gifts.

Chapter 5

SAILING IN THE WAKE
OF THE BOUNTY

"It seems to me that the places where men have loved or suffered keep about them always some faint aroma of something that has not wholly died. It is as though they had acquired a spiritual significance which mysteriously affects those who pass."
"Red" by W. Somerset Maugham

Nov. 16, Barbara: Mid-ocean landfalls are magical. It seems impossible that dirt and rock can withstand the constant force of wind and waves, and yet here stands Pitcairn Island — small, solitary and steep. We approached at night, the full moon cloaked in gray squall clouds, yet giving an eerie light. The half dozen lights of Adamstown seemed to wink on and off as we slid up and down the steep swells. The friendly voice of Betty Christian, making a blind call to any ships in the vicinity, came across the VHF radio. She contacted Brian Young who advised us of the best anchorage in present wind conditions. Then invited us, sight unseen, to stay with her when we arrived on the island.

We anchored in Western Harbor, paralleling 1,000-foot cliffs. I remembered the story about the four original settlers who died by falling or jumping from these cliffs.

The whistling wind and the low hiss of breakers on the jagged rocky shore were my companions as I stood anchor watch. The land seemed close and savage. Located at 130° W. longitude and 25° S. latitude, Pitcairn is more than 2,000 miles west of Santiago, Chile, 1,350 miles SE of Tahiti and 3,000 miles NE of New Zealand, her administrative center. The closest inhabited island, Mangareva, is 300 miles WNW of Pitcairn. There is no place to land a plane on rugged Pitcairn; therefore all these distances must be covered by ship.

One can understand why Fletcher Christian picked Pitcairn as his hideout from British justice. Remote and tiny it would be an unlikely spot to hunt for mutineers. In 1789 Christian led the mutiny aboard the *HMS Bounty.* He landed on Pitcairn in 1790 along with nine other mutineers, 12 Tahitian women and six Tahitian men. What first appeared as a tropical paradise to Christian soon became a nightmare. Fighting between the two very different races, alcohol, disputes over land and women caused the violent deaths of 15 people in ten years. After a decade only one man, John Adams, remained with ten Tahitian women and 26 children. Adams took the only book available to him, Fletcher Christian's Bible, and taught the children to read and write English and to live together peacefully. Eighteen years after settlement, the little colony was discovered by Captain Folger on an American sealing ship. The ship's crew were impressed by the simplicity and piety of the islanders and astonished that they spoke English.

Nov. 17: John dived to check our anchor this morning and before he could change out of his wet suit, seven men in bright yellow slickers appeared aboard one of the famous Pitcairn Island longboats. They brought all ten tons of motorized aluminum alongside and tossed us a bunch of bananas, before Brian, a young barefoot magistrate, came aboard. A powerful Tahitian-looking fellow with a wonderful sense of humor, he helped us board the pitching longboat.

We took off for Bounty Bay, sheer volcanic cliffs topped in verdant green and eroded in fascinating shapes rising steeply to our right. To the left, square black rocks called Young's Rocks rose 100 feet.

We noticed looks of alarm from the men as the coxswain steered us between Young's Rocks and the island, through the breaking surf up the crest of a wave. The longboat leapt skyward, then crashed down; spray stung my face and my upper teeth smashed against my lower teeth. One of the men shot me a concerned look, but I replied with a smile. I was enjoying myself; this was the adventure of a lifetime — following in the wake of the *Bounty.*

We surfed into Bounty Bay and veered sharply left just as I thought we might crash into the rocks ahead of us. We stopped short of the concrete landing where all 37 feet of boat was attached to a cable and hauled to the safety of the boat shed. A big yellow and red sign above us read, "WELCOME TO PITCAIRN."

I felt shy and conspicuous once we landed. It was as if we'd landed on someone's private estate. A few jokes broke the ice and the islanders soon made us feel welcome. Hitching a ride on a Honda three-wheel tractor, we were taken up the steep narrow path called "the hill of difficulty," the same path used by the mutineers when they landed. Our legs were wobbly when we met Betty Christian in front of her house.

The first order of business on Pitcairn is to make sure guests are well fed; eating is the national pastime. Betty accomplished this in her rustic kitchen on the site of her ancestor Fletcher Christian's original house. Then, wasting no time, we were given the grand island tour. The unpredictable weather, punctuated by violent wind changes, curtails many a yacht's time ashore and is responsible for dozens of lost anchors and shipwrecked sailors. Not knowing how long we could stay ashore, we tried to pack as much as we could into our first day.

So, all aboard Betty's three-wheeler and in danger of tipping over on the turns, we threaded our way up washed-out red dirt paths to a cliff from where 1,000 feet below, we watched *Mahina Tiare* dancing in her exposed anchorage. Through groves of banana trees, past pineapple patches, rows of carrots and cabbages, we wound our way around the island. Betty explained as she handed us a peach from her father's tree, "If you smoothed out the bumps, Pitcairn would take up a lot more space than one by two miles. There is lots of usable land on the hillsides and, depending on the time of year, Pitcairn gardens can produce just about any tropical or temperate weather fruit or vegetable."

Returning to Adamstown, we visited the "U"-shaped town square. The Seventh-day Adventist Church, library, dispensary, post office and town hall border the square on three sides. Beside the town hall is the bell — five rings signal the arrival of a ship and two rings is the call to prayer. In front is the *Bounty* anchor retrieved by Irving Johnson. Johnson stopped many times at Pitcairn during his seven circumnavigations aboard the *Yankee* and was much loved by the islanders. The square is neat and European in appearance but as one meanders through Adamstown, past fragrant Plumeria trees, purple morning glories and a grove of creeping Banyans, the similarities to a European village fade.

We observed many empty houses, a reminder that Pitcairn's population has dramatically declined from a high of 233 in 1937 to about 55 people today. Changes in shipping routes make it difficult and costly to get supplies to the island. Also, the lure of an easier lifestyle and available medical help inspired many islanders to move to New Zealand.

On our way to Betty's we passed the Browns' house, a sprawling affair with an open front workshop. Nig Brown and his brother Dave, wives, friends and family all sat around joking and working on what they call curios — anything from sleek woodcarvings of sharks, birds or *Bounty* replicas to baskets and painted leaves. They sell these items for modest prices to passengers on the occasional cruise ships or passing freighters that stop at Pitcairn.

When we reached Betty's, her long kitchen table was crowded with homemade breads, a roast from her freezer, fresh vegetables and a Tahitian dish called pillhai, a vegetable pudding wrapped and baked in banana leaves. Our hostess's sister, Daphne, and their four girls surrounded the table. Our preconception that Pitcairners were too devoutly religious to have fun was soon shattered. As the meal progressed we heard more and more good-natured bantering. Obviously a well-developed sense of humor is as necessary for survival on Pitcairn as hard work.

Nov. 15: The swells subsided, so Brian was able to pick us up in *Rubber Ducky*, the island's 20-foot rigid-bottomed inflatable raft instead of the aluminum long boat. Riding over the waves was terrific fun.

Brian took us to his home overlooking Bounty Bay. Kari, Brian's stunning Norwegian wife, spread avocado on homemade bread as we exchanged sea stories. Our nine-day passage covering 1,200 miles from Easter Island was a speedy one. Brian recounted trips of 29 days or more to make the same usually stormy passage. He wistfully told us of his dream to sail the oceans of the world, a dream which would necessitate his leaving Pitcairn to earn money to finance the trip.

Kari, perhaps because she had chosen to live on Pitcairn, seemed to love the island more than those born here. She understood that many of the things which make for a rugged isolated existence also make Pitcairn special. Although her household and many others on the island had video players, she regretted that people spent more time watching than talking about island history or telling sea stories as they had in the recent past.

Marilyn, Darilyn and Dean Warren, Pitcairn Island

71

At Pulau, on the far side of Adamstown, we shared our slides of Galapagos wildlife with the 14 children in the one-room schoolhouse. When I asked, "Has anyone seen one of these?" as a slide of a Galapagos tortoise flashed on the screen, a chorus of voices answered: "Yes, it's Mr. T!" Leon Salt, the soft spoken, bearded school teacher, explained: "We do have a Galapagos tortoise on the island, named Mr. T., short for terrapin. Mr. T. and a mate, now dead, were brought to the island by Irving Johnson aboard the *Yankee*."

At the age of 15, Pitcairn Island children can elect to further their education in New Zealand. Most do; only a small percentage return to live on Pitcairn. Leon had come on a two-year contract as Pitcairn's education officer, but he and his family enjoy the island and so he has extended his contract for a third year. He is a distant Pitcairn descendant himself, his relatives live on Norfolk Island. His wife Brendda is part New Zealand Maori. Together they publish the monthly *Pitcairn Miscellany* newsletter which enjoys worldwide circulation. Overlooking the manicured lawn above the schoolhouse, we had tea with Leon and Brendda in their recently remodeled house.

Amazed that 55 islanders could support the upkeep of the school, teacher's house and salary, and other public salaries and buildings, we asked Leon about the island's two-tiered economy.

The islanders' private income, he explained, comes from selling carvings, baskets, lobster and, occasionally, vegetables to visiting ships and yachts. Many adults also have some type of government job — radio operator, policeman, dental technician, postmaster — which pays them about $3.00 (U.S.) per hour for a few hours of work per week. The public income (nearly $500,000 U.S.) comes mostly from stamp sales. Printed in England, the colorful stamps are shipped to the island, where, once they are hand-cancelled, are highly valued by stamp collectors worldwide. Revenue from the stamps covers all shipping costs for food and building supplies from New Zealand, plus fuel for the generator and medicine for the clinic. Shipping is expensive and infrequent; Pitcairn must pay for a freighter to stand by for a few hours while they unload supplies into the longboats. They usually charter only two freighters a year.

As dusk approached, Leon and his family gave us rides on two Honda three-wheelers down to the rocks near where we had left our dinghy in Western Harbor. Descending through the vegetation of the tropical valleys was more fun than any ride at Disneyland. An island law prohibits more than two adults and three children riding a three-wheeler at the same time. With a total of ten of us on two Hondas, we were barely within the law.

Nov. 18, John: We awoke on a pitching boat. I discovered we were now on a lee shore with squalls headed our way. Hoisting our 35-pound CQR anchor and 200 feet of chain out of 70 feet of water, I was glad we had spent the money for an oversized windlass to crank it up on deck. We motored into Bounty Bay which, since the wind had changed direction, was for a time semi-protected and we were able to anchor in only 50 feet of water. Despite our shorty wetsuits, the 65-degree water chilled us when we dove to check the anchor and then swam against the current and swells to *Bounty's* final resting place.

Trying to avoid detection of his island hideout by passing ships, Fletcher Christian burned and sank *Bounty* here, forever isolating himself and his followers on this tiny rock. Little remains of *Bounty*. All we could find were her ballast rocks.

Barbara: I had lost about eight pounds on our rough passages, but was quickly putting them back on sitting around Pitcairn's groaning dinner tables. Tonight Betty Christian's table was laden with seven different entrees. Her mom, Millie, joined us for dessert. She told us that the majority of Bounty descendants now live on Norfolk Island, north of Australia where the entire Pitcairn population was resettled in 1856. However, 43 islanders grew lonesome for Pitcairn, they returned in 1864, and today's descendants are from these families.

Nov. 22, 1:00 a.m.: The wind had shifted until Bounty Bay became too rough for safety or sleeping. So in the darkness, helped by decklights and spotlight, we raised anchor and carefully felt our way around the corner and anchored in Western Harbor again.

Brian and Nig called on the VHF in the morning, worried about us, thinking we were still anchored in Bounty Bay. I was asleep when they called, but John was already out in the dinghy trying to find a better anchorage farther around the island.

We had our roughest dinghy ride yet into Bounty Bay and needed to tack our Avon dinghy into the waves, since they were too big to crash straight into. Totally soaked, we took showers and changed into

73

church clothes in the boathouse. After separate Sabbath Schools, the children and adults met for a simple service consisting of a couple of hymns and an obscure Old Testament reading and interpretation by Ollie Simpson, the Seventh-day Adventist minister. Then everyone gathered on the benches around the town square to chat. Andrew Young intrigued us, his snowy long hair and beard making him resemble a prophet. At 87, he was in superb mental and physical shape. A treasure trove of island lore, he recalled the days when he was young and the square rigged sailing ships visited the island. He stressed the importance of ships stopping at Pitcairn, not only in the past but also today, as the islanders' only link with the outside world. During his youth Andrew persuaded a ship's wireless operator to show him how to build a spark-gap transmitter. He became Pitcairn's first radio operator. Whenever a ship was sighted he would send out a message in Morse code, identify the island and invite the ship to stop. Before the radio, the only way to get a ship to stop was to launch a longboat, weather permitting. With more than a dozen men at the oars, they would row after the ship. The radio now allows Pitcairn to contact passing ships for medical evacuations or to purchase or trade for supplies. The radio station keeps a daily watch on VHF, AM and SSB frequencies, and transmits daily weather observations to New Zealand. Several of the islanders have ham radios and keep in touch with friends in New Zealand and the United States.

After church Betty brought out her well-worn photo albums. She pointed out relatives now deceased or living in New Zealand. I began to feel close to her and her daughters, and I admired her choice to stay on isolated Pitcairn to care for her aging parents.

In the afternoon, seven of us hopped on Betty's two three-wheelers and took off on a Sunday outing. We had to abandon the overloaded bikes on a steep grade and set out walking through a taro patch. Rain fell and, grabbing the plant's huge heart-shaped leaves to use as an umbrella, we made our way to an area so steep it is called "Down Rope." Here, curious Polynesian petroglyphs cluster on the cliff sides. These, along with burial sites, earth ovens, stone adzes and statues were the relics of an abandoned Polynesian settlement, artifacts the mutineers found when they arrived on the island.

Hiking along a ridge, then dropping down a jumble of volcanic boulders and cliffs — the barefoot girls our guides — we came to the two rock pinnacles known as St. Paul's Rocks. These towering sentinels flank a blue pool. Sea water, forced between the rocks and through submerged passages, surges and foams up in the pool. Islanders know the place as a favorite fishing hole.

En route to Adamstown, we stopped to pick strawberries at one of Betty's numerous garden patches. And here we overheard Pitcairn dialect as Betty spoke to her daughters about the strawberries. The dialect sounds like Old English peppered with Polynesian words. Unique to Pitcairn and later to Norfolk Island, it developed between the English-speaking mutineers and their Polynesian wives.

Nov. 23: The wind had shifted during the night, making our anchorage rougher; we decided to stay aboard in case we needed to move. Around noon, we saw Leon and Brendda and their four kids clambering over the boulders toward the landing place in Western Harbor. John took the Avon and picked them up. They enjoyed their visit aboard, except for getting slightly seasick. Leon told us how some of the older Pitcairn women get sick on their way walking down to the landing, seasick before they even board the longboats to go out to the ships for trading. A classic case of conditioned response.

I went ashore with the Salts and caught a ride with them up to the village. It was Betty's birthday. While she was out of the house, her daughters, Darlene and Shari, and I blew up balloons, and hung streamers. As we wove flower leis, Darlene, seven years old, confessed she couldn't wait to be old enough to leave "the rock."

I had baked a lopsided birthday cake on our gimballed stove and decorated it with trick candles. But before we got to dessert, Nig showed up at the door and said that the wind had freshened; John needed me to shift to a safer anchorage. While Betty was insisting that I take a box of hot food with me, I was silently praying that this hasty farewell not be the last time I'd see my Pitcairn friends.

Aboard *Mahina Tiare*, we hoisted anchor and followed Nig and Brian around the western tip of the island into the Ginger Valley anchorage. Dark when we anchored, we wished Nig and Brian a safe return to Bounty Bay.

Nov. 24: We awoke to a calm day at Ginger Valley. Brian called around 10:00 a.m. on the radio to invite us for lunch. Ashore, Betty's girls asked if I'd like to hike up to Christian's cave. They guided me up the incredibly steep, lichen-covered rocks to the cathedal-like cave. Andrew had related that Fletcher Christian would climb here daily to scan the horizon, ready to alert the islanders to put out cooking fires and hide their boats should he spot a ship.

Drenched with sweat after the tortuous descent from the cave, the girls — I called them the little mountain goats — led me down to the landing. We all jumped into the surf to cool off but the strong current pulling seaward scared me. The young girls laughed; they were used to it.

After dinner at the Salts we launched our Avon and headed back to *Mahina Tiare*. Our anchorage at Ginger Valley was the farthest point on the island from Bounty Bay, and the trip was spooky, with fog hiding the higher points of the island, no moonlight and choppy seas. We had trouble finding the boat, and were briefly stricken with fear that she might have dragged anchor and drifted out to sea.

Nov. 25: The young island men sped out to our anchorage in two plywood skiffs and invited us to go diving. Floating on the surface, it was beautiful to watch them 60 feet below spearing fish and lobster in the cold, blue waters. The bubbles from their regulators appeared like convex mirrors as they wobbled to the surface. My distorted reflection in them intrigued me. The guys had a great time playing in their homemade "jon" boats, and we followed them in our Avon in and out of caves along the surf line.

We were racing Steve Christian through the surf at Bounty Bay when he buried the bow of his boat coming off a wave wrong. It nearly sank. We surfed in, made the turn, dropped our beaching wheels and caught the next wave. It sent us surfing right up the slippery concrete surface of the landing. Meanwhile, they were struggling to winch their boats up the landing. Steve's comment when he finally made it ashore, was "That little bastard (our Avon) can really fly, can't it?"

Steve invited us to his huge new home at "Edge", just above Bounty Bay, for showers. Then he and his wife, Olive, took us to their weekend house in the interior of the island, an informal cabin with an open wood-burning grill (called a bolt) for cooking. Younger islanders have weekend houses where privacy allows them a more relaxed attitude away from the Seventh-day Adventists' strict laws regarding smoking, dancing, drinking. We have never heard anyone use swear words as colorfully as the younger Pitcairn Island men.

Nov. 27 (Thanksgiving), John: We suited up in foul weather gear to come around the island by dinghy, a wild, rough and wet trip. The heavy rains had washed deep ruts in the Hill of Difficulty and the gooey red mud caked inches deep on the bottom of our sandals, made the climb more difficult than usual.

Somehow Brian and Kari produced a turkey (the only one on the island, I think) and trimmings for a Thanksgiving feast. Their gesture honored us; normally they do not celebrate American holidays. Looking around the room, I felt thankful for such a warm welcome from people who had been complete strangers until two weeks ago. And I felt incredibly blessed to be among them as friends.

Nov. 28: Terrible weather. I put two bow anchors down for the first time on Pitcairn, and they are tangled. Plus our main chain rode is wrapped around a coral head. Now, for the first time in years, I put on my scuba tank to try to save the anchor and chain. In 84 feet of water, the surge and currents are horrendous. I might have to abandon our main anchor gear. I try to unwind the chain from the coral head, but the chain jerks tight with a bang as the boat pitches in the swells. A finger can get pinched off. When I finally get the last of the chain clear I am on my reserve air and shaking with cold. Back aboard, we hoist both anchors and motor around the corner into Bounty Bay, a slightly more protected area.

Nig and Dave Brown come down to the landing to bring us freshly baked bread and a pound of frozen New Zealand butter. I fill our water jugs and tell them that we will probably leave the following day. The seemingly endless squally weather is exhausting.

Nov. 29: Conditions in Bounty Bay were worse this morning, and in some of the swells our anchor roller would touch the water. Getting into the dinghy required good timing and a lot of luck. Ashore we had a great going-away feast at Betty's. Warren, Betty's father, brought the hand-carved miniature Pitcairn wheelbarrow we had asked to buy. By the time we started loading the dinghy to leave, half the island's population had showed up to say good-bye.

It took us three fully loaded trips in the dinghy to ferry out all of the gifts we received from friends: bananas, carrots, cucumbers, sweet potatoes, watermelon, green beans, onions, fresh bread, hot meals in plastic boxes, and a box of granola bars that Brendda had baked for us. Barbara and Betty were crying, Nig and Dave clowned around and threatened to come with us. If we had made no other landfall during our entire trip to the South Pacific the visit to Pitcairn made it all worthwhile.

Postscript, Barbara: Most recent accounts of Pitcairn conclude that population will dwindle, that soon there will not be enough people to handle the longboats. Severing this lifeline to the outside world will force an evacuation of the island. But I believe this community will survive. A fierce love of the island runs through Pitcairn's history. Twice in the 19th century the island was completely evacuated, only to be resettled a few years later by homesick islanders. People like Andrew Young voice that love when they declare, "I was born here, I'll die here." At 87 he had announced that he would refuse any attempt to evacuate him for medical reasons, fearing he might not make it back to Pitcairn alive. He died on the island as he had wished, two years after our visit.

For myself, I look forward to returning to my friends here, strolling through Adamstown past the creeping banyan and colorful plumeria trees. Certainly the legacy of Fletcher Christian and the *Bounty* will continue to flourish.

Taiohae Bay, Nuku Hiva, Marquesas

Chapter 6
LANDFALL IN THE LANGUID MARQUESAS

Dec. 1, John: We left Pitcairn at the right time. The worsening weather that had been forecast, materialized. Last night we had winds to 45 knots, forcing us down to a storm jib and four reefs in the mainsail. None of the anchorages at Pitcairn would have been safe in these conditions. The heavy overcast and squalls ruled out any chances for sextant sights; we had to rely on the accuracy of our SatNav fixes and a vigilant deck watch as we passed 11 miles from tiny Oeno atoll, a Pitcairn possession. By dawn the weather improved; by dusk we were back to working sails and making 5 knots in better sea conditions.

Dec. 9: We sighted Fatu Hiva, the southernmost Marquesan island, at dawn. Another scorcher of a day. A golden sunset silhouetted angular Tahuata and Hiva Oa islands as we sailed in their lee.

Dec. 10: A seabird flying off our stern quarter kept pace with *Mahina Tiare*, as if a messenger sent to welcome and guide us into land. As we passed between the triangular stone islands which serve as sentinels at the entrance to Taiohae Bay on Nuku Hiva, the mountains rose up to form a verdant amphitheater.

Unpacking our best clothes from zip-lock bags, we dressed to clear customs at the Gendarmerie (Police Station) in Taiohae, the main port in the Marquesas. Inside a furnace of an office, the French Gendarme explained the bond and stamp requirements for obtaining a visa. We had worried that we might have to go straight to Papeete to get a visa. Instead, the Gendarme radioed Papeete for a three-month's visa for us.

Since the bank where we needed to post our bond had closed for the afternoon, we headed to Maurice McKittrick's store. Maurice greeted us with cold drinks and five months worth of mail. Simple things, monumental pleasure.

For me, coming back to Taiohae and visiting Maurice seemed like coming home. This was the fifth time I'd sailed to these islands since 1974, and in 1977 I spent several months living ashore. Maurice and I had helped each other out in different ways over the years, and I had become quite fond of his lovely daughter Corrine. His father was a Scotsman who set up one of the earliest stores in these islands; his mother was German-American from San Francisco.

Barbara: Maurice and John chatted while a steady stream of Marquesan customers filed in and out of the tiny store. Skinny cats jumped on and off the ancient counter and mosquitoes swarmed around my ankles.

When we walked along a road following the arch of the bay, John commented on changes in the villages since his last visit — part of the road paved, a new store and a bank, a few more jeeps. Still, the village appeared sleepy, even deserted, despite its 850 residents. The locals are early risers and try to get their hardest work done early in the morning when it's cooler, then take things easy during the hottest hours of the day.

We wandered back to the dinghy staying on the shady side of the street. Horses were tethered here and there along the road, and a free-roaming mother hen scratched up bugs for the incessantly peeping chicks surrounding her. Waning afternoon light slanted over the mountains into lush Taiohae valley, the colors glowing intensely. I was reminded of the golds and greens in Gauguin's paintings.

Dec. 11: We walked up the steep valley behind the village to the plant-filled yard of John's friends, Maxine and Jeannie Tehuatua. John had helped lay the foundation for their fiberboard house in 1974. Since then they had had three more children (a total of nine) and added a sleeping area onto the house which was enclosed on two sides and had a double bed, picnic table and a couple of tattered chairs inside.

Jeannie, a tall, classic Marquesan beauty of royal bloodlines, appeared through a curtain which serves as one of their doors. Her large dark eyes, arching eyebrows, and high cheekbones gave her the appearance of the women in engravings from Cook's expedition to the Marquesas. Jeannie's husband, Max, had soft brown eyes and wild rastafarian hair. We gave them gifts of perfume, T-shirts and vegetable seeds and were embarrassed by the gifts they showered on us: rare shells, a handwoven purse, a tie-dyed pareu (sarong), and the largest papayas we'd ever seen. Jeannie looking at John, kept saying, "Oh John", her voice filled with affection and pleasure at seeing him again.

We had dinner at Maurice's home, his son Jimmy preparing a semi-traditional menu for us: kumera, feii (cooking banana), and lamb chops steamed in coconut milk. We celebrated our arrival and friendship with a bottle of champagne from us, and a litre of ice cream from Maurice's store.

John: It seemed like nothing had changed since I had lived up the hill from Maurice's store. Since Maurice and I both lived alone, many nights I'd come over to the store, fix us dinner, then we'd sit around the kerosene lamp, drinking tea and catching the news from Tahiti between the static crashes on his old shortwave radio. It was sure good to be back.

Dec. 14, Barbara: Today we rode over to Taipivai Valley with Max, Jeannie and family in their Suzuki jeep. After driving the tortuous route surmounting the Taiohai valley walls, then dropping down to the next valley, we arrived at the village of Taipivai. The village stretches along a lazy river, and the main dirt road is lined by small houses, their yards overflowing with colorful ti plants, hibiscus and poinsettias.

Before the arrival of Christianity, the Taipi people were notorious warriors and cannibals. Traditional enemies of the people from Taiohae Valley, their prowess in war has been chronicled in Herman Melville's book *Typee*. Today their rivalry takes the form of fierce soccer matches. The Taipi often win, although their population is one-fifth that of Taiohae.

Jeannie and the kids stopped to watch the soccer match while Max, John and Jeannie's brother took off in the jeep. It was clear women were not welcome to accompany them. Jeanette, an Australian women who had ridden over with us, and I started out for a stroll along the river. But the heat became unbearable so we slipped out of our clothes and into the cool river. A 16-year-old Marquesan surfer paddled up on his board and nonchalantly spoke with us in English, then politely headed downstream on hearing we would be getting out of the water to get dressed.

The circuitous road back to Taiohae was made more treacherous by the jeep's engine cutting out whenever we approached the really steep places. Max said the fuel from Taipivai must have a lot of water in it. The starter didn't work, so Max rolled the jeep backward to get it going. We closed our eyes and held our breath, hoping he wouldn't back off a cliff.

Back at Max and Jeannie's home, they served a great delicacy — the amber-colored head of a roasted pig. Cut up for us, we tried not to notice what parts we were actually eating. But it was difficult to ignore the thick black hairs still attached to the skin. Jeanette got part of an ear and I'm sure I ate the snout. After eating, I was handed a bowl with lime squeezed in it. I thought it was for washing my hands. But then noticed stifled smiles on the faces of our hosts and a spoon in the bottom of the bowl. I had washed my hands in a bowl of limeade. Everyone had a tremendous laugh and my faux pas became a standing joke.

Dec. 17: John rowed over with fresh fruit for a yacht that had just sailed into the bay. It was a Danish yacht, arriving after a rugged 17-day beat up from the Tuamotus. She was crewed by three women whom John invited over for tea and banana bread. I was excited about the prospect of meeting other women sailors.

When the crew of the *Suliema* showed up, there were six, five Danes and one Swede. The three men and three women aboard had met for the first time a month earlier and were traveling on a primitive, borrowed, 39-foot ferro cement ketch. All were fluent in English and French. We developed a great rapport, eagerly trading reading material.

Dec. 18: A snorkeling expedition outside Taiohae Bay turned exciting when a black manta ray with six-foot wingspan came powering by beneath us. As it rippled its wingtips, it resembled a black-cloaked Dracula. Trying to keep pace on the surface above the ray, we swam into a mass of nearly invisible stinging sea nettles. We sped back to *Mahina Tiare* and rubbed on papaya skin, the local remedy, to stop the itch and burn from the nettles.

We had dinner on the *Suliema* in a worn, wooden cockpit lighted by a kerosene lamp that showed up hundreds of unabashed cockroaches. It seemed like we had traveled back in time to one of the whaling or sandalwood ships that had anchored in the same bay a century earlier.

Dec. 20: We rose at 7 a.m. to escape the heat. I had decided to handle the boat myself on our sail to Hakatea Bay. Up to this point on the trip John had been captain, sailing master and navigator. I'm not gung-ho about taming flying sheets and sails, especially when the motion of the boat takes away my willpower and makes me sleepy. Now I would assume responsibility for everything, so should something happen to John I would be more confident to sail alone. I raised the anchor, hoisted the mainsail, set up the autopilot. Everything was fine until leaving the protection of Taiohae Bay where the boat was slammed by gusty winds and rough seas.

John watched. It was my baptism by fire. I rigged the preventer for the main, then it was violently backwinded by the gusty following winds and choppy seas. I was mad and frustrated, but I was determined. An hour after sailing out of Taiohae, I dropped anchor in 14 feet of water in Hakatea Bay, the most protected anchorage in the Marquesas. I had proved to myself that I could handle the boat alone.

Hakatea was about 90 degrees and more humid than Taiohae. High mountains block the tradewinds and I felt like someone was slowly smothering me in a thick warm blanket. Finally, the boat put away, I swam in the bay and showered in the cockpit three times. I still felt hot — it was that kind of heat. I helped John sew up a large sun awning. I hoped it would keep the boat cooler. Otherwise we would have to move to a cooler anchorage.

Dec. 21: We finished our awning/raincatcher by pounding in the grommets. We hung it up as a light drizzle fell, the day's heat now bearable.

Speedboats dropped people off on the deserted beach all morning, and around noon a small dinghy rowed by a middle-aged Marquesan couple approached *Mahina Tiare*. Danielle and Antoinette, friends that John had met 12 years ago, recognized our boat's name and came to take us to their nieces' birthday feast. Under the shade of a tin-roofed lean-to with cows grazing nearby in the uninhabited valley of Hakatea, we feasted on roast pork and breadfruit out of an underground oven, poi (paste from ripe breadfruit mixed with coconut milk), roasted bananas and chicken, a bottle of Mumm's Cordon Rouge champagne, and a cake decorated with plumeria flowers.

Feeling full and lazy, we went for a leisurely walk up Hakaui Valley, on shore west of Hakatea. The valley is a half mile wide where it meets the beach, nearly flat, and walled in on the western side by 1,600-foot sheer volcanic cliffs. Seemingly inaccessible small caves in the cliffs had served as a refuge for the royal families in time of war and as burial caves. Danielle told us that earlier inhabitants had carved steps in the vertical cliffs, hoisted the dead chiefs and their canoes into the caves and then had destroyed the steps as they descended.

A month before our visit Jacques Cousteau had anchored the *Calypso* in Hakatea and had persuaded Danielle to accompany him as a guide in the ship's helicopter. Evidently it took some persuading to get Danielle into the helicopter since he hadn't seen one before. But together they found a new set of burial caves not visible from either above or below the cliffs.

We rounded a bend in the trail startling a pink and black sow and her six piglets. She grunted threateningly, then crashed off into the brush followed by her brood. Then we were stopped by two frisky horses, one biting the other on the rump. They, too, hurried away.

Beneath the canopy of coconut trees we saw dozens of paepae, stone house foundations. Some had precisely cut stones, like the ceremonial platforms we had seen on Easter Island. An odd sensation passed through me as we walked by the remains of so many deserted dwellings. I could visualize this area bustling with activity in a time long past.

Our path joined a raised stone-paved historic road. More than eight feet wide and up to 20 feet high where it bridged gullies and rivers, the road spoke highly for the engineering abilities of the Taioa people who had once inhabited this valley. Danielle estimated the population at 3,000 when their civilization was at its peak. Today all 12 inhabitants live down near Hakaui Bay.

Throughout the Marquesas once thriving valleys are now empty and silent. The strong, handsome race described by Captain Cook as the most splendid islanders of the South Pacific had succumbed to imported diseases. In 1774 when Cook visited he estimated the population at 50,000. The census dropped to a low of 1,200 before starting to rise again. Today it stands at 6,000.

The Marquesas as a place to live have long appealed to artists and writers, including Pierre Loti, Paul Gauguin, Herman Melville, Robert Louis Stevenson, Jack London, Jacques Brel. At the turn of the century when London and Gauguin arrived, the race was dying out. Leprosy, smallpox, tuberculosis, influenza, measles took their toll on these people with no immunity.

At 750 miles from Tahiti, 3,600 miles west of Peru, and 2,000 miles SE of Hawaii, the Marquesas remain isolated today. Although theoretically you can to fly from Tahiti to Nuku Hiva or Hiva Oa, local school teachers or government workers book the few seats on the weekly plane six months in advance. Tourism essentially is limited to the few yachts that sail here from Panama, Mexico or California, and a few Russian cruise ships that stay a maximum of four hours in Taiohae Bay.

One of the copra schooners, the *Aranui*, takes a few passengers in cabins on its month-long trip from Tahiti to the Marquesas and back, but this limits them to a couple hours in most of the villages.

Dec. 22: We resumed our hike up the valley today. Our goal, the waterfall at the head. We pass though a mape (Tahitian chestnut) forest. The trunks of the mape trees consist of vertical slabs which circle the base like flat-sided, above-ground roots. The huge trees block out the sunlight and the trek through the forest becomes damp and gloomy.

Presently stone cairns (trail markers) lead us through a maze of paepaes, stone walls, and fallen trees to a delta in the river. Stepping from stone to stone, we make our way up the slow flowing western branch into the fern-lined mouth of the Hukui river valley. The towering cliffs slowly close in on us as we walk closer to the waterfall. I have a soaring sensation when looking skyward, much like I've felt when looking up inside a Gothic cathedral.

At last we hear the cascade. Leaving on only our tennis shoes, we scramble over the boulders, then swim through the icy brown water toward the base of the torrent. The thundering water feels like a fire hose turned on full blast. We swim into a side grotto to catch our breath, then head back under the cascade for another rush. Emerging into the warm air, we lean our dripping backs against the curve of a boulder and look up from our shady brown world. The sky seems a faraway abstract blue shape cut from the high jagged cliffs. A pair of snow-white tropic birds circles in that patch of blue. I feel so alive as John embraces me.

How did I get to this enchanted valley? How did I go from wearing plaid to pareus? I think back 18 years to Katonah, New York — a gray winter morning. I stand on the corner of Kelly Circle, our dead-end street, waiting for the school bus. I am 15. I wear an itchy wool plaid skirt. I am allergic to wool and hate the pantyhose which bind my legs when I try to run for the bus. The ride is the same every morning. I stare out the window. I know every stone wall, mailbox and grave stone as we wind along for 45 minutes. I am a good student until 12th grade. At this point I am tired of my two major occupations, studying and watching television. The studying doesn't have much relevance and I realize I have spent years watching others lead their lives on television. I stop watching TV and decide I have the choice to make my life meaningful, as exciting as anyone's on television.

All my decisions have led to this valley; the choice to move from half a dozen places I could have called home, the choice to let go of jobs, security, friends. Spurred by restlessness they were hardly choices at the time but compulsions toward something missing, a constant surrender to the unknown.

Dec. 23: The notorious Marquesan no-no's (tiny bloodthirsty sandflies) drilled me from head to toe yesterday while I was otherwise occupied near the cascade. Last night the itching and heat kept me tossing and turning. We agreed to sail back to the cooler anchorage of Taiohae.

Dec. 24, Taiohae, John: We took turns going ashore for some last-minute Christmas shopping at Maurice's store. When I told him that I was trying to find a present for Barbara, he rummaged around under the counter and produced a beautiful hand-printed pareau and sold it to me for half-price.

Barbara: We celebrated Christmas Eve with Max and Jeannie and their large family. Balloons and tinsel streamers hung askew on the skinny aito (ironwood) tree — a feathery evergreen — set up in their 10 x 12 foot livingroom. Under the tree were several expensive toy trucks and dolls, gifts from Tahitian politicians eager for Marquesan votes. The Tehuatuas were shy about accepting our gifts, Marquesan adults usually do not exchange gifts on Christmas.

As the evening progressed, the rest of Max and Jeannie's children arrived with their own kids. Their nine children range in age from two to 25 years old. With such an age range, the generations overlapped — some of Max and Jeannie's grandchildren were older than their own children. Jeannie says: "No more babies." She named her ninth child Sunday. "On Sunday," she told us, "God rested, and now I want to rest and travel to the other islands. I want to visit all of my family."

Dinner was in their open air kitchen and, in typical Polynesian fashion, we, their guests, ate only with Max; the family would eat later.

When we finished, men and boys collected around us at the cleared dinner table but the women hung back in the shadows and took care of their children. We received a stalk of bananas and papayas as a parting gift, then they took us down to the bay.

Back on the dark boat I recalled the magic of Christmas at home — the sparkling lights on a Christmas tree and the aroma of pine. Still I wouldn't trade this Christmas Eve for one back home. Here I was like a child again; everything was new and exotic. Instead of pine the scent of plumerias, pareaus instead of sweaters, new friends to fill the void of missing the old ones.

Christmas Day: We slid through the white water of a breaking wave like a sleigh on a snowy hill, and landed safely ashore. Changing clothes in the bushes, we walked to Notre Dame des Iles de Marquises, a massive wood and stone cathedral. Inside was a congregation of colorfully dressed Marquesans. Leis of tiare and plumeria flowers hung in white and pink lines from the altar and draped the intense faces of the locally carved statues of saints. The air was fragrant, humid and hot - about 80 degrees.

The Catholic mass was sung in French and Marquesan. But the haunting melodies and harmonies were pure Marquesan. The songs gathered force until they seemed to become a living entity, vibrating through us and the wooden pews as more and more voices blended in.

The powerful Polynesian melodies were haunting, but I longed to hear just one familiar Christmas carol, or hear my friends at home singing "The Messiah", a tradition in Friday Harbor. The press of damp bodies leaving the church brought my thoughts back to the present.

We stopped in the courtyard to examine an exotic creche that beautifully blended European and Polynesian traditions. The ceramic figures were standard European issue, but the creche was a native-style fare (hut), with thatched roof and woven walls. The Holy Family, Wise men, sheep and cows were nestled amid tropical flowers and draped in miniature leis.

Max and Jeannie drove us up to Toovii, an experimental agricultural station on a plateau in the island's mountainous interior. The rolling grassy meadows and experimental pine forest reminded me of our home in the San Juan Islands. While we were enjoying the delicious cool 68 degree weather, our hosts were shivering despite their jackets. The area is and always has been uninhabited.

We cooked Christmas dinner for Maurice at his bachelor pad where cats roam freely and kill cockroaches the size of mice.

Dec. 26: A new boat sailed into the bay and we invited its skipper Jean Casalis, a French cruiser-schoolteacher from Hiva Oa, over for dinner. His observations about the Marquesan people after two years of teaching introduced us to their world-view. While some of the French teachers are lured to the Marquesas by the bonus pay for teaching in an isolated area, Jean was in the Marquesas to learn from and about the people. The last place he taught was in the French West Indies and, unlike the students there, he sensed that the Marquesan students had no inferiority complex since their relatives were never slaves. The Marquesans still own and inhabit the land of their ancestors.

In this culture, he explained, people neither put on a facade of friendliness nor cover up their bad moods. If you are a guest in a Marquesan home, they don't feel the need to talk or entertain you constantly. At social gatherings in villages there is often little conversation. Not much happens in these small places, and what does go on is quickly known by the villagers.

Jean mentioned that the Polynesians love babies and small children, but once reaching their teens they are usually left to fend for themselves. Teenagers are expected to help in the care of their younger brothers and sisters. Often a child is raised by grandparents, and when the grandparents grow too old to be self-sufficient, the grandchild will look after them. Frequently the last child in a family is raised as a girl (even if this child is a boy). This youngest sibling is dressed in girl's clothes and taught housework instead of fishing and hunting. This child is expected to remain close to home and care for the parents when they become infirm. Referred to as a mahu, when male, this person holds a respected place in society, never ridiculed as effeminate.

Dec. 29, John: We had a difficult beat to Ua Huka, east of Nuku Hiva, to windward against a 1 1/2 -knot current and fresh tradewinds. Although only 28 miles away, this short, difficult sail discourages all but a dozen yachts a year from visiting Ua Huka.

When Motu Manu (Bird Island) appeared on our starboard beam, thousands of terns reeled overhead. The crescent-shaped white sand beach of Haavei Bay was on our port beam, and we began looking for the narrow, hidden entrance to Vaipaee Bay (Invisible Bay) not seen until you're directly abeam it. We were greeted by a cool, stiff breeze coming down the valley as we entered Vaipaee Bay.

We anchored bow and stern in 15 feet of water with a firm, sandy bottom in the cliff-lined bay, about a quarter mile from the beach.

Barbara: Children played in the gentle surf near a boat launching ramp, and a man tugged his reluctant chestnut horse into the water for a swim. When the horse reared up on its hind legs, pawing the air with

Landing with a little help from our friends, Vaipaee, Ua Huka

its forelegs, the children laughed.

Ashore, we hopped into a local jeep for a ride into town, passing a dozen or more fancy plywood speedboats in a community boathouse. In typical Marquesan fashion, the main road of Vaipaee village follows the winding course of a lush river valley cut deep into the surrounding hills. We followed the river up past the red-roofed Catholic church, literally and figuratively the center of the village, and houses of wood, cinderblock and fiberboard. Pausing to sit on a bench under a canopy of mango trees, the river murmured past us and a tethered horse whinnied nearby.

Horses were introduced from Chile in the 1850s and have adapted well to the Marquesas. Used for hunting expeditions into the hills in pursuit of wild boar, goats and cattle, they also transport copra (coconut meat) from isolated villages.

About 250 people live in Vaipaee. The post office, mayor's office and museum share one building. In the space awarded the museum is a collection of stone adzes, poi bowls, ear plugs, and etchings of old Marquesans, their bodies totally covered with tattoos.

Our progress through the village had not gone unnoticed, for when we wound our way back down the hill, Jean Baptiste Brown motioned us into his small, neat store. The stolid middle-aged Jean Baptiste gave us red New Zealand apples and cold sodas, his conversation sparse but his manner sincere. Then we were called across the street, to the old blue, two-story house where Jean's parents and brothers lived. They presented us with a bag full of cucumbers, green beans, pineapples and bananas. Most of these delicacies were either unavailable or prohibitively expensive in Taiohae. The Browns told us that they were part American, perhaps descendants of a Thomas Lawson from New England who in the 1850's had set up a ship's repair and reprovisioning service in Vaipaee.

When the village children heard my name was Barbara, they would repeat, "Santa Barbara, Santa Barbara." I was perplexed by this, until I realized this came from an American soap opera which the Marquesans had been eagerly following on their three hours per evening television reception.

We noticed a very large Marquesan woman submerged to her waist in the river. She was doing laundry with a big square of coconut soap and the ample supply of rushing water. She called to us, then pointed to her pretty teenage daughter who spoke to us in French. "Could she visit *Mahina Tiare* the following day?"

Dec. 30: A throng of eight honey-colored Marquesan girls hailed us from shore. John fetched them in the Avon, and I really wouldn't have blamed him if he had motored off into the sunset with these giggling beauties. They came bearing mangoes, pamplemouse, papaya, oranges, and a large spiny fruit called soursop. We played a tape of Tahitian tamure dance music and they showed me how to gyrate my hips to the beat until most of them succumbed to seasickness and had to be ferried back ashore. Before they left, they used our typewriter to type a thank you note in English. Their visit was probably the closest we'd come to the days of Captain Cook when the vahines (young women) swam out to visiting ships bearing fruit, and making gifts of themselves to the sailors.

The cooling afternoon enticed us ashore for a sunset walk up through the valley. Sunset doesn't last long in these lands only nine degrees from the equator. Along the road the pink and gold plumeria blossoms seemed to breathe extra fragrance into the humid night air, perhaps to lure lovers into the velvet tropical night. For surely no one loves flowers more than the Polynesian.

Dec. 31: The mutoi (local village policeman) came to the boat this morning to invite us to the New Year's Eve celebration in the next village. He offered us a ride over the mountains in his Toyota Land Cruiser, one of the few vehicles on the island. We were on the beach at the appointed time but he wasn't. We've learned that you can't be sure when making a date with a Marquesan. Sometimes the invitation is just to please you, and certainly their concept of time is looser than ours.

We started on foot, threading our way out of Vaipaee valley. As we emerged from the valley, the land ceased to be green. Instead, herds of wild horses and goats grazed on hills covered with golden grass. The road, etched into the sides of steep hills, was hot, steep, dusty. We rounded hill after hill only to realize we still had much further to go.

Jean Baptiste Brown passed us in his jeep. He stopped, turned around, and gave us a ride back to Hane, even though he had just come from there.

The festivities were in the brightly lit Catholic church. It sounded like a rock concert. A fully amplified band played, and hymns were being sung in French and Marquesan. It looked as if half the population on Ua Huka, about 300 people, were in attendance. All in their finest clothing they had jammed into the church, spilling out the doors and windows. We were the only non-Polynesians, but we were welcomed into the church despite our inappropriate dress. Having no idea what sort of festivities we were attending —it could have been a beer bash on the beach — I had worn sailing pants and a long sleeved shirt to ward off the ubiquitous mosquitoes and no-no's. When the singing stopped at 7:30 p.m., a dynamic, dark, middle-aged woman stood in front and lectured, sang, and shouted in French for an hour. It was hard to decipher her rapid-fire French but "Jesus-Christ" and "Dieu" figured heavily in it. Later she lectured the teenagers on the dangers of drugs and fornication. Her volume and vehemence seemed to embarrass the two Marquesan men who flanked her on stage. When the crowd broke for cake and coffee, served in glass bowls with lots of sugar and milk, the band set up on the grass outside.

A string of bare white light bulbs illuminated the two dozen teenage girls wearing flower crowns and bracelets. Assembled in lines in the shape of the cross, they performed a graceful dance, hips gently swaying and arms waving colored squares of fabric (this was the church-approved version of the sensual hip-gyrating tamure dance the girls had shown us a few days before). At 11 p.m. it was back into the church for more speeches and singing. By now we had sung the songs several times and knew the words. At midnight, everyone clamored to wish us "Bonne Annee," especially the older women whom I thought would be most shy. They kissed us on both cheeks, their skin slightly damp and smelling of perfume.

We squeezed into the back of the mutoi's truck along with seven teenagers. On the trip back to Vaipaee the night sky was alive with stars, and the Southern Cross lay over the water far below us. In the distance the headlights of the other cars defined the shapes of the black hills. The teenagers, who braced against the back of the cab, were silhouetted by our headlights, and the wind carried back the fragrance of their flowers. The harmonies of their songs hung in the warm air.

Jan. 1: Jean Baptiste gave us a box of wild oranges today, the sweetest oranges I'd ever tasted. The skins were greenish brown and the pulp inside looked fluorescent orange. I decided to keep them for gifts to the other cruisers so they could discover how outrageous an orange can be.

Jan. 3: Walked up the valley to visit Rose and Norbert, the odd couple. Norbert is small and muscular, his eyes steely blue, his hair thinning and blonde. German by birth, he had joined the French Foreign Legion after completing an apprenticeship as a pastry chef in Vienna. His tour of duty included a stint as a security chief at Muraroa, the French nuclear testing area in the Tuamotus. Here he'd met and married Rose. They had moved to Vaipaee, Rose's hometown. Norbert told us that all Marquesans were untrustworthy: "They smile to your face, but will put a knife in your back." He made a stabbing gesture that convinced me he knew how to use a knife and probably had. Personally, I would trust any Marquesan over Norbert with his mercenary background.

He asked repeatedly if we would bring him a gun from the States on our next trip. But he couldn't understand that our boat would be confiscated by the Gendarmes who are quick to hear if any yachties are bringing guns or bullets to these islands. Gendarme or not, we would never put a gun in Norbert's hands. Rose, a jolly Marquesan, is twice Norbert's size. They have eight children, none of the kids resembling Norbert in the least. Two of Rose's children were adopted, one a two-year-old boy (actually her grandson) and an adorable four-year-old, her sister's daughter. The little girl, whose father was an African from Martinique, has wooly hair and large eyes. Rose and the other children mocked her because she was different and darker. I wanted to take her home with me.

We were served some delicate cake Norbert had baked and decorated. It could have come out of the window of a Viennese pastry shop — except for the cloud of tiny black flies surrounding it.

Rose sent us on our way with as many tomatoes and avocados as we could carry. The vegetables came from the extensive gardens of a Frenchman named Paul, who had been a stockbroker in Paris and had come to the Marquesas seeking solitude. He lived a reclusive life in the mountains between Vaipaee and Hane. He and Norbert were the only European residents on Ua Huka.

Jan. 4: We went to early mass at the Catholic church and sat one seat away from a tall woman who wore her dark hair twisted up and held tightly against her skull with a comb, in the manner all mature Marquesan women do. She appeared annoyed by her four-year-old son who sat next to us and kept looking at John, making circles with his fingers and putting them to his eyes. John, wearing swimming goggles, had played with him in the surf yesterday. When the offering plate was passed, John dug in his pockets for change and came up empty. I hadn't brought my purse. Without a word the stately woman handed her small son a 50-franc piece to give us.

At 9:00 a.m. the service ended and already the sun was burning its way through the overhead canopy of trees. As we walked from the church, a small boy rode up on a bicycle and handed us a bag of donuts and freshly baked raisin bread. We didn't know who they were from, but this simple generosity left a lump in my throat.

Late that afternoon when we went up the valley for our daily hike, I stopped across the street from the church to enjoy the singing of the evening mass and to sketch the church. There is nothing like drawing to slow me down, allowing the land, buildings and plants to speak their unique language. Engrossed in sketching I see vividly and experience deeply. When I looked up I was surrounded by ten children. Apparently they considered my drawing some sort of magic. I was instantly elevated in their eyes. The kids spoke to each other in the throaty Marquesan language which lacks the softer consonants of English. It often sounds as though they are mad or impatient about what they are saying. Their language sounds primitive in a thrilling way. English and French sound tame in comparison.

Jan. 3: After several days of brutally hard work sanding all our old cracked and peeling varnish down to bare wood, we finally applied the first coat of varnish today. Working in the equatorial sun is a killer.

We offered to cook dinner for Jean Baptiste and his children today, wanting to return his generosity. Jean Baptiste has five children —a crippled 11-year-old daughter, three sons, and a four-year-old daughter who, severely burned and crippled as an infant, was in Taiohae with her mother undergoing an operation to help her walk.

Although the arrangement was that we would provide dinner, Jean contributed goat stew (he'd shot the goat that day), rice, bananas and

94

pineapple juice to the menu. We sat on wooden benches at a plywood table enjoying the open-air porch of Jean's new house. He and John conversed about mutual Marquesan friends. He suggested we visit his sister-in-law and family when we reached the island of Hiva Oa, and we promised to visit his wife and daughter at the hospital when we returned to Taiohae.

Jan. 7: We completed the second coat of varnish on the exterior teak, and I cut up bananas to dry in the sun. I cooked a custard for Mrs. Lichtle and her granddaughter who had been giving us eggs and cakes. When I presented the custard the granddaughter gave me a freshly baked loaf of bread. You can't win with these people. Mrs. Lichtle's granddaughter explained that her grandmother's mother was from San Francisco, so she loves to give gifts to Americans. She also told us that since you can't buy fruit or vegetables in the stores in Vaipaee, it is acceptable to ask for them. So far we hadn't asked for anything. And, no way could we ever eat all that we'd been given.

Tonight was a lovely, star-studded night. Standing on the bow in the cool ocean breeze and looking out at the narrow entrance of the bay, I felt like I was on the edge of the earth. Safe where I was, yet constantly being beckoned by the vast ocean, the cool breeze enticing me to discover its source. Perhaps the early Polynesian navigators felt this pull, this restlessness, before they set sail to discover other Marquesas Islands – Easter Island, Pitcairn Island, Hawaii. Archaeologists believe that Ua Huka was the gateway to the other islands; the remains of the oldest settlements have been found here.

The sound of goats crying on the cliffs drifted down to us as the surf pounded on the cliff walls. I felt tired, but happy from another full day.

Jan. 12: It rained, and the wind funneled down the valley last night causing our stern anchor to drag and leaving us beam on to the swells. The bay was still rough in the morning, and we opted to head back to Taiohae. We went ashore to say our good-byes. Mrs. Lichtle, who had heard we were leaving, had beaten the bushes all morning for eggs and handed us seven when we bid her farewell. She kissed our hands and said in rough French, "When you return in a few years, I'll be gone." She gestured out the doorway and continued, "I'll be resting on top of that hill in a grave next to my mother's." As she spoke, her granddaughter stood in the background crying softly.

95

Jan. 30:
We heaved to Hiva Oa
where scientists rarely goa,
with serious porpoise in mind
plusieurs especes d'araignee to find.

Betsy Berry

Arriving back in Taiohae, we noticed a pale-skinned middle-aged couple wandering the streets trailing a butterfly net. Lost tourists? They were a spider scientist from Indiana and his pharmacist wife in the Marquesas to collect spider specimens for a study of species distribution throughout the Pacific Islands. Jim and Betsy Berry weren't having any luck getting from place to place in the Marquesas where public transportation is non-existent and the locals aren't concerned about time schedules. The Berrys had been trying to get to Hiva Oa, 100 miles southeast, for several days and were running out of time. We offered them a ride on *Mahina Tiare* since we were headed that way. Little did we know what we were getting into as Jim and petite Betsy, both plied with Dramamine, stepped aboard *Mahina Tiare*. This was their first sailing experience, and my first encounter with people seriously debilitated by seasickness.

We sailed from Taiohae at 3:00 p.m. and I felt helpless as Betsy turned a whiter shade of pale, threw up, then became cold and clammy and beset by dry heaves. Jim got sick in sympathy and I, a bit squeamish, tried not to breathe through my nose. Betsy slept in the cockpit, and we had to awaken her and get her to shift her eighty-pound weakened body each time we changed tacks going to windward. The night was long and rough, and in the morning we persuaded her to try a Scopalomine patch behind her ear. In a half-hour she was standing on the bow with me enjoying the antics of bottlenose dolphins who rode our bow wave, coming within inches of my dangling feet. Then a pod of acrobatic spinner dolphins appeared astern of us, leaping into the air with a series of flips and twists. They were a hit with our passengers, and seasickness was forgotten.

As we rounded the last headland before entering Hanamenu Bay, the wind and seas kicked up and I got soaked clinging onto the forestay, riding the bow like a bucking bronco. Hanamenu (near the NW tip of Hiva Oa) appeared two-toned: greenish in the middle and brownish near the beach where sand and silt were suspended in the ferocious surf.

Rather than risk losing our outboard should the dinghy get tumbled, we left it aboard and John rowed Betsy and some scientific gear into the shallows between the breakers.

Meanwhile, aboard *Mahina Tiare*, when Jim grumbled to me about not expecting such a difficult landing, I laughed: "Think of this as an adventure, something to tell your grandchildren." He commented, "I'm too old for this type of adventure." When it was our turn to go ashore, I carried one of their bags and John dropped me first. Jim with his 60-pound backpack followed quickly, jumping off in waist deep water just as cresting breakers appeared seaward of us. I ran forward to meet the swell, instinct from years of playing in the surf, but Jim stood his ground, backpack held high as the wave broke around him. He staggered, but made it ashore. John was waiting for one of us to retrieve the second backpack from the dinghy before he landed on the beach. Tiny Betsy, a real trooper, headed out with me to help. We didn't reach him soon enough. Before he could retreat behind the surf line, a wave caught the stern and lifted the boat until it was vertically standing on end, facing us. Seemingly in slow motion, John tumbled head first into the surf, along with oars and backpack. He grabbed the dinghy as it surfaced in the breakers, but the backpack did a perfect job of surfing in on its own. It landed high up on the beach in its plastic garbage sack.

Ashore John and I ran for the pool he had visited and written about 12 years earlier in his book, *Log of the Mahina*. By surrounding the base of a small waterfall with smooth flat lava rocks, the ancient dwellers of the valley created the pool. The hibiscus bushes and fruit trees they had planted created a shady, bird-filled paradise, enjoyed only by the occasional yachtsperson or Marquesan hunter. We splashed and laughed and cooled down in the frigid water, while freshwater shrimp nipped our toes. Lest I give the impression that all was perfect, a throng of no-nos and mosquitoes eagerly hummed around our heads, an inducement to stay as much underwater as possible.

While we explored the ruins back up the valley, the whistles of hunters tracking wild boar echoed off the valley walls. Returning to the beach, we met a couple of young hunters sitting at a rough wooden table with a bottle of "chateau plastique" (cheap French red wine).

The pool at Hanamenu, Hiva Oa, Marquesas

Three pig carcasses swung from the roof beam of a primitive thatch house nearby. The fire which the hunters had used to singe the hair off the pigs was smoldering and smelled of bacon.

One of the men proudly posed for a photo by his kill. Then, drawing a long sharp knife from his belt, sliced off a hind quarter of fresh pork for us. But what was I going to do with a quarter of a pig? I ended up cooking the meat in the pressure cooker in several batches, then stored it in a tight plastic container with lots of salt. It lasted unrefrigerated for a year. We left the Berrys busy shaking spiders out of trees onto a tarp, and sailed 15 miles south to Hapatoni Bay on Tahuata Island.

Ashore for the afternoon, we returned to the dinghy in darkness, the tide now way out. Waves were breaking in two phosphorescent lines, three feet from the shoreline and another 30 feet further out. We waited for the breakers to ease before launching the Avon. John manned the oars and I stayed in the water to push the stern. After four steps I slipped on a rock and clung onto the stern while we crashed through the first line of breakers. John kept rowing as fast as possible to get through the second set. I couldn't regain my footing, so I hung onto the transom and kicked behind. Clear of the breakers, John stopped and I climbed in over the side of the dinghy, panting. I'll always remember that insecure feeling of scrambling over submerged stones into the dark turbulent ocean on a moonless night.

Feb. 8: We rose early and headed for Hapatoni church. The mass was celebrated by a young woman dressed in white; the village isn't large enough to rate a priest. The 57 people in attendance were among the most attractive we'd seen in the Marquesas — the men tall and hard-muscled, the women stately and surrounded by lively kids. The age of the lighter-skin children would seem to correspond to the late '70s when Hapatoni was visited by many single-handed European sailors, including John.

After church the older women sat under a huge mango tree dressed in bras and brightly-colored pareu skirts. They embroidered pillow slips and quilts. A few decades ago these women would have been bare-breasted. Now they wore armor-plated cross-your-heart bras in public. "The Pope must have stock in Playtex!" was a friend's comment.

Feb. 9: We left Hapatoni by early morning moonlight to make it through Bourdelais Strait (between Tahuata and Hiva Oa) before the afternoon winds and currents picked up. The moon lit up the clouds like fleeing specters and illuminated Hopatoni beach until it glowed like snow on a clear winter night.

At Atuona on Hiva Oa, we anchored behind the breakwater. Three French yachts were moored here, their owners teaching school to replenish cruising funds.

We provisioned at an old Chinese store, rumored to be where Gauguin had shopped. Pierre, the young Chinese-Marquesan owner, had an unquenchable desire for anything American. We traded him a short wave radio and some Jimmy Buffet tapes to pay our grocery bill.

As we rowed back to *Mahina Tiare,* the setting sun turned the clouds rose, the hillside glowed a deep tropical green, and mist collected on the hills above Atuona where Gauguin is buried.

Feb. 11, John: We set out hitch-hiking early in the morning to deliver letters from our Ua Huka friends, the Browns, to their family who live down the road from Atuona. When a rusty truck stopped for us, we told the driver that we were going to visit Antoine Lacharme. He indicated with a gnarled hand that he was Antoine. He turned out to

Hanavavae Bay, Fatu Hiva, Marqueasas

be a salty old Frenchman who, with his daughter, her husband and child, lived in a sprawling, unpainted wooden house on a hillside overlooking the bay. Thirty years earlier, when finished with his military service, Antoine had gone to Tahiti and tried to make a living as a planter. Finding the competition from numerous Chinese vegetable growers too stiff, he moved to Atuona, married, and for 20 years has been making a living out of his crops. He gave us five beautiful cantaloupes, and we bought five cabbages. When I asked for permission to photograph his price list, scribbled on a piece of cardboard tacked to the wall, he thought I was photographing a wooden sword next to it. He insisted on giving me the intricately carved sword as a gift. It was carved by Jean Baptiste Brown.

Feb. 13, Barbara: Made a last minute mail, food and ice run to Atuona, and sailed for Fatu Hiva around noon. It was night when we finally ghosted into Hanavave Bay (Bay of Virgins). Lights from a new generator in the village served as a reference point as we anchored. Huge, phallic stone pinnacles silhouetted against moonlit clouds looked like overgrown tikis standing guard over a charmed bay.

Feb. 14: As soon as we were ashore, a figure appeared in one of the schoolhouse windows and desperately motioned us inside. The doors were all locked, but in a minute a side door opened and a petite French school teacher, obviously starved for European companionship, greeted us. In her cassette-course English, she told us how lazy the Marquesans were, how they had no use for books and reading and that their children's school work averaged three years behind the children in France. "All they do is fish, hunt, sleep and make babies!" she commented. We asked her why she had chosen to teach in such an isolated place. Her response: she receives a substantial bonus for teaching on Fatu Hiva, but counts the days until she can return to France.

The education she spoke about had to do with facts and figures, not about natural wisdom, connection to family or earth. What could she teach these people, she who had come here only for the money? There was no humility, no curiosity, in her knowledge.

Feb. 15, John: Up at 5:00 a.m. for a last run ashore to fill our water jugs and deliver gifts to an old man who had loaded us down with 20 pamplemouse (grapefruit) the day before. We then left the Marquesas Islands headed for the Tuamotu Islands.

Chapter 7
THE TUAMOTUS:
NECKLACES OF CORAL

John: The Tuamotus' low visibility combined with unpredictable and strong currents between islands, have given the group a nickname, 'Dangerous Archipelago'. I've seen the remains of 20 yachts, fishing boats and ships scattered on the four islands of the northeast part of the Tuamotus.

The current at sea between the Marquesas and Tuamotus averages one-half to three-quarters of a knot but this increases, sometimes up to 4 knots when approaching the atolls. Almost without exception, the wrecked yachts resulted from crews not on watch at landfall.

At night it's impossible to see the reef in time, so I never plan a landfall in the dark. When squally weather has prevented getting an accurate position, I've headed back to sea on a course that took me 180 degrees away from land. I would sail slowly under reduced sail until either the weather and visibility improved, or daylight came.

The Tuamotus are directly in line between the Marquesas and Tahiti, but some cruisers choose to bypass this fascinating group; they sail around the northeast corner, then straight south to Tahiti. The majority stop only at the islands of Ahe, Manihi, and Rangiroa. Central islands may receive only one yacht in several years.

Each of the five times I've sailed through the Tuamotus, I've taken a different route, visiting new islands. Looking at the chart and sailing directions, I decided to make Raroia our first stop this trip. Thor Heyerdahl cracked up here with the *Kon Tiki* in 1947. I had never met anyone who had stopped at the island, but the charts and sailing directions detailed a fairly safe pass and a fair anchorage near the village.

The Tuamotus (actually only one island, Pukapuka) were first spotted in 1521 by Magellan, but Taiaro was not discovered until 1935 and the French Navy just completed the charts of the Archipelago in the 1950s.

These islands were first settled 1000 to 1500 A.D. by warriors vanquished from Tahiti and the Marquesas. Few islands had permanent populations and life was more difficult here than in Tahiti or the Marquesas. The inhabitants resorted to digging pits in the sand to grow taro and fruit trees. By 1850 the influence of the missionaries and churches had changed the nomadic lifestyle of the Tuamotuan people. Coconut plantations were started to encourage the inhabitants to become more settled. Hundreds of tons of copra were exported to the coconut oil refinery in Tahiti. Income from pearl shells meant the islanders could change from a subsistence lifestyle to a trade-oriented one. Now they could build ornate colonial-style houses with Douglas fir from Oregon, eat canned salmon from Alaska, even import Model T's.

Today most of the islands have a basic lifestyle and economy. On a few islands the famous South Seas' black pearls are cultured. Two of the islands (Manihi and Rangiroa) have expensive, small hotels, but most of the people work copra or fish. Transportation ranges from several flights a day between Rangiroa (pop. 1000) and Tahiti, to only one or two visits per year by trading boats to the smaller islands, some populated by only four or five persons.

The French provide teachers and nurses trained in Tahiti, and medical clinics on all but the smallest of the inhabited islands. Solar-powered radios link nurses to Tahiti and they can call for directions or evacuations. Several islands now have gravel airstrips and a flight or two from Tahiti by a Twin Otter (a twin engine DeHaviland short take-off and landing airplane).

Cyclones devastated some atolls in 1878, 1905, 1906, 1958 and eight were hit during 1983. The increase in cyclone activity has a direct correlation with increased water temperature or "El Nino". Cyclone season runs from late October through the end of March. Therefore the government asks cruisers to leave the Territory by September. Since 1966, two of the southeastern Tuamotu atolls, Moruroa and Fangataufa, have been the French government's "Nevada Test Site" for nuclear weapons. Due to political pressures, they may soon move part of the test site to the Kerguelen Islands in the south Indian Ocean.

Feb. 17, Barbara: The thermometer at the chart table read 100 degrees today. The oppressive heat drove me on deck; in the shade of the mainsail, I felt a 5-knot breeze generated by our motoring. From the deck I spotted my first coral atoll, Napuka, a barely discernible frayed green band on the horizon. Motoring closer, the island's six-foot high white coral sand base became evident. Salt spray clouded the shoreline where swells, long at sea, crashed in frothy masses on the sharp teeth of the coral. Even during the day in excellent visibility it is difficult to distinguish a distant atoll from a wave, and the tops of the 70-foot palm trees were visible only from seven miles at deck level.

We passed a small village peeking out from the palm trees and a few children ran along the beach. They waved and followed our progress until they reached the end of the islet we were paralleling. I got thirsty just thinking about living on an atoll in the equatorial sun.

Feb. 18: Motorsailing with the main up to steady us, the roiling waters of Raroia Pass suddenly appeared before us. I was scared by the prospect of entering.

Deferring to John's judgment, we made our approach with the waves breaking on the coral shelf on either side of the pass. Swells rolling in from astern met with the swift ebb current from the lagoon ahead of us, creating confused seas in the narrow confines of the pass. Whirlpools bubbled and surged to the surface, whitecaps and overfalls formed a rapidly moving mass of water. *Mahina Tiare* was locked in a tug-of-war between surf and current, twisting under the strain. But the 25 horsepower Volvo engine prevailed and within minutes the still waters of the lagoon surrounded us. A rooster crowed ashore, and after four days of motoring in windlass conditions we were struck by the quietness of our surroundings. We have never motored for so long a time. We asked the locals when the trades had last blown, and they answered, "six weeks ago."

Feb. 19: The nutrient-rich water by a pass is an excellent place to find abundant coral and sea life. The pass at Raroia was a good example. I had never seen such a variety of tropical fish in one place, nor had I seen such large examples of common species like parrot fish. Schools of small fish darted into their coral head sanctuaries when scared, then all shot out at once. These emerging bright bits of color resembled underwater fireworks. As we slowly glided with the current past a large coral head, the fat speckled head of the largest fish I had ever seen looked at me from a hole in the coral. His overslung jaw and protruding teeth gave him a brooding expression, and I kept my distance.

Later, ashore, by jutting out my lower jaw I did an impression of him for the locals who told me he was a grouper, harmless unless speared. His best defense when speared was either to bite the skin diver with his powerful jaws, holding the diver until he drowned, or else back into his coral cave where it was virtually impossible to pull him out.

John retrieved the Avon, which was drifting out the pass, but was cruised by an inquisitive 12-foot shark. We decided to called it a day and climbed back into the dinghy.

The smaller, black-tipped reef sharks common to these waters are rarely a problem, but often larger pelagic sharks will loiter near the passes. They are more aggressive and make spearfishing a challenging operation for the locals.

Raroia's village was a mixture of impressive coral-limestone cement structures and old, often vacant, colonial-style wooden houses. The large, whitewashed church with stained glass windows hinted of Raroia's prosperous past when oil from coconuts was a valuable commodity and pearl shell was abundant in the lagoon. The population has dwindled from around 200 at its peak to roughly 60 now. Many of the islanders have moved to Papeete for better school and job opportunities. The price paid for coconut oil on the international market has steadily declined, but the French government subsidizes the prices to ensure a living for those who continue to work copra.

Sitting on the steps of a once-grand colonial-style house by the wharf, 63-year-old Etienne Estoll motioned us to follow him into his kitchen, a room detached from the main house. Pointing to a dusty photograph of a Tuamotu woman dressed in a Victorian wedding gown, arm-in-arm with a Caucasian man, he explained these were his parents; he was half American. Then he pointed to a photograph of Thor Heyerdahl and Bengt Danielson, taken when they were young men; he told us they were his friends.

We sat around his kitchen table transported by his story to a night 40 years earlier. The year was 1947; the men, home from fighting in

Europe and Africa; the village, quiet except for a couple of barking dogs. Then came the cry through the village, "Fires on the motu, lights on the motu!" In a village so small, everyone knew where everyone else was. No one had visited the motu furthest to windward for several months, no ships had entered the lagoon in months. What could the glow of distant bonfires mean? The people of the Tuamotus are superstitious, and so they assumed that ghosts or spirits camped on the tiny motu (islet).

The next morning the tradewinds washed cans of pork and beans and a few battered crates onto the beach in the village. And then the bravest — and least superstitious — launched their sailing canoes and set out to meet the spirits. They were shocked to find Thor Heyerdahl and the crew of *Kon Tiki*. The battered balsa log raft had been thrown high on the reef on the windward-most part of the atoll.

The local men and women wasted no time in helping Heyerdahl's crew salvage the equipment. Then, using muscle power and a high tide, they dragged the unwieldy raft over the coral reef and into the lagoon.

Eventually *Kon Tiki* was towed to Tahiti by a government schooner, then shipped on deck back to Norway where it is still on display in the Heyerdahl museum. Bengt Danielson stayed in Tahiti and occasionally returns to Raroia where his adopted son was born.

Although Heyerdahl's drift voyage proved the feasibility of an east-west migration to Polynesia, scientists believe the migration was from west to east in Polynesian catamarans, some up to 100 feet long and capable of speeds over 15 knots under sail.

We left Etienne and walked to the ocean side of the motu. I absent mindedly picked up a pink cone shell, dropping it like a hot potato when a tiny claw pinched my finger. Someone was home. Hermit crabs seem to like the same shells I do, and I don't have the heart to evict them.

Heading back to *Mahina Tiare* at sunset, we heard the women singing in the church, while several of the young men were getting boxing lessons from the policeman. They were moving black shapes against the aqua background of the lagoon.

Feb. 20: Three island men stopped by in their plywood speedboat. They were returning from a fishing trip outside the pass where, using hand lines, they had caught 40 bonito in half an hour. They gave us

106

three fish, then visited in the cockpit. Cleaning our fish on the wharf drew several three-foot long black-tipped sharks. I tapped one on the back with a stick, sending him shooting off into the distance. This was a small triumph, for I have always swum away from them.

We took a long swim around the boat in the afternoon. The incredible water clarity is a mixed blessing. Although we can see over 200 feet, this view often includes sulking sharks and the skinny, brazen remora fish which attach themselves to the sharks. Several remoras had attached themselves to our keel and others kept approaching me. It seemed they thought I'd be a good candidate to attach their flat sucker heads to. In a way I prefer cloudy water which hides some of the sinister creatures around me. What I can't see, I don't worry about.

Feb. 22, John: Despite full throttle, we were standing still, occasionally slipping backward as we fought to enter Taenga's pass against the 7-knot current. The Sailing Directions state, *"There is an almost constant outflow through the pass. This can attain a rate of 10 knots … the brief inflow rarely exceeds 3 knots."* We found out later that the current often ebbs continually for days, even weeks depending on the amount of water coming over the reef.

Why was I risking *Mahina Tiare* to battle against such strong currents in a dangerous pass that didn't even provide a passage all the way into the lagoon of Taenga? Maybe I was being a bit crazy, but ten years ago when I was between boats, I had stayed in a cheap Papeete hotel, the Mahina Tea. There I had met Bill, a fellow wanderer and surfer who traveled on local trading boats to find the most outrageous surf and diving spots in the world.

Somehow Bill had ended up on a tiny island in the Tuamotus — Taenga — which had only 40 inhabitants. In the evenings Bill told me intriguing stories of life on this isolated atoll which had never had any permanent European residents. He told of a custom: When an island woman died, the Taengans did not bury her for over a week, but kept the body in its coffin in a house where women sang haunting chants over it. He also recounted stories of the supernatural. If this wasn't enough to get me all fired up to see Taenga, he mentioned that the island had a pass. Although this pass didn't go all of the way up to the wharf where the fishing boat from Papeete had dropped and picked him up. Bill gave me the name of the mayor and encouraged me to visit the island. I took notes and decided that some day I would visit Taenga.

In Papeete at the French Naval headquarters and later in the States, I tried to find a chart of Taenga only to be told that none had ever been made. But a large-scale French chart of the general area of the Tuamotus was available. Now, after ten years, I was finally going to experience Taenga, IF we could make it through the pass!

Barbara: Absorbed in battling the current and trying not to scrape the coral, we were surprised to look up and find 40 people crowding the small concrete quay. One, an islander named Tahura, yelled to me in three different languages. He also pantomimed that I throw him our bowline. Meanwhile, the crowd roared with laughter at his antics. If we had tied the bow line ashore before a spring line, the current would have rammed our bow into the rough dock. John kept the engine in gear and running even after we were tied alongside because the current, still registering 4 knots on our knotmeter, tended to push the boat heavily against the wharf.

As soon as the dock lines were secure, Tahura hopped into his plywood speedboat and carried our anchor and chain up current in the pass. Once he had set the bow anchor, we were able to take much of the strain off the lines and shut the engine down. It was a tricky mooring at best, and could easily become a dangerous trap with a change in conditions.

Before I had time to catch my breath, Vaiea, a vibrant young schoolteacher from Tahiti, had me by the hand and was leading me into the village where I was guest of honor at a rousing game of volleyball. All young people on the island were players.

As the sun set my eyes were on the glow of color around me, not on the volleyball. The island is carpeted with white sand and crushed coral. The houses are painted pastel colors and bright squares of fabric dry on lines between pink-blossomed plumeria trees. All the fallen leaves had been raked up and the island had a park-like appearance.

Vaiea and her 18-year-old brother, Farani, suggested we join them in their comfortable government-supplied schoolteacher's house after the game.

Vaiea and Farani are "Demis" — half Tahitian and half French — and had only recently come from Tahiti. Vaiea explained in flawless French that a single young woman from another place should not live

Speared sea turtle, endangered species

on the outer islands alone, so her brother volunteered to assist her for one school year in preparing and correcting the lessons. Vaiea was starved for new conversation and contact on this tiny island.

Feb. 23: By sunup villagers were departing for the surrounding motus to work copra and tend their pearl shell farms. Kids were bringing wheelbarrow loads of fallen leaves and flowers to dump into the current. A speedboat was about to take off out the pass on a fishing trip when excited shouts of "HONU, HONU!" were heard. Within seconds the five men aboard had donned fins and masks, grabbed their spearguns and were in hot pursuit of a green sea turtle. In less than a minute, the youngest of the divers broke the surface near the side of the pass and thrust the speared turtle in the air as he swam against the current to the wharf. Bright red blood foamed where the turtle's lung had been punctured and its large, lidded eyes looked human and intelligent; they seemed to blink in pain. Turtle meat is the top delicacy on this island where corned beef, fish, rice, coconut — and occasionally dog — form a monotonous diet.

Tahura, the clown who had helped take our anchor out when we arrived, invited us to go work copra with his family on the motu across the pass. I think he never anticipated that we would accept his invitation. His small, homemade plywood speedboat was overloaded by the time he'd put his parents, children, wife and us in the boat (nine people). The coconut sennit twine that he used to start the engine didn't inspire confidence, but we knew that if the motor broke down and the boat was swept out the pass, somebody would probably see and rescue us. Ten minutes later we approached the motu and Tahura edged the boat gently into the coral shallows. We hopped out in three feet of water and waded ashore.

Five of us went to work gathering fallen coconut branches and old husks into piles to burn while Farani spiked fallen coconuts and threw them into vague piles. Tahura, dark, trim and very fit, swung an axe over his head time after time, splitting hundreds of coconuts in half with one blow. The opened nuts were then piled face down in lines eight feet long and three feet high to dry for several weeks. In the older nuts a spongy inner core, the nau nau, was removed and saved to feed the pigs. Once dried, the white meat (copra) would be removed from the husks and placed in 100-pound sacks to await the next trading vessel. The empty husks would be burned.

The work was exhausting but fun. A strong breeze kept us cool and the canopy of trees filtered the sunlight into a latticework of small bright patches on the ground. Occasionally an overturned branch would expose the purple-blue body of a tree-climbing coconut crab. These crabs are collected to prevent them from damaging the young nuts on the trees. Roasted, the crabs are eaten as a delicacy. Meanwhile the small children sat in a circle, smashing the shells of hermit crabs, the animals inside to be used as fish bait. When we stopped for a breather, Tahura reached high into the trees with a long harpoon to pry down refreshing green drinking coconuts called viavia. The cool liquid was thirst-quenching, but the best part was the sweet custard-like coating (nia) on the inside of the nut. Everyone shared a lunch of rice, corned beef and sweet coffee heated over a coconut husk fire.

Madeline, Tahura's four-year-old daughter, sat on John's lap at every opportunity. Tahura asked quite seriously if we would like to adopt her. Although Madeline was one of his five children and his young wife Peline would probably have many more, the offer was made out of generosity, not as an attempt to get rid of an extra child. Children, considered a blessing, are very much loved in the Polynesian

John and Madeline

culture. When islanders find out that John and I don't have children, they are saddened, unable to understand why anyone would choose not to have a child. Tahura jokingly offered to swap his wife for me for an evening, in case John was having trouble figuring things out.

Late afternoon, Tahura's jovial 200-pound mother set the piles of downed fronds ablaze in a spectacular show of orange against the green palm background. When the fire had consumed the debris, Tahura's patch of coconut forest looked like a manicured park.

By the time we arrived back at the wharf, I couldn't wait to swim. Diving off the wharf I was tugged instantly by the strongly ebbing current. I had to fight to get back to shore downstream where the kids and fish clustered in a small back eddy. Viewed from underwater I observed a strange seascape of fish, children's legs, and assorted jetsam from the village.

That night we had a dinner at Tahura's house: fried red snapper, baked parrot fish with rice, coconut bread and crepes. We sat at a low table with benches — the only furnishings in the large one-room house built on a concrete slab. He told us that everyone in the village slept outside on the ground or on the wharf. "Cooler, and fewer mosquitoes outside," he explained.

Peline didn't sit at the table but waited, nursing her baby, until we were through. She had thick, wavy hair and large eyes. Attractive, but stout, she looked older than her 24 years.

Feb. 24: We accepted Tahura's invitation to go diving on the outside of the pass, and shortly after breakfast piled into his speedboat with him, Farani, two other islanders and a visiting Frenchman named Yves.

While the others were spearing fish, John and I watched from underwater. A wall of translucent blue-green water would suck seaward in a concave arch, then rotate up and down in an explosion of white frothy bubbles near the reef.

After a tub had been filled with fish, Tahura headed the boat back in the pass. Yves joined us for lunch.

John: Yves, a fit man in his mid-forties, had worked for more than 15 years as a registered nurse in the most isolated islands in French Polynesia, postings no one else wanted. Intrigued by Polynesian culture and history, his idea of a vacation was volunteering for Medicins sans Frontiers (Doctors without Borders) in Africa.

He told me about his being an 18-year-old draftee in the French Army during the Algerian war of independence, and asking himself: "Why am I here, trying to kill these people who want freedom?" He remembered that the French government had decided to withdraw from Algeria but the generals refused to leave. The soldiers went on strike against the generals. After his experience in Algeria, Yves became a nurse, took a job offered at a Papeete hospital, and has made French Polynesia his home ever since.

He has a commercial pilot's license and has competed in aerobatic competitions in Europe, the U.S. and Tahiti. We traded old aviation magazines, and he promised to help me get my reciprocal French pilot's license once we arrived in Tahiti.

Barbara: I took up Vaiea's invitation to sleep ashore, but it was a fitful night. The wind in the palms and rushing current in the pass kept me worried about the safety of the boat. Chickens scratching in the brittle coral outside the open window sounded like approaching footsteps. After eight months of living aboard, the boat was home now, and I was uneasy sleeping on land alone.

Feb. 25, John: Yves was waiting at the boat and as we reduced the number of docklines from eight to two, he dove and freed our anchor; I took up the strain by putting the engine into gear. We recruited Peline, who had been getting her hair de-liced by a friend on the wharf, to cast off the last bowline as Yves and Barbara fended *Mahina Tiare* off the concrete.

Everything was going as planned until I increased power and the engine died. We were completely out of fuel. There wasn't even a drop left–not even in our extra jerry jugs–and none on the island. While Yves and Peline helped pull in the lines again, I poured our last two gallons of stove kerosene into the main tank, bled the fuel system, and we tried to leave again. Peline released the bowline first, and in seconds the current grabbed the bow, swung the boat 180 degrees and shot us out the pass like the cork out of a champagne bottle.

Feb. 26 - March 3: The rest of our tour of the Tuamotus: Makemo atoll where the mayor gave us ten gallons of diesel, and Tahanea, an uninhabited atoll with navigable pass. One could spend months tucked away in the lagoon of one of these uninhabited necklaces of coral but Tahiti beckoned.

Chapter 8

TAHITI & MOPELIA:

TRAFFIC, TURTLES AND TROPIC BIRDS

"Seen from the sea, the prospect is magnificent. It is one mass of shaded tints of green, from beach to mountaintop; endlessly diversified with valleys, ridges, glens and cascades. Over the ridges, here and there, the loftiest peaks fling their shadows far down the valleys... upon a nearer approach, the picture loses not its attraction..." Herman Melville, 1842.

March 4, Barbara: Seen from a distance, the island of Tahiti is every bit as green, undulating and alluring as the romantic South Seas writers portray. But it is with a bit of sadness that I approach Tahiti; I foresee my time off the "beaten track," my time of living carefree and incommunicado, will be ending. Our goal of reaching Easter and Pitcairn Islands is behind us, our food stores and cruising kitty are getting low, so Tahiti and her capitol of Papeete means phone calls, bills, and a return to a somewhat hectic pace. The last eight months of escapist cruising have been by far the happiest time of my life. Will the return to reality end my newly-found serenity?

Near midnight, in a cool drizzle, we eased through the red and green flashing buoys marking the entrance to Papeete harbor. The distinct "city smell" of diesel fumes from the buses and generators hung in the night air. The hulls of a dozen yachts at anchor were silhouetted by the blaze of street lights. We made out the shape of the 76-foot Norwegian ketch *Svanhild* which we had met months earlier in the Galapagos, and a flood of happy memories accompanied the recognition.

March 5, John: I went ashore, hoping to get our checking-in paperwork out of the way quickly. But I was told that the day was a religious holiday, to come back in three days. The immigration officer said we could move a few miles around the corner to the quieter anchorage off Maeva Beach Hotel, and gave us permission to go ashore. The island of Tahiti has dozens of secluded, protected anchorages SE from Maeva Beach, but very few yachts ever visit them.

March 6, Barbara: *"Upon nearer approach, the picture loses not its charm..."* It's at this point that the modern day traveler landing in Papeete would beg to differ with Melville.

Papeete is first and foremost a city, a bustling international port, the largest in the eastern South Pacific. It is noisy, traffic-packed, chic, tropical, exotic and exciting. Papeete is — an unlikely blend of French colonialism and Polynesian culture in transition. Having visited here by plane a few years ago, I knew not to expect the innocent paradise which draws so many visitors. I could freely appreciate Papeete and Tahiti for their present-day charms without the letdown of a first-time visitor.

A fifteen-minute ride in a colorful wooden-sided bus called "le truck" cost 90 cents and landed us midtown next to the market. The excitement of a city and the anticipation of mail along with seeing old friends dispelled my earlier reservations about our Tahiti landfall.

Heaps of letters and several packages awaited us at the American Express office plus a big hug for John from Marie Helene, the office manager who has collected mail for John during his many visits.

That night we enjoyed sunset drinks aboard a friend's boat tied to the quay. Here we met more cruising friends from the Marquesas and Galapagos. After drinks, a dozen of us strolled along the quay to "Les Brochettes," an eclectic collection of about 50 vans that have been converted into mobile restaurants. We walked the length of the vans trying to decide between homemade pizza baked in a wood-fired brick oven, couscous, shish kebabs, barbecued chicken or steak, Vietnamese or Thai food or poisson cru (marinated raw fish). Papeete, the crossroads — coming out of isolation was becoming more fun by the day.

March 7, John: My birthday. Barbara spent the afternoon baking a birthday cake, and in the French tradition I invited friends to join us for dinner in town. New friends, Tommy and Lynn from Belfast (they'd built their Tahiti ketch in their backyard nine years ago) and old friends of mine, Earl and Irene and their daughter, Maimiti, joined us at Lou Pescadou's — a raucous Italian pizza and seafood joint near the cathedral in downtown Papeete.

Suzy, the daughter of the owner of Acajou's restaurant, happened to be at the next table. Acajou's is the Papeete restaurant where Tuesday-go-to-meeting luncheons are a tradition. For years Earl Schenck has invited visiting cruisers to join him there for beer and lunch and it's become a tradition. Many a Tuesday over the years Earl and I plus a bunch of cruisers have sat at Acajou's solving the problems of the world while Papeete's street life bustled by.

Suzy bought us a bottle of Moet champagne, served in frosted glasses. We shared cake and champagne with the people seated at nearby tables; what a great way to turn 35.

March 9, Barbara: For a few months we'd been talking with Earl on his "Coffee Klatch," an informal ham radio get-together three times a week. He'd been telling us of his Tahitian wife Irene's all-night fishing trips in Tahiti's lagoon. Pleasantly surprised that any fish survived so close to town, I asked Irene if I could tag along. At 10:00 p.m. she met me ashore, carrying her 30th birthday present, a shiny new Coleman pressure lantern. The lantern is the most important tool for successful night fishing, and one of the most prized possessions of Polynesians on the outer islands.

Irene's brother, Timmie, and sister, Marguerite, carefully primed and lit the lantern, then Timmie stood at the bow of the family's well worn outrigger canoe dangling the lantern from one hand. Next, Irene took up the oars and Marguerite and I stepped into the stern and sat down.

The lagoon was black and mirror-calm. The oars made small splashes as Irene rowed away from shore. She stood, wielding a long, light harpoon tipped with three small spikes. Needle-shaped silver fish darted and jumped one or two at a time toward the light. Irene expertly speared these fish — the length of my little finger — and Marguerite removed their wriggling bodies into a bucket. Pointing to the fish, I asked incredulously, "Pour manger?" (For eating?). "Oui," they replied. I had to ask again, "You mean these aren't for bait?" "Non, pour manger." I thought to myself — all of this effort for sardine-sized fish; speared one by one we'll be here all night! Timmie took his turn at the spear and I marveled at the accuracy of his aim. Just about every second throw resulted in a fish. And now it was my turn. After several unsuccessful stabs, two fish with a death wish impaled themselves together on the end of the spear. I was an instant hero, and Irene and Timmie made unceasing fun of Marguerite, who never catches fish.

Slowly it dawned on me that the least important part of Irene's fishing expeditions with her family were the number of fish caught. They did agree that this night was not a good one for fishing, either the moon or tide to blame. After two hours I was tired and they dropped me at *Mahina Tiare*. But they continued fishing until the early hours of the morning, more than half filling their small pail. Then Irene spent the rest of the morning cleaning and scaling the minute fish to make poisson cru.

March 11, John: Hoisted anchor and motored a half-mile south to Lotus Marina, to the only floating fuel dock in the territory. The marina is just a few years old and the fuel dock has reasonably priced and very clean diesel fuel, plus engine oil, a few outboard parts and pretty Tahitian girls to help you tie up.

March 12, Barbara: To appreciate the activities of the tropics, one must visit the towns and villages either at sunrise or sunset. We caught an early morning bus to the heart of Papeete to visit the public market. It was only 6:00 a.m., but the pulsing beat of reggae music blaring from large speakers in the back of the bus had us completely awake by the time we reached the market. The entire area is packed with people, buses, Chinese shops, snack bars and hole-in-the-wall restaurants.

With the arrival of fresh fish at 5 a.m. and 6 a.m., the Papeete market is at its liveliest. Some of the fish are still flopping as they are hung by either head or tail in long rows for sale. Fresh pork and pigs' heads, live chickens and tons of fruit and vegetables are symmetrically displayed in rows and pyramids. The market is washed down with fire hoses each morning and night eliminating clouds of flies and fishy smells.

What would Tahiti be without flowers? The overpowering fragrance in the market is the natural perfume of freshly cut flowers,

Sea Cloud tied to Papaetee's wharf

bundled and standing in buckets of water. On display, not only indigenous exotic tropical flowers, but large arrangements of roses and carnations. Handwoven hats, mats, grass skirts, shell leis and scented coconut oil in old whiskey bottles are displayed on tables, especially for the tourist trade.

Fish and watermelon are the big sellers at the market. Weekly, islanders come from Huahine and Maupiti with their watermelon and produce. They camp out next to the market in temporary shelters of cardboard packing cases with blue plastic tarps as walls and ceilings. When they've sold all their produce, they catch the next boat home — prices for everything are posted and there is no bargaining.

Tourists come to the market to capture the elusive "native look" of Tahiti with their cameras. The vendors aren't enthusiastic about having pictures taken. But after buying vegetables, then asking permission we were graciously accommodated and a 210 mm telephoto lens allowed us close-ups photos without being pushy.

To seaward of the market is Quai du Commerce, the waterfront boulevard where larger yachts tie stern-to. Dozens of little stalls sell shells, shell jewelry and wood carvings on the inland side of the street. Also available, colorfully dyed and printed pareus, a cool and versatile attire for women in the tropics.

March 15, John: Earlier in the week we received a relayed and garbled message via radio from our friend Nig Brown that the *Sea Cloud* had just departed Pitcairn for Tahiti with one of our friends from Friday Harbor aboard.

We couldn't imagine who among our friends could afford to sail on *Sea Cloud* as a passenger, but were delighted to find out that Tom Hook, an old friend of mine and former co-worker of Barbara's, was cruise director.

Moored alongside the cruise ship wharf in Papeete, the *Sea Cloud* was a magnificent sight. She was built in Germany in 1931, by E.F. Hutton as a wedding gift for his bride, Marjorie Merriweather Post. Today the 316-foot, four-masted square rigger is owned by eight German businessmen who occasionally sail aboard with their families and paying passengers. Her normal compliment of guests is about 55 who, for up to $1,000 per day, sail in luxury on the largest private classical sailing ship in the world.

Since the next set of passengers hadn't arrived, Tom poured us drinks in the posh panelled lounge, then played jazz tunes on the grand piano in the saloon. Below deck, Marjorie Post's former cabin was complete with gold fixtures, Italian marble vanity, fireplace and a secret passage through to her husband's cabin. Tom's own cabin was tiny — a desk, single bunk and a copying machine that took up half the space. His job was to arrange events, tours, play the piano and generally keep the guests entertained. The most difficult aspect of his job was finding piano tuners on short notice.

Tom had opened up a jazz club in Avignon, France and served as an interpreter-guide on exclusive balloon tours of the French wine country. He'd come a long way from playing piano in Friday Harbor bars on rainy winter nights.

March 16, Barbara: Sleepy-eyed, we met our friends Jim and Kathy Bybokas at the Faaa airport which was totally darkened, then, miraculously, came alive at 4:30 a.m. when the international flights began arriving. We brought fresh flower leis for them from women who camp out all night next to the airport. For us, it seemed like Christmas. Only true sailing friends would bring a large duffel bag plus an extra suitcase crammed with spare boat parts from West Marine, medical supplies and treats too expensive to buy in Tahiti.

March 17 - June 19: We took Jim and Kathy on a tour of Raiatea, Tahaa, Huahine, Moorea and Bora Bora, islands westernized and highly receptive to tourists.

June 19: We left Bora Bora around noon with steady tradewinds on our stern quarter and passed Maupiti at sunset. When the sea is kind, the long quiet times alone on watch breed memories and snippets of poetry. Perhaps the clear night air distills thoughts like morning dew. I find myself remembering people and events that I had long forgotten. Defining one's journey is a solitary pursuit, companionship and the day's distractions stem the flow of thoughts and free associations. More and more I realize this voyage is more than a string of unending adventures. It is nourishment for the soul.

June 20: By noon we were nine miles off Mopelia, and by standing on the boom we were able to see the dark green tops of coconut trees. Mopelia, also known as Maupihaa, is the Society Islands' only atoll with a navigable pass into the lagoon.

Marcia Davock, in her book *Cruising Guide to Tahiti and the French Society Islands* states, *"When you are in the right position (to enter the pass) you may take one look and change your mind about entering!"*

As we inched into the pass, it seemed the current could spin us around, sending us crashing into the jagged coral on either side. We weren't making any progress, but then as the pass widened our pace and confidence increased. As we entered the lagoon, clouds of frigate birds and terns from the nearby motu wheeled and squealed overhead.

Once inside the pass, the lagoon was deep except for a few spots where mammoth coral heads grow to within inches of the surface. We anchored in ten feet of water on a sandy bottom and near the only village.

Mopelia's village is a collection of abandoned cement houses covered with moss and graffiti and two thatch houses on stilts by the edge of the lagoon. There isn't a Gendarmerie or radio transmitter on the island, so it isn't possible to check in or out of the territory here.

Several cisterns provide water for the island's present population of three, and there is often enough water for visiting yachters, after asking permission, to top their tanks up.

John: From our anchorage near the village we saw a man unloading copra from a speedboat on the beach. Michelle, a strong looking

Tahitian in his mid-20s, met us in front of his thatch stilt house and helped us pull our boat out of the water. He welcomed us in French, then went back to effortlessly lifting his 100-pound sacks of copra from the bottom of the speedboat to his shoulder, carrying them up the beach and dumping them in a dilapidated copra drier. When I offered to give him a hand, Michelle just sort of chuckled.

Mopelia is leased until 1999 to the Compagne Francaise de Tahiti and has been planted in coconut trees for the past century. Once a thriving plantation, Michelle is now the only permanent copra cutter, but workers from Maupiti and Huahine visit periodically. Since working copra is the only steady means of support on the island, life gets monotonous, and we sensed that Michelle was happy for our companionship and the fresh fruits and vegetables we brought him.

Barbara: Michelle prepared drinking nuts for us after which the three of us ambled down the beach to meet Adrianne and Marcello, the only other inhabitants. They immediately invited us to join them on a lobster hunt at nightfall.

Exhausted from our passage the last thing we wanted was a late night, but sensing this might be an adventure and my only opportunity to taste the much talked-about but so far elusive South Pacific lobster, we accepted. If nothing else, I learned on this trip to grab opportunities when they present themselves — often they will not be repeated.

At 7:30 p.m. we were on the beach in long pants and boots. We expected to walk a hundred yards or so to the ocean side of the motu for our lobster; instead, the five of us piled into Michelle's leaky flat-bottomed plywood boat equipped with a tired-looking 20 hp Johnson motor. But no oars or paddles. A moonless night is ideal for collecting lobsters, and it was pitch black as we headed across the lagoon. The engine kicked up as we ran over shallow coral patches invisible in the darkness and I thought, if these people wanted to dump us in the middle of the lagoon, or if the engine conks out, all of us would be swept out the pass and who would know what had happened? We could feel the current grab the boat once we were in the pass. Michelle found the edge by carefully running the boat aground, then backing off and looking for a place where there was enough water over the coral for us to pull the boat by hand away from the pass and onto the fringing outer reef. As he carefully set three homemade re-bar anchors in holes in the coral, it was obvious that they frequently had gone lobster fishing in this area at night.

Michelle said a brief but serious prayer in Tahitian before we left the boat, and Marcello primed and pumped up the Coleman lantern whose brilliant light would attract the lobsters.

Stumbling along the coral shelf, John and I tried to avoid stepping in the deep holes filled with spiny urchins. The knee-deep ebbing current from the lagoon blurred the water and tried to tug our legs out from under us. As we headed toward the breakers on the outer edge of the reef, Marcello warned us to stand still, sideways to the waves as they tumbled over the reef. Presently, a few large combers crashed in, hissing foam around us to our thighs, and nearly sucking us out to sea.

Adrianne told us: "Look out for two moving orange spots (the eyes of the lobster reflected in light), then step quickly on the lobster's body. I'll pick it up with gloves." Sure, I thought, the only way I'll trap a lobster is if I accidentally step on one. In two hours our friends caught 15 lobsters and John and I managed not to get sucked out to sea. Tired and soaked, I swore to never again complain about the high price of

Adrian and Marcello's house, Mopelia

lobster.

Back at the village, a cooking pot over an open fire was quickly brimming with lobster, while crabs caught earlier in the day were steaming over the coals. A passing midnight squall drove us up steep wooden stairs that spiralled around the trunk of a palm tree and into the shelter of Adrianne and Marcello's simple thatch house. Rice, crab and lobster heaped our plates. Michelle offered around a bottle of Johnny Walker Scotch, and when we all declined, in true Tahitian style he drank the entire bottle himself over the course of the evening.

Radio Tahiti provided our friends with current world events; they knew about warships amassing in the Persian Gulf. Closer to home, they told us of their trips to neighboring uninhabited Scilly Island to collect green sea turtles and their eggs.

Scilly is one of the few islands in the Pacific supporting large numbers of endangered breeding sea turtles, a species hunted to near extinction on most inhabited islands. Michelle illegally sells the adult turtles to visiting fishing boats from Bora Bora, the fishermen then smuggle them to Tahiti where they are unloaded at night on deserted beaches and illegally sold to restaurants or families. The turtles bring up to $800 each.

The turtle eggs they bring back from Scilly are hatched in an enclosure on the sandy beach in front of the village, safe from wild pigs and sea birds. The baby turtles are raised in saltwater pens until they reach a size which allows them to outswim most of their predators. Released, these turtles eventually return to the same beach where they were hatched to lay their own eggs. Although those involved know it's illegal to kill the turtles, eating turtle meat always has been part of Polynesian culture, and today financial gains are terrific compared to cutting copra.

We mentioned that on nearly all islands turtles were either very rare or non-existent because of overfishing. Michelle explained they were careful not to take all available turtles, and they hoped that as a result of their efforts to protect the babies, more were surviving.

Marcello gave us two cooked lobsters to take back to the boat for breakfast, then placed the remaining live lobsters in a chicken wire cage which he tossed into the shallow water of the lagoon: "There's your refrigerator. When you want more lobster, come and get them."

June 21: *Solveig IV,* a Swedish-built 42-foot Hallberg Rassy ketch, braved Mopelia's narrow pass to anchor next to us. Her German owners, crusty Rollo Gebhart and his elegant young cruising partner Angelica Zilcher, invited us aboard. Rollo, a former actor, captivated us with tales of the German Count Felix von Luckner's exploits during World War I in his pirate/raiding ship the *Seeadler.*

Von Luckner, by disguising his heavily armed sailing ship as a merchant vessel, was able to sink 11 Allied ships in the Atlantic, and four in the Pacific. Most of his victims were unarmed trading schooners. He would transfer their crews to *Seeadler,* strip the schooners of any useful supplies, then sink them with time charges. His prisoners were treated well, and no one was ever killed or confined during or after his raids. When a French ship carrying champagne was sunk, both prisoners and crew shared equally in the bubbly. But after seven months at sea, the last three spent near the equator, his crew became bored and listless. Lack of fresh food caused an outbreak of beri-beri and scurvy among them. An island with fresh food had to be found — but where? The British, French or Americans claimed all of the islands in this part of the Pacific. Mopelia, an uninhabited French atoll 150 miles west of Bora Bora, seemed to fit the bill.

On July 31, 1916, *Seeadler* dropped anchor half a mile from the pass to Mopelia's lagoon. Although the lagoon's water was deep enough for them to anchor, the depth in the pass could not accommodate their 18-foot draft. *Seeadler* was left anchored off and a ship's launch full of hungry men entered the lagoon and landed on the eastern motu. Like us, they found three friendly Tahitians on shore who welcomed them with a feast of roast pork, broiled lobster, turtle soup, and sea bird omelets. Treacherous currents and changing winds made it difficult to keep the *Seeadler* anchored close enough to the pass to easily reprovision, but after three days she was nearly loaded. What happened next is debatable. Rollo's version is that the *Seeadler's* anchors dragged in the sudden squall, sending the ship crashing into the reef. The gentlemanly von Luckner, who was ashore at the time, changed the story to protect the career of the lieutenant in charge.

The Count's story goes like this. Some seismic disturbance caused a 20-foot tidal wave to pick up his ship, lay her over on her beam and smash her down on the reef. Masts snapped like toothpicks. Although his lieutenant saw the wave coming and weighed the bow and stern starboard anchors from the reef, the two engines would not start.

Whichever story, the *Seeadler* was wrecked but radios, guns, charts and navigation instruments were salvaged before she sank. Everyone settled into life on the island except the Count. He grew bored after three weeks. Transforming an 18-foot motor launch into a gaff rigged cutter/motorsailer he set sail with five other men to capture a sailing ship. He planned to use the pirated vessel to return to Mopelia to pick up his men and resume his raiding. He made it as far as Wakaya Island on Fiji — 2,000 miles away — before being taken a prisoner of war.

Rollo told us about two big diving expeditions using sophisticated equipment to wrest the *Seeadler's* safe from its watery grave. Treacherous currents almost took the lives of several divers and the expeditions ended in failure. His conjecture was that the clever von Luckner had time to remove the safe and bury it in the sand of a nearby motu. After the war the Count did sail back through the Pacific as far as Tahiti. If the safe containing treasure from the 14 ships was buried on Mopelia, I think he would have sailed the few extra hundred miles from Tahiti to retrieve it.

The rest of the afternoon Rollo talked about his teenage years spent as a soldier in the German army on the Russian front during World War II. Heavy listening.

The laughter and lighthearted conversation we had with our Mopelian friends over dinner made a pleasant contrast. Adrianne, Marcello, and Michelle devoured the spaghetti, cabbage salad and poisson cru I had prepared, but the stale bread from Bora Bora was the hit of the evening. They told us they tire of their own diet, even if it does contain lots of crab and lobster, and they appreciate visits aboard yachts.

June 22: Our second wedding anniversary. What a surprise these last years have been. Before I met John I was afraid of marriage. It has turned out to be the most liberating choice of my life. John is nurturing and encouraging; secure in his own achievements, he is proud of mine.

For an anniversary present, Marcello gave John a lemon shark's jaw replete with successive rows of needle sharp teeth emerging from the bone, then curving inward. Adrianne gave me a long, thin, crimson bouquet of tail feathers from tropic birds, I believe, but I wasn't asking questions. Emily Post says the proper second wedding anniversary gift should be something cotton — nowhere does she even mention shark's jaws or tropic bird tail feathers.

June 23: A cool rainy day. As the rain drummed on deck, we sipped tea with rum in *Solveig IV's* classy mahogany cabin. Rollo's eyes came alive and his face younger and more animated as he told us of his three circumnavigations.

"As you get older, time speeds up and you realize you probably won't have time to do everything. Sailing makes the time go slower because one has time to think and remember," he said. "The days are long with adventure in new places, with different people.

"When you are on land doing the same thing day after day, time goes quickly — one day blends into the next. You look back over the years and can't remember anything about them, so you say, 'Where has the time gone? What have I done with my life?'"

His words made me think back over our last year under sail. Yes, many times we had more adventures in one day than in a year of living on land, days when so much happened that I became exhausted trying to capture it all on paper.

Back on board *Mahina Tiare*, I was drowsy from the rum and heavy German food served on *Solveig IV*, so went right off to sleep.

The wind had changed direction and come up fresh from the southeast. John checked the anchor, then flopped down hard on the double berth next to me. He flopped down again and again.

Finally I yelled, "WHAT ARE YOU DOING?"

No answer.

Louder, "STOP DOING THAT!"

No reply.

Turning over I realized the spot next to me was empty. John wasn't flopping down on the bed. *Mahina Tiare* was jumping up and down on a coral head. On deck, John managed to clear us by using the windlass to haul in some anchor chain.

June 25: Last night we saw the light of a sailboat hove-to off the island. This morning, *Nordkaperen*, a 55-foot steel gaff-rigged ketch, sailed into the lagoon. When we rowed over, adults and children kept popping out of hatches like rabbits out of a hat, until seven mostly naked Danish adults and four children stood on deck. *Nordkaperen* has been famous in Denmark for decades. Built in Poland in 1905, a previous owner had written about his circumnavigation. The present owners have used her to film TV specials on the South Pacific as well as write and illustrate wonderful children's books about cruising the world.

The present crew were friends of the owner. They had borrowed *Nordkaperen* with the understanding that if she were returned in the same or better condition than when she left, there would be no charge. Their philosophy is that everyone should be able to cruise, regardless of their finances.

This was the third Scandinavian communal boat we had met. On board were some of the most adventurous and ingenious people cruising the world. They are out to meet the natives, hike the mountains, swim the seas and arrange the most outrageous parties. Cruising with few luxuries and no fancy gear, they are among the happiest folks we've met.

One child on *Nordkaperen* had been crippled since birth. At seven, he had never been able to stand without support. But in his bunk, to keep himself from falling out when *Nordkaperen* was under way, he had developed muscles not used before. These muscles now gave him the ability to stand on his own and take a few tentative steps. It was a breakthrough, and the pleasure and pride were obvious on his handsome young face.

June 26: A fishing boat from Tahiti stopped by briefly and dropped off a local family before heading to uninhabited Scilly Island to collect sea turtles. Marcello, Adrianne and the family came by in their skiff on their way to Motu Manu (bird island). Would we like to join them?

Sure. I assumed they were on an egg-gathering mission and had visions of finally seeing the downy white sea bird hatchlings featured in sailing magazines and South Pacific slide shows.

I hadn't long to wait. We motored into the shallows, cut the engines and drifted to shore. I was the last ashore. As I jumped onto the beach the children were yelling "Barbara, Barbara." Suddenly I heard a long frightened throaty scream coming from the bush where Marcello was plucking a beautiful red-beaked white bird from its nest. Nearby kids were pointing to a fluffy chick with a big head and helpless body.

Captured tropic bird chicks

Marcello wound the tropic bird's outstretched wings around each other, essentially crippling the bird and, carrying it by the wingtip feathers, deposited the bird in a heap on the beach. The process continued until 20 screaming birds lay in twisted heaps on the beach. Adrianne now started plucking out their long red tail feathers. The scene was too vivid in the glare of noonday sun, bright blue sky, white birds, red blood and the sound — their screams of fear and pain.

Meanwhile the children were picking up the unattended chicks to take home as pets. The eggs were tested in the lagoon for freshness. A floating egg meant the embryo inside was too far advanced to eat and was discarded; eggs that sank were kept. I walked away as the birds were slaughtered and cleaned in the lagoon, hoping to find just one nesting bird alive on the sun dappled floor of the tropical bush. But I heard the engine start and ran to catch the boat. The screams had stopped. The only sound now was the hum of the outboard.

June 27: We talked to Rollo and Angelica this morning. I was saddened by yesterday's slaughter of birds. Angelica was upset over seeing giant sea turtles tied up, kicked and thrown on the beach by the Tahitian fisherman. She offered to buy one at the going rate of $800, planning on turning it loose. Her offer was rejected. I tried to forget all

128

this as we rowed ashore to celebrate my birthday.

One of the village's previously empty houses had been swept clean and decorated with a palm fringe and fragrant tiare flowers. A long table had been laid out. The 12 Tahitian fishermen sat together silently on a wooden bench facing the table. We and the Europeans sat opposite them. It was like a high school dance — no one wanted to make the first move. John added a bottle of tequila and some cut up fruit to the juice of green coconuts. Our Danish friends handed out guitars and ukuleles for the Tahitians to play, then broke out in a rousing Danish birthday song. The ice had melted, the party began.

There were 33 gathered in the open porch under bright Coleman lantern light. I worried about enough food, but the table was suddenly laden with two kinds of poisson cru, thick fried caron fish steaks, hearts of palm salad, bean salad, fruit salad, rice. The big surprise was the mound of turtle meat steaks, tender and delicious. Earlier we asked that they not kill a turtle for us, not only because we didn't want one to die but because it would represent so much lost income for them. But they considered it an early celebration of their Independence Day.

Everyone got looser and looser as the evening progressed. The fishermen brought out "bush beer," a nasty concoction of yeast, sugar and water which according to the Danes packs quite a wallop. Everyone danced, the Tahitians mimicking the way the 'popaas' danced — as we all erupted in laughter.

The Danish and Tahitian children played together with the captured baby tropic birds, then curled up and fell asleep side by side on mats inside the house.

John passed out birthday cake made with the infamous sea bird eggs. Adrian bestowed upon me a necklace which she had made of light round shark's vertebrae. The Danes presented me a black-lipped pearl shell polished to rainbow brilliance. At 10 p.m. we left, not wanting to delay the dinner of the Tahitian fisherman. They hadn't eaten with the rest of us. The Danes, who stayed on, said that another whole table of food had been laid out and that they had eaten again. This was my most memorable birthday and an incredible send-off from French Polynesia. When people say to us that French Polynesia is crowded, that the people are unfriendly, we think of Mopelia and shake our heads.

Chapter 9

PENHRYN:

TRADING FOR GOLD PEARLS

June 29, John: Our second day at sea, a beautiful sliver of a moon is setting. A freshwater shower in the cockpit feels good. Seas are the mellowest in seven months. Only 388 miles to Penrhyn, one of the Northern Cook Islands.

Barbara: Wind freshening, Milky Way Galaxy arching overhead from horizon to horizon like a luminous mist. An easy passage so far, but after four months of settled anchorages I am having trouble finding my sea legs. The smell of decaying shark's jaw and shells, gifts from our Mopelian friends, do not make sitting in the cockpit pleasant. My harness has gotten moldy from disuse and, as always at the beginning of a passage, I don't get much pleasure from the sailing, but view it as a necessary evil to get to the next place.

June 30, first light: Honolulu AM radio stations are booming in over the air waves, the first commercial radio I've heard in almost a year. It gives the impression that America is a nation of loud, fast talkers, consumers and sports fanatics extraordinaire. After experiencing the simplicity of our Mopelian friends, I question Western materialism, preoccupation with time-saving devices. What do we do with this time-saved? Watch television, watch what is going on across the globe yet have little connection with our neighbors.

As one of our Swedish cruising friends put it, "One of the nicest freedoms of cruising is meeting people onshore and on other boats and neither prejudging nor being prejudged. We often know so little about each other's cultures, we can't pigeonhole by accents, clothes or surface appearances. Friendships which cross economic and educational boundaries are the rule. At home we choose friends like ourselves because its

130

easier, but by selecting unusual people our lives are enhanced."

July 2 : For the first time since we left on this trip a year ago I find myself wanting to live on land, sleeping in a stationary bed instead of having to lower our cabin table and add cushions every day. The weather on this passage has been easy but it's been hard mentally. For some reason I haven't been able to relax and enjoy the rhythm of our days at sea. Perhaps I'm out of practice.

July 3: John stayed up with me on my early watch (3 a.m. to 6 a.m.) because of a nasty dry squall and our closeness to Penrhyn Island.

7 a.m.: Land-ho after five days and 525 miles at sea. Even though we had excellent visibility, Taruia Pass was difficult to detect from more than half a mile away. It finally appeared as a small break through miles of barely visible reef coral, with markers on the south side of the pass, a coral shelf on the north side. With a good chart, binoculars and bow watch we had no problem entering.

We anchored in heavy chop at the main village of Omoka. An island women, Sophie, married to the American captain of the inter-island copra boat, met us on shore. Fluent in English, she escorted us through the village to the cinderblock house belonging to the customs official and his wife. An hour later, and only after surrendering our passports, we were officially cleared. I think the customs official held onto our passports to make sure we didn't skip out owing the exit fee, or the daily fee for anchoring in the lagoon.

Our next stop was the post office which changes money, sells liquor and gasoline and Penrhyn Island stamps. Old wooden counters and iron bars separated us from the clerk; it felt like being in a bank from an old-time western.

I expected to see dugout canoes on this remote island; instead, every family owned a shiny aluminum speed boat equipped with a powerful outboard engine. Their 174-square-mile lagoon is one of the largest in the Pacific and affords some of the best pearl shell diving in the world. Harvesting the black pearl shell makes them wealthy in comparison to most atoll dwellers.

Six hours, four cups of tea and two drinking nuts later we made it back to our pitching boat. It was afternoon and I stood bow watch as we headed for a calmer anchorage across the five-mile lagoon to the village of Tetautua. The afternoon light slanted across Tetautua,

forming blue shadows. The still, hot air created a surreal scene. We walked on the village's one crushed coral road, straight and lined with pink and yellow plumeria trees glowing in warm intensity. Little girls sat sewing flower crowns, holding one end of thread by their toes. Deftly they added soft blossoms. Older sisters swept up fallen leaves and flowers with switch brooms, while nearby their mothers sat on cement porches weaving pandanus mats.

The sounds of pigs, children playing volleyball and the steady chip, chip, chip of men knocking barnacles off of pearl shell, was the song of the village.

The children became less shy as we walked through the small village, eventually bestowing their flower crowns on us and telling us the Maori (Polynesian) words for pigs, chicken and breadfruit. A white-haired man with blue eyes extended a hand of welcome and introduced himself as Nikau. He insisted we visit his house where he offered us as much fresh water from his family's cistern as we needed. With darkness approaching and our entourage growing, we headed back to *Mahina Tiare* for a good night's sleep.

July 4: We had barely finished our breakfast when two of the village's aluminum skiffs drew up. Nikau and two young men came aboard with papayas, drinking nuts and shell necklaces. In pidgin

English, 73-year-old Nikau stayed on to tell us stories of Penrhyn's past. When he was young many more ships from all over the world called on Penrhyn to trade for the black pearl shell then so abundant in the lagoon. During his boyhood the shell grew on coral heads in the shallows and was easy to collect. But continuing harvest has meant that islanders must now free dive — scuba gear is not allowed — 10 to 20 fathoms to retrieve the shell, less abundant but still valuable. Today, a good diver can make more than $100 a day collecting shell which is shipped to Japan, made into buttons and ornaments, and ground into metallic paint. The shell sells for $8,000 N.Z. a ton. It is so much more profitable than cutting copra at $350 a ton that the islanders have virtually stopped cutting copra. The shells are 8 to 12 inches across when harvested and a shell can weigh up to three pounds. Divers go in groups for safety. Usually three work below the surface using stones as weights, while three are above resting. The temptation to make more money by staying down too long cost two young divers their lives that year.

In addition to the black-lipped oysters, the nutrient-rich lagoon also grows the much smaller pipi oysters. About the size of a quarter, the pipis have a lustrous gold shell and, unlike the black oysters, they frequently contain natural (uncultured) pearls. The pipi pearls are what the islanders love to trade to yachties. Nikau was no exception.

John had visited Penrhyn four years ago and was familiar with the skill of Penrhyn's pearl traders. Going below, he brought out the highest quality pearls he had traded for back then. Nikau immediately put away the misshapen pearls he'd been about to show and fumbled around for the pearls cruisers don't always get to see. An hour later another set of traders motored out to *Mahina Tiare*. John told them I was asleep, so they left. Pearl trading is at least a three-hour process and can take all day.

Kiwi cruising friends, Peter and Jenny told us that when they'd been in Tonga there was a steady stream of Tongans wanting to come aboard their yacht *Southern Cross*. After days without privacy and trying every excuse to deter the all-day visits, Peter, out of desperation, told the Tongans, "It's our time with the Lord." He would sit cross-legged on the foredeck with a big Bible-ish looking book in his lap, reading solemnly to Jenny who would be listening reverently with bowed head. The pious Tongans respectfully acknowledged their "special time," and paddled away silently.

I took a long swim in the clear water surrounding *Mahina Tiare*, and for the first time since we left Mopelia a week ago I feel really energetic. John and I have been suffering from exercise withdrawal and passage blahs. A phenomenon we've noticed is that a new anchorage always revives our energy. *Mahina Tiare* gets new varnish and her hull waxed. But the longer we stay anchored in the same spot, the more our energy dwindles until we spend most of our days turning pages.

July 5: Dressed in a floral sun dress, I arrive with John at our friend Nikau's house to accompany his family to church. My outfit creates a commotion. Nikau's granddaughter, Aloha, tries to find me a white dress and hat to wear to the service. They explain that today is communion Sunday and all the women must wear white. I hurry back to the boat. When I return in broad-brimmed hat and white dress everyone nods in satisfaction.

Inside the large cement Protestant church (Cook Island's Christian denomination), the ceiling and wainscoting is dark varnished wood which contrasts with white walls. Tall open stained glass windows allow the prevailing winds to sweep steadily through.

The young women sit together in the center section of the church in a sea of fancy white hats and yards of white lace and ruffles. The men squirm in their wool and polyester suits and white shirts. Some wear leather shoes, others come barefoot.

But the singing is what strikes me most, so strong and resonant that the church vibrates as if an organ is being played. The harmonies weave in and out, their spell intoxicating. The people seem to approach a trance-like state when they sing, sometimes soft and sweet, other times harsh and nasal. I look out the window at the blue sky and green palms and wonder if this is a dream.

The Maori minister, standing atop his 20-foot high traditional pulpit, gives his sermon first in English solely for our benefit. He repeats it in Maori for the rest of the congregation. When the service ends the young people run from the church, but the older people stay, singing and praying continuously all afternoon, breaking once for lunch.

Aloha prepares a feast for us and the extended Nikau family after

Natural gold pearls grown in Penrhyn's lagoon

church. The Nikaus are one of seven families who live in this village (population 300) but, they assured us, they are related to everyone in the village one way or another. Nikau tells us that only in the last century have Penrhyn's people lived in two villages. In fact, before contact with Europeans 2,000 people lived on the motus scattered around the atoll. In 1863, four native London Missionary Society ministers stationed on Penrhyn sold their entire congregation to Peruvian slavers, who took the islanders to work in the mines of Peru. Since the entire ruling class were among those taken, Penrhyn today is the only Cook Island without a paramount chief. A few islanders eventually made it back from Peru. They described being treated like pigs and showed their ears notched to identify to whom they belonged. By the end of the 19th century only a few hundred islanders remained on Penrhyn.

Nikau said that when he was a young man the Americans came and built an airstrip near the other village. "We were very poor at the time and wore flour sacks for clothes. When the first airplane came the people, afraid it was a monstrous bird, hid in the bush."

From 1943 to 1945, six thousand American soldiers camped out in tents on the motus, and the lagoon frequently contained several large gray warships. Five children with Yankee fathers were born in the village of Omoka during the war years.

Recently an American arrived by yacht looking for his brother. The man's father had been stationed on Penrhyn during World War II and had left a Penrhyn Island woman pregnant. But his brother and all the other war babies have left, most likely to live in New Zealand where Cook Islanders have free entry. In truth, there are more Penrhyn Islanders in New Zealand than on the island.

Faira trading Penrhyn's natural gold pearls aboard Mahina Tiare

July 6: The lagoon was a glassy lake as we rowed ashore to visit Tetautua's village store, a place well stocked with food, clothing and plastic flowers. When we asked the store's hours the storekeeper laughed, "It is open when you want something."

In the village, graveyards take up most of the space around the houses, old ones crumbling heaps of grey coral blocks, new graves a shiny granite complete with a screened color photo of the deceased.

The coral cement houses display few furnishings, often just an iron bed, a treadle sewing machine, a chest for clothes. All surfaces are covered with embroidered throws and crocheted doilies, something you'd expect to find in your grandmother's linen chest. We sensed that we were visiting the past — a small town in America fifty years ago. An era when there was more time to make visitors welcome.

July 7: We spent the day with Faira Nikau, the tall, handsome son of our friend Nikau. As a young man, Faira left Penrhyn to join the New Zealand army. Eight years ago, in his mid-30s and divorced from his New Zealand wife, he returned to the island and married a local woman. His excellent English and gentle manner made Faira a wonderful island guide. He explained the techniques of traditional pearl diving as well as island superstitions. Faira said that sharks would bother us only if we were "bad" on Sunday. Sunday taboos include swimming, moving our boat, working or conducting business, and acting disrespectfully in church. As an example, he told of the time when his uncle kicked a pig that had wandered into the church during a Sunday morning service. The next day, while he was diving for pearls, a shark bit his uncle in the foot.

Over breakfast on *Mahina Tiare* we traded with Faira for a flawless natural gold pearl the size of a small pea. The trade involved some cash, clothing, snorkeling gear, perfume and lots of goodwill. To celebrate a successful trade, Faira took us and Pilala, his barefoot five-year-old son, in his aluminum skiff to the far side of the lagoon. We dove in an area with a white sandy bottom studded with coral heads. Current from breaks in the island's fringing reef had made deep paths in the sand. Swimming against the current even with fins was difficult but when we turned around we had a wonderful 3 knot free ride back to the skiff. On the way back to the village, Faira glided the skiff to a stop

Pilala and Faira with drinking nuts

on a motu overgrown with fallen palm fronds and coconuts. Machete in hand, he cleared a path. When the island's population was greater, this motu had supported a village. All that now remains are the crumbling coral walls of the island's first church and its present congregation: coconut palms. Faira climbed up one of the tall palms and whacked off a couple of green drinking nuts for John, me and Pilala. For himself, he rolled and smoked a cigarette. He must be like a camel, I thought, adapted to the hot, dry climate.

John: Many ships have wrecked on Penrhyn, perhaps the best known is the Chatham (1853). One survivor, E.H. Lamont, spent 18 months on Penrhyn chronicling his adventures in the classic *Wild Life Among the Pacific Islanders*. Faira took us to the most recent wreck, a Korean fishing boat which had gone aground at night a few years ago on the windward side of a motu. Villagers from Omoka, attracted by distress flares, came across the lagoon to help evacuate the crew.

According to Faira, the captain of the Korean boat was drunk when they plowed into the island in the dark, and had refused to leave his ship or allow the islanders aboard. After a hasty conference, the islanders on shore decided to string a life line from a palm tree to get to the ship. They then sent out a one-man delegation, a policeman, to persuade the captain to abandon his ship so that they could strip it. The policeman used his boxing training to knock out the captain with one carefully timed blow, and then carried the unconscious man, slung over his shoulder like a bag of copra, through the breakers ashore. The captain's dignity remained intact since he had not voluntarily given up his ship. The islanders put up the crew in their homes while they unloaded everything they could carry from the ship. They camped out on the beach near the wreck and after a week, the ship broke in half, fishing line and equipment washed into the shallows. There wasn't any way to salvage the fifty tons of frozen tuna which rotted in the tropical sun.

Barbara: To withstand the heat I tied my shirt around my head as we sped back to *Mahina Tiare*. We gave Faira and Pilala a snack of corned beef and crackers (corned beef is a big hit with Pacific islanders) before heading ashore to do laundry at one of the island's many cisterns. Faira told us that there was plenty of water this year. However, in 1985 the island had completely run out of water. The islanders took salt water baths and made a nasty tasting tea with the juice of green coconuts. The situation became so bad that the Australians airlifted drinking water to Penrhyn. Since then the Australian army has built new cisterns for every island family. As long as the cisterns are properly covered so that no stray animals can fall in, the catchment rain water is good tasting and safe to drink. We prefer it to the ground water of unknown origin available on volcanic islands.

Twenty kids crowded around to watch the "popaas" doing laundry, amazed that John and I work as a team.

We walked back to *Mahina Tiare* in the dark, the moon reflecting off the crushed coral pathways. Palm fronds seemed sheathed in silver as they rustled in the trades.

July 8: The Nikau family prepared us a going-away feast: chicken, fish, breadfruit, papaya, coconut cream sauce, rice and bread baked in an earthen oven. Aloha stood by fanning away the flies and the children waited in the shadows for leftovers.

Our after-dinner stroll took us past a group of adults and children watching a Hollywood video that depicted gruesome murders. I asked Aloha what she thought of the videos. She answered, "They are especially bad for the children." The minister, she said, was angry tonight because some of the people didn't come to "debate night", an evening of Bible study, games and singing. Instead they watched the video.

Often a village will only own a couple violent videos which they watch hundreds of times. At one time Western diseases nearly wiped out this race. Now videos exposing them to violence and the disintegrating side of our society threaten to wipe out what is left of their culture. The kids grow up seeing all the things Westerners own, but rarely have the skills to obtain them once they leave their islands.

July 9: John hoisted himself to the top of the mast in a bosun's chair to check the rigging, something he does before every passage.

Faira and Nikau sped out to *Mahina Tiare* as we were leaving to give us a couple of gold pearls as a farewell present. John had made old Nikau a new gas tank out of a spare jerry jug to replace his rusted steel tank. We weren't sure if they wanted something in return (Nikau had been wanting one of our anchors which we couldn't spare) or if the pearls really were a gift. Maybe they weren't sure either. In either case they wanted us to have the pearls.

At Omoka John took off to clear customs and I sat on the floor of a cooking shed with a group of ladies. Two old women smoking cigarettes were alternately working on a pandanus floor mat. A young woman was putting together a switch broom, while in the doorway a very old woman sat working an ancient treadle sewing machine which resembled the arched back of a frightened black cat.

After getting our passports back, we visited Sophie's house. She welcomed us with shell leis, then explained how she was boiling down the juice of ground coconut meat on her kerosene stove to make oil. The coconut oil is called "monoi" and villagers use it to make their hair shine, as a skin softener, and for cooking. Sophie loaded us down with papayas, bananas and pumpkins, rare delicacies on coral islands where fruits and vegetables are scarce.

July 10, John: We got up before 6:00 a.m., replaced the frayed control lines on our Monitor windvane, folded up the sun awning and took a quick sportboat trip out the pass just north of Tetautua village to check conditions. Although the tide book said it was slack water, we experienced large breakers on either side of the pass and a lot of confused water in the middle. I decided to take *Mahina Tiare* out that way, as it put us five miles further east than the more protected pass on the lee side by Omoka. Motorsailing to windward through the pass, we took heavy spray on board. As Penrhyn sank into the horizon, we tossed our flower leis into the ocean along with a silent wish to return.

Chapter 10

IN FIELDS OF MOLTEN LAVA

Barbara : This is our longest passage in eight months and the last South Pacific passage before we re-enter U.S. waters after a year's cruise. I dread most passages, yet I look forward to this one. It is as if for the last year I have been feasting and now need time to digest, to arrange the colors, feelings and faces of the voyage into a pattern. While passages can be frightening and uncomfortable, they also offer large blocks of time for reflection.

John: The wind is backing from NNE to NE. Hawaii lies due north of Penrhyn, so we are close-hauled, trying to get as much easting as possible before we reach the stronger winds and westerly-setting currents of the northeast trades on the other side of the equator. We also are trying to stay close enough to the wind to pass Starbuck Island, 230 miles NNE of Penryhn.

A poster at the post office on Penrhyn asked for information on a missing 40-foot sloop named *Marara*. The sloop had disappeared a couple of months earlier en route from Tahiti to Hawaii with singlehander Manning Eldridge on board. Looking at the chart, I figured Eldridge, if he was dismasted, might have ended up at Starbuck or Malden Islands, both uninhabited. I asked Fred Boehme, one of the net controllers for the Pacific Maritime Mobile Ham Net out of Hawaii, if anyone had checked the uninhabited islands between Tahiti and Hawaii. He agreed to ask the Coast Guard in the morning.

July 12: This morning Fred told me that the Navy had steamed by each of the islands on which Eldridge could have been shipwrecked, that the Coast Guard had flown over them, and that a group of Eldridge's friends had rented a private jet in Honolulu to overfly the islands as well.

Even sailing as closehauled as possible, we were not able to lay Starbuck. We passed 21 miles west of the island in the afternoon, out of sight of the low atoll. The only signs of the nearby island were hundreds of birds and a change in the swell pattern.

July 13, Barbara: I develop a voracious appetite on passages, but nothing on board seems very appetizing and when it's rough, no matter how much we eat, we lose weight. The longer the passage, the skinnier our thighs and rumps. It seems the constant adjustment to the movement of the boat tones the muscles. John's once meaty thighs have become muscular matchsticks.

John and I spent the day planning what we would do first on reaching Hawaii after being absent from the U.S.A. for a year. Most of our anticipation involved food — huge salads, fresh orange juice, frozen yogurts, dinner out. Also on the list was a movie, all night in bed together, and laundering in a washing machine. And although we looked forward to a return to these luxuries, going back also meant a return to telephones, TVs, hurried and competitive situations, key rings heavy with responsibilities. The urgencies of our former lives have slowed, dimmed, and we prefer it that way. In *The Log from the Sea of Cortez*, John Steinbeck conveys the feelings of many sailors as he describes the end of his cruise in a sardine boat:

"We had been drifting in some kind of a dual world — a parallel realistic world; and the preoccupations of the world we came from, which are considered realistic, were filled with mental mirage... And in us the factor of time had changed: the low tides were our clock and the throbbing engine our second hand. This trip had been like a dreaming sleep, a rest from immediacies."

July 14: We claw our way north through squalls, grumpy seas and leaden skies. The last few days at sea have reduced John and me to eating-reading-sleeping machines. For us, sailing is self-imposed con-finement with the reward of limitless horizons and welcome landfalls. But what about those people who are institutionalized, whose confine-ment offers no rewards or options? I often wonder, how many people confined in nursing homes regret the lack of adventure in their earlier lives. Before leaving on this trip, one of my older friends said, "Good for you. Explore now while you are young. If you wait too long, life throws up obstacles and a trip like yours looms as too difficult. If I had the chance to live my life over again I'd take more chances, be more radical."

People often ask us, "Do you feel out of it? Is life passing you by while you cruise?" No, just the opposite. By slowing down, we have time to develop a world view, to challenge and compare our values with other cultures, to savor small things — the reflection of the moon on a calm sea, the aroma of earth as we make landfall. The busy person is run by thousands of details in their day-to-day life. So who, really, is life passing by?

July 15: The tendency to become boat-bound is a common occurrence among cruisers and I'm sometimes guilty of it. I long for a passage to end but, upon landfall, I become reluctant to go ashore. When I do go onto land, it is to fill our water jugs and quickly return to *Mahina Tiare*, my floating sanctuary. To me, the phenomenon is like prisoners, who upon finally gaining their freedom, quickly commit a crime to ensure their speedy return to the controlled environment in which they're comfortable. To stay free involves too many choices and challenges from the unknown. Although it involves some minor challenges, to go ashore and spend time with the Pacific Islanders one does experience a slowing down of time, a lack of urgency, a window into another culture whose occupations are fishing, diving for shells, cutting copra, singing and family life. Family extends to anyone who fits in.

But all is not ideal in island cultures. Marital discords, pressures from encroaching Western culture, health problems all exist. Still, much can be learned from islanders even as they learn from us.

July 16: When on the high seas, it's easy to imagine myself in different periods of history; there are no points of reference, no buildings, no other boats. The possibility of a time warp becomes real. The sea on which I sail is the same as Captain Cook's. I imagine his *Endeavor* or *Resolution* on the horizon and fantasize what he would think of our sleek plastic boat. What would his speech be like? Would we — could we possibly — understand one another?

At one point, our batteries were not holding a charge, threatening to wipe out our SatNav, electric lights, and engine. A wave of fear washed over me until the reassuring thought of Captain Cook came to mind. For thousands of years people have sailed in ships and catamarans, with only the wind. Of course *Mahina Tiare* could sail without engine and batteries — her sextant, her strong suit of sails, and kerosene lights and stove would stand us in good stead.

July 17: Squeaky-voiced seabirds, probably from Christmas Island 190 miles to starboard, dive and soar around us. At night their wings reflect our masthead light and they look like luminous white butterflies against the dark sky. While on watch, the moon jumped out from behind the clouds to starboard as if someone had suddenly switched on a searchlight. Startled, I turned around to make sure it wasn't some freighter about to bear down on *Mahina Tiare*.

July 18: The equatorial sun lived up to its reputation today. The heat in our cabin was worsened by the running engine and a steady stream of heat from the stove as I baked bread. Fresh bread but unbearable, closed-hatches heat. We were driven out to the cockpit for cooler air, but the sun leering down on us offered little relief and roasted us pink, radiating our own thermal energy. Why can't I convince John that we need a sailing awning?

Woke up at midnight from a deep sleep to help reduce sail. I panicked while John was on the foredeck and I was in the cockpit. Where was the other person? For a second time on this passage I sensed a teenage boy on board. It startled me when I realized the boy was in my imagination and that John and I were quite alone.

July 21: Warm starry evenings stir the soul; sitting in the cockpit during these velvet nights, I recall my father, a wonderful story teller who instilled a sense of adventure in his four children. Yet he suffered the nine-to-five necessity of supporting a family and never made time for his own adventures. I wonder whether he ever thought of a "great escape" as he commuted by train two hours each way into New York. He chose the long commute from the country over living in the city in which he grew up, a city he despised. His sister, my Aunt Mary, has told me that, as a young girl in the 1910's, her father used to take her to the New York Public Library. He would choose children's books for her and South Pacific adventure stories for himself. (His father was an English seaman). Then they would sit for hours reading and dreaming.

Gazing at the stars, I felt that my father and grandfather were enjoying my adventure from their place in the universe. It was not hard to imagine them as part of the beauty of the night sky. I thought, "If you really are there, send a shooting star." Seconds later, two parallel shooting stars streaked across the dome of sky.

I believe that my ancestors paved the way for me to live as they were not able to, to live their dreams, and answer the questions they left unanswered. I don't feel alone on my journey, especially not at night at sea. It is not such a strange belief. Hawaiians and Hopi natives believe their ancestors' spirits dwell in mists and clouds, and Renaissance physicians believed each person's soul originates in a star.

July 23: It was mostly sunny today but cooled as we traveled north from the equator. Blue sky and strange dry squalls which looked like patches of fog extending down to the water. Like the innocent-looking clouds you fly through which cause turbulence in airplanes, these clouds were windy inside, but short-lived. Sailing on a passage creates much the same feeling as looking down from a jet during a long flight. A wonderful sense of detachment and freedom exists in the knowledge that you are not involved in and cannot affect the distant land; you can only observe.

On land, I lack the detached perspective I feel in a boat or on an airplane — the symptoms of being unable to see forest for the trees.

3:30 p.m.: LAND-HO! Spotted the low, gray lava finger of Cape Kumukahi barely discernible from the leaden sky.

7:30 p.m.: Night descended, the island dusted with tiny winking orange lights along the shore. Then a big bright cluster from Hilo. Cool moist air carried the rich aroma of volcanic soil out to us. The island's black mass made me feel small and vulnerable.

9:00 p.m. We risked entering Hilo Harbor at night in a drizzling rain and almost ran into the one-and-a half mile breakwater which is unlit except for a tiny white light on the end. Threading our way buoy by buoy, we entered Radio Bay, where half a dozen yachts were tied stern to the wharf. We soon recognized the silhouettes of friends' boats. Once tied up, the absence of sail, wind and water noises made the stillness overwhelming. Our sleep was like the sleep of the dead — long, deep, uninterrupted.

Shortly after our arrival in Hawaii the local radio stations and Honolulu newspapers reported that the *Marara* had been found, the boat drifting about 600 miles south of Hawaii. A Coast Guard cutter towed the sloop to Honolulu. Eldridge's body lay below, and the news reports theorized an accident.

John: Sailing to Hawaii was a compromise. Barbara didn't want this trip to end yet. I, on the other hand, felt the need for some challenge and stimulation and was ready to try something completely different. In the flying magazines that had been forwarded to us during the cruise, I kept reading about a shortage of commercial pilots. So, I considered getting my commercial pilot's license.

Hawaii was a place to leave the boat safely, go back to work for a few months and take time to check out flying job prospects. We never expected it to be one of our favorite cruising areas. We chose Hilo as our first landfall since it is the furthest east of the Hawaiian Islands, any other islands a downwind sail. Hilo is one of the four Ports of Entry for Hawaii along with Kahului on Maui, Honolulu on Oahu and Nawiliwili on Kauai, and has the only small boat harbor (Radio Bay) reserved solely for visiting yachts. From my previous visits I remembered Hilo as one of the most friendly and traditional towns in the islands.

On a personal level, while we were in Tahiti I had learned that relatives of mine who'd sailed from Boston in 1831 on the whaling ship *Averick* had built the first school and frame house in the town. The New England-style house they built in 1839 is still standing. Lyman House is the only museum in Hilo today.

July 26, Barbara: Radio Bay is a square cement basin half-full of still, greenish water. You have to climb up a wooden ladder to get out of the basin and once out, you are in the midst of an asphalt and container landscape. Matson Lines leases the land around the bay, and twice a week makes an incredible racket as they unload and load container ships all night long. Many exhausted sailors with thoughts of emerald waters and swaying palms tie up in Radio Bay after their first ocean passage — and are incredibly disillusioned. They should not be. Hot showers are available a few yards away, also a laundromat and small store within walking distance. But more importantly, the island of Hawaii has hot pools; waterfalls; acres of orchids and anthuriums; snow-capped Mauna Kea (highest peak in the Central Pacific); Mauna Loa, the largest volcano on earth; desert; rain forest; black, green and white sand beaches; massive stone ceremonial temples (heiaus); and evocative petroglyphs from the time when native Hawaiians settled on the coast and in the valleys of the Big Island.

Radio Bay also has an eclectic collection of cruisers eager to explore the island with each other. Les, the Hawaiian harbormaster, spots arriving yachts on the horizon and is often on the wharf to take their stern lines and welcome them to Hawaii. One morning he brought a load of ripe papayas from his farm and made sure that the crew of each yacht had more than enough.

I found myself giving pep talks to several women in the bay who had just made their first ocean passage. They had experienced the discomforts and frustrations of sailing, but none of the rewards yet. They vowed never to make another passage. I explained that sailors have bad memories, that by the time they're ready to make the next passage they have forgotten the discomforts of the preceding one. Their minds become occupied by the fun they have had on shore and the anticipation of the next landfall.

Two boats in the anchorage had only husbands aboard; their wives had left and were suing for divorce. Then there was *Tiva*, Greg and Leslie Olson's 37-foot Brown trimaran, their passage from Southern California so smooth they had not needed to change sails once. The potted geranium in their cockpit stayed upright the entire trip. Leslie joked, "I expected a rough passage and I'd lose weight. Instead I'm the only one who's gained weight on a passage."

Hilo is an easy ten-minute bike ride from Radio Bay, past expanses of park land gently sloping to lava-edged Hilo Bay. We detoured on Banyan Drive, a street canopied by creeping banyans. These mammoth trees drop their rope-like roots vertically from high branches in an ever widening sphere, the kind of trees in which you might expect to find elves.

Hilo's downtown retains the charm of old Hawaii. Many buildings were washed away in the tsunamis of 1946 and 1960, but what remains is part wild west frontier town with wooden false-front buildings and part prosperous sugar town with stores and banks in Renaissance Revival and Art Deco styles.

There is a sprinkling of hotels and guest houses; the pace is slow. But Hilo is the state's second largest city, its outskirts filled with shopping centers and fast food restaurants. People of Japanese descent outnumber those of Polynesian or European ancestry. Their influence

Pu'o'o vent Kiluea volcano

is felt in the acres of traditional Japanese gardens, restaurants and the occasional old sign in Japanese and English. Suisan Fish Auction caters to their love of fish. Every morning fresh fish is unloaded from Sampans and speed boats, then at 8:30 visitors gather around the open-sided building as the fish is auctioned off to restauranteurs and market owners.

Although bicycles are a great way to see Hilo, you need a car to get around the Big Island. After spending days walking to town in the rain, Greg and Leslie bought a roomy 1967 Chevy Impala for $350. Four thousand miles later they sold the car for the same price.

One night six of us piled into Greg and Leslie's Chevy with the carefree feel of a bunch of high school kids cruising in their parents' car. For 25 miles, as we drove in the dark from Hilo to Kalapana, the site of the Kiluaea Volcano's latest eruption, we watched an eerie red glow in the clouds. Suddenly Route 13 stopped. The lava which had recently flowed over it had formed a black crust on top. Passage was impossible. Through cracks we could see red and feel the heat of the molten lava below. Looking up to the right of the road, ohia trees were exploding in bright orange flashes and red snakes of molten lava crawled down the slope.

July 28: Last night's volcanic landscape whetted our curiosity. Today we hiked over acres of brittle shiny lava, carefully skirting the unattended civil defense barriers to get to the active area. Strange shapes, like an arm or leg encased in a black cast, lay before us. Bubbles with jagged cracks looked like eggs spawned in a fiery underworld. Some lava glittered gold or silver like jewels, some resembled ropes or sinuous vines. It made a hollow sound like broken clay pottery and crumbled as we walked across its hot surface.

We finally reached the area where heat waves shimmered above a slow moving river of lava, 2,000 degrees of molten rock a few yards from where we stood. It was liquid earth, creating a metamorphosis of the landscape as it flowed by us into the sea.

The scene was somehow familiar, as though the power of the image was already etched into my unconscious. Perhaps as mankind evolved along with the landscape, the smell of sulfur and glow of red hot rock became an indelible part of our memory.

As the wind changed, a blast of heat and fumes from the flow sent us scurrying away. There was a house we hadn't noticed in an untouched pocket of land (kipuka) amid the sea of lava. Shrill words telling us "Get off my land, you are trespassing" came from the house. We were reminded that a few weeks earlier where we stood was green, not black, and that the land, however altered, once was someone's yard. What for us was a natural wonder had meant the loss of homes for 46 families during the last year.

Ten miles east, along the coast from Kalapana, we

Beneath surface cracks, molten lava flows to the sea

149

stopped to soak in a warm mineral pool at Isaac Hale Beach Park. The pool is sunken in a lava grotto where black rock contrasts with the green of fern and philodendron vines. The chill of sunset and a light rain kept us soaking in the warm pool for hours. It was quite dark when six shriveled bodies slipped from the pool.

July 30: An International Day. The Japanese goodwill/sail-training ship Nippon Maru was about to leave port in Hilo. As we passed, dozens of men climbed up the four masts and out onto the yardarms, like so many ants following a trail. They waved their yellow hard hats in a gesture of farewell. Elderly Japanese couples lining the dock waved in return. Long blasts on the air horn sounded as a powerful tug turned the *Nippon Maru* toward the open sea, her white hull and delicate rigging silhouetted against a patchwork of green Hawaiian landscape.

That evening Greg, Leslie, John and I visited another ship, the *Acadamik Crolius,* a Russian oceanographic research ship which had been hosting American and Russian scientists. The few areas of the ship our Russian guide showed us looked clean and orderly, despite smells of sweat mixed with stale cigarette smoke and vodka. We ended up on the aft deck with our guide, an unsmiling man in a khaki uniform who

The Japanese goodwill/ sail-training ship Nippon Maru

claimed he was the pilot. Later we were told he was the ship's Political Officer. When two-middle aged women appeared on a bench behind us, we thought they were fellow tourists. Leslie started talking to them, but they appeared bewildered. Then through pantomime and select words, they communicated to us that they were Russian scientists and had traveled to Australia, Spain, Germany, Tahiti and the U.S.A. aboard the ship. Leslie, through exaggerated gesturing, indicated that something cooking below smelled good. Comprehending, they nodded; we were invited to dinner.

Surprised looks followed the four of us as we were guided to a table in the ship's dining room. A tureen of chicken soup, fresh bread and hot mustard was laid before us on a checked table cloth. Roast chicken and rice followed. The room was large, the chairs comfortably upholstered, and a loud color TV drew the interest of some of the scientists.

As we were leaving the ship, we passed the women who had arranged for our dinner. We invited them to come for a visit on *Mahina Tiare* moored nearby. The Political Officer refused permission. When I asked why he deferred to someone else, and the ladies took off with our group before he could get back with an answer. They were like excited school girls playing hooky. We gave them auger shells and leis from French Polynesia and got them to write their addresses in our guest book. We told them, "Some day we may sail to your homeport of Vladivostok and look you up."

John: The following day three of the scientists that we'd met came by *Tiva* for beer. They spoke some English and told us that we would be welcome at their sailing club in a small port near Vladivostok. We were all in our mid-30s, and each of them had two children. They asked us for one favor: a trip to the nearest grocery store. Greg decided it would be a lot more fun to take them to the huge Safeway a couple of miles away than to the corner Chinese store, so all seven of us piled into the Impala and roared off.

At first they just stood around, sort of bewildered . "This isn't at all like food stores in the Soviet Union," they murmured. After spending more time with them the subject of politics inevitably sprang up. We decided that if the people, not the politicians, of both our countries had the opportunity to meet and decide policies, there would be far greater understanding.

Barbara: Thirteen months of cruising had taken us 12,000 miles, through some of the most remote anchorages in the South Pacific. We needed to replenish our cruising kitty. But I was unwilling to give up the freedom of cruising life. I knew that if we sailed the boat back home, we would be sucked back into our former workaholic lifestyles; it might be years before we could get away again. So we left *Mahina Tiare* in Hawaii, and flew back home. Looking back on the voyage is like looking at a precious gem with the face of someone we had met along the way reflected in each facet. Carlos from the Galapagos, Monica from Easter Island, Betty Christian from Pitcairn, Greg and Leslie in Hawaii.

The most special places were those anchorages where we had gotten to know someone. While we had forgotten most of the sea conditions and many of the landscapes, the memory of adventures with friends stay clearly etched in our minds.

VOYAGE TWO

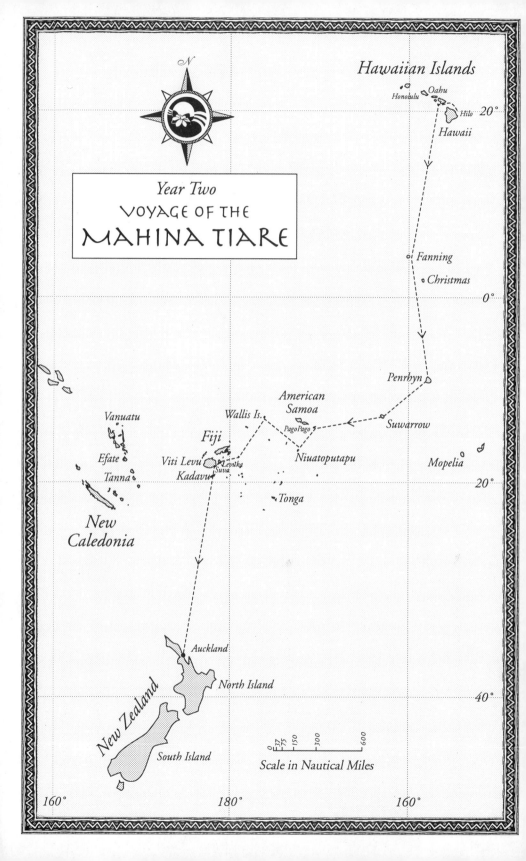

N

Hawaiian Islands

Honolulu ○ ○ Oahu
Hilo 20°
Hawaii

Year Two
VOYAGE OF THE
MAHINA TIARE

Fanning
○ Christmas

0°

Penrhyn ○

American Samoa

Wallis Is. ○

Fiji PagoPago ○ ○ Suwarrow

Viti Levu ○ Levuka
Kadavu ○ Suva

Vanuatu

Efate Niuatoputapu

Tanna Mopelia

20°

New Caledonia ● Tonga

Auckland

North Island

New Zealand

40°

Scale in Nautical Miles
0 37 75 150 300 600

South Island

160° 180° 160°

Chapter 11

FANNING ISLAND
SHIPWRECK ON SUWARROW

June 9, 1988, Barbara: We had hauled *Mahina Tiare* at Honokohau Harbor near Kona, Hawaii and returned to the mainland for seven months of work. When we returned, the only evidence of our absence from *Mahina Tiare* was a layer of volcanic dust on deck and a cloud of wasps that had created papery wasp condos in our boom and anchor locker. Ants had crawled aboard, but the two large roaches that flew in had fallen prey to our roach bait. They lay supine on the carpet.

While on the mainland, plugged into a frenetic lifestyle, it seemed our cruise had been something I had dreamed. But as I looked around *Mahina Tiare,* I saw a shell from the Tuamotus, a postcard from Pitcairn Island, a somber wooden Tiki from the Marquesas. *Mahina Tiare's* familiar scent also made the cruise seem real again. Back on board I felt unencumbered, ready again to keep a journal. Things appeared clear, simple, able to be expressed. Off-the-boat life had seemed complicated, too mundane to paint with words.

John: We spent two days sanding and touching up the epoxy barrier coat we'd put on *Mahina Tiare's* bottom a year-and-a half-earlier; we also added a fresh coat of Petit Trinidad 75 bottom paint. Although the Travelift at Honokahau Harbor was new, so apparently were its operators; a couple of boats had been dropped. The management was adamant that we sign a release before they would touch our boat. Nevertheless *Mahina Tiare* slipped unscathed into the water, and we wondered where she would take us this trip.

Barbara: We sailed to Honolulu on the island of Oahu, stopping briefly at Lanai and Molokai. Tied up as guests at the Hawaii Yacht

Club, we provisioned and prepared for our next jump into the South Pacific.

June 25: Looking back at the city from a mile out, the gray mountain mist descends from the peaks to fill the valleys, then creeps down to the shoreline. Stark white Honolulu high-rises stand out from it, appearing disembodied. Thirty-seven miles out. The glow of Honolulu lights fades and we are left alone with the three-quarter moon and vast black ocean.

June 27: My birthday present: a disagreeably lumpy sea. I spent the day in my birthday suit trying to stay cool. If I hadn't known better, I would have wanted to go back to Hawaii, to never set foot on a pitching, noisy boat again.

June 28: The ants reappeared, foraging for stray corn chips in the cockpit. Up until now they had been hiding out. I suspect that they'd been seasick and visualized them with the dry heaves. Now I guess they've gotten their sea legs. Maybe it takes them longer than humans because they have more legs.

July 4: We approached Fanning Island. The bases of the clouds gathered above the island were tinged green, a reflection from the shallow lagoon below. We skirted the western side of the atoll, past a radio antenna and the rusting hulk of a Banks Line freighter in the shallows. The only pass is on the southern side and unmarked, but at 200 yards wide, 25 feet deep, it is easy to find and negotiate. We were nine days out of Hawaii and the land looked lush and inviting. But the passage had made the boat feel like home again. We anchored in the western corner of the lagoon in six feet of water. Grey and Sarah Wicker and their three-year-old daughter, Stacey, on *Vamanos,* their C&C 38, were our neighbors. They had had a stormy passage from Hawaii to Christmas Island. Grey's father, Tom Wicker, who is a political analyst, TV journalist and neophyte sailor had accompanied them on the passage.

Sarah had allowed herself to be talked out of stocking up on the amount of provisions she thought she would need; her list had seemed excessive to Grey's father who was helping buy the food. He had flown home from Christmas Island instead of Tahiti as planned. By the time we met Grey and Sarah, two months after their Hawaii departure, they were living off fish, coconuts, french fries made of breadfruit, and catsup.

They were also low on propane, which was unavailable on Fanning. To conserve, they often cooked on coconut husk fires onshore, and had borrowed a one-burner kerosene stove from one of the locals.

But the crew of *Vamanos* was having a blast. Stacey played with the kids on shore, and Grey and Sarah, who spent a lot of time foraging, were thrilled with their self-sufficiency. "The only thing I worry about is running out of catsup," Sarah remarked, "because I'm not sure Stacey will eat without it."

Shortly after anchoring, Tony, the customs official, confirmed our belief that the smaller the island the more self-important the officials. Fanning's population was 600 and only a dozen or so yachts visit per year, yet Tony apparently delighted in keeping yachts in waiting. When frustrated owners went ashore looking for him, they were reprimanded for leaving their boats without clearance. We were charged a $20 Australian exit fee and $10A for the skiff he'd used to come out to *Mahina Tiare*.

Ashore we saw several wooden plantation houses as well as small cement houses, big sheds with old wooden sailing cutters rotting inside, and generator houses containing Perkins diesels rusting into oblivion. A small graveyard contained the ornate gravestones of the Greig family, people from England who had owned the prosperous copra plantation on Fanning at the turn of the century.

The island recently had been sold to the nation of Kiribati (formerly Gilbert Islands) by a subsidiary of Burns Philp & Co., Ltd., Sydney, who had used Gilbertese workers on their copra plantation on Fanning. Although the islanders still cut copra, organization and production had drastically declined since independence.

We met Perry Langstrom in the former plantation manager's house. Perry's high forehead accentuated his bright blue eyes and long nose. He wore a yellow sarong, and his local residence was furnished with lovely old chiffoniers and cheap couches. An elaborate picture of the Virgin Mary was thumb-tacked to the wall and a framed pencil drawing of his I-Kiribati wife hung nearby.

Perry's home was actually on Christmas Island (also owned by Kiribati) but he was on Fanning to survey and stake out 100 one-acre plots of land, advance preparation for 1,000 I-Kiribati people from

Tarawa Island, the fledgling nation's overcrowded main island 1,600 miles away.

When the island was discovered in 1798 by Captain Fanning, no one lived here. But in the 1930s, archaeologist Kenneth Emory had found the remains of a Polynesian dwelling, similar to those built in 16th century Tonga. Other artifacts discovered suggested that Hawaiians and possibly Marquesans had visited Fanning.

Perry watched our outboard engine's gas tank (kids on the island stole gas) while we wandered off looking for the postmaster. We needed to change our money into Australian currency to pay Customs. The coins we received in exchange were green with age and came out of the official safe — a shoe box. While searching for Tony to pay our customs fee, we met a husband and wife drying fish fillets. A night's catch of 75 fish lay on the crushed coral in front of their house. They would send the dried fish on the next supply ship to relatives on Tarawa where the lagoon was fished out.

We also met the Protestant minister, a short man with rich brown complexion and high cheek bones. His house was a raised wooden platform with a thatch roof; mats rolled down to form walls. His wife was sewing on an old hand-crank sewing machine. Her mother, with feet cracked like dry earth, lay stretched out asleep nearby.

The minister offered us tea. "This is Kiribati tea," he told us in English. "We make it sweet with the coconut sugar." It was so sweet I could hardly choke it down. "The supply ship from Tarawa is three months late, so we have no grain sugar." He gave us a stalk of bananas and some papayas and we offered to bring them granulated sugar the next day.

When we asked where to find Tony, the minister replied "Ah, Tony is a toddy man. Some of the men here drink too much toddy. The wives don't like them to drink toddy. The men do no work all day, strike their wives and children. Tony is maybe drinking toddy with the men."

Toddy, he explained, is made by cutting the fruiting stalk of a coconut tree, tying a bottle to the end and collecting the sap. It takes about a day for the sap to ferment but connoisseurs say the longer they allow it to ferment, the stronger and better the alcohol formed. We found Tony high up in a breadfruit tree, knocking down the football-sized fruit for a woman who waited below. He climbed down and checked us in. It was the only time we saw him sober.

Maurice and Heather off *Nereus,* the other yacht on Fanning, came over for drinks. Like the islanders, they were low on provisions. A few months earlier, as a favor to the islanders, they had taken their 46-foot cement ketch and eight I-Kiribati men to Christmas Island. They had returned with five tons of supplies. The supplies they had brought were mostly gone by now, but Heather and Maurice had learned fishing secrets from the locals. Trolling a hand line with a lure of chicken feathers, they fished during an incoming tide in the pass. In ten minutes they could catch enough fish for dinner.

When they wanted larger fish such as bonita or shark, Maurice and Heather accompanied the island men on fishing expeditions outside the lagoon. He described their ingenious system. "Using a flat rock as a sinker, the islanders cut up pieces of chum, place them on the rock, then wrap the rock with banana leaf. They wind a baited hook and line around the entire package, the hook secured to the package with another piece of leaf. They toss this package overboard, sharply tugging the line when they feel the rock hit bottom. The tug releases the baited hook and lets the chum fly." Fish caught this way, Maurice said, were shared among the fishermen. Heather related how an islander had reached in through the gills of a live fish and, tearing out the still-beating heart, offered it to her. When she turned away in disgust, the islander popped the heart — considered a delicacy — into his mouth.

July 7: The shallow wells in the main village were not recommended for drinking water, and the clean catchment water was too scarce to use for laundry. Our need for fresh water took us out to Napari, a half-hour tractor ride through uninhabited coconut forest. Accompanying us were sixteen wild-looking boys who sat in the back of the tractor and stared at us. They cut copra and worked on the village site while we collected water.

Ten solid cement western-style structures, including a large office building, several multi-family houses, swimming pool and tennis court were laid out in an orderly village. All were deserted, and most of them were locked up but in surprisingly good shape. The Chinese/Kiribati caretaker allowed us to take water from the overflowing cement cisterns which formed the cellar of each house. The island was

Kiribati flag, Independence Day, Fanning Island

Independence Day parade, Fanning Island

annexed to Britain in 1888 when it was found to be in line with a proposed Trans-Pacific cable. From 1902 to 1963 the island was the connecting point for this cable, which ran from Fiji to Canada. The buildings, built in the early '50s by British Cable and Wireless Ltd., were abandoned a decade later when the new British Commonwealth coaxial cable was opened. Since then, they have been used sporadically by the University of Hawaii.

July 8: Ashore, the heat bred a slow pace. When we passed a house we were invited to sit for a cup of tea, some fish or breadfruit. Whatever food the islanders had, they shared. We delivered some photos to Tabia, an islander who had befriended a cruiser we met in Honolulu. We declined his offer of a turtle meat dinner, but accepted a bottle of kamaimai, a sweet amber-colored syrup made from boiled-down coconut sap. Grey and Sarah swore that it's the best replacement for maple syrup around.

The setting sun headed us back through the village, past a copra dryer, that emitted the soapy rancid smell so much a part of the tropics, past an old woman collecting coconut husks in a burlap bag for her cooking fire. And past a young man, intoxicated with toddy, who was singing his heart out from the top of a coconut tree.

July 10: The *MV Nei Momi*, the government freighter from Tarawa, three months overdue, finally arrived. The excited islanders waited on the shore to see if they would have relatives, supplies or mail coming from the ship. What they unloaded was about two month's supply of sugar, flour, rice, and biscuits. Also several bicycles, cases of baby powder, matches, twist tobacco, and two bags of mail.

Two little girls, arms slung around each other, remembered my name, saying "Babua." Then one placed her index fingers on either side of her nose and giggling, pushed in, imitating my long pointed nose. I took a finger and flattened my nose to look like hers, and we all laughed.

July 13: Independence Day: At 11:00 a.m. we heard the parade approaching. One of the school teachers had made a drum out of an old cabin biscuit tin and was beating out a rhythm with sticks. About one hundred children, marching in unison and clad in orange and white, followed. They remained in formation perhaps five minutes, then dissolved into chaos, looking around for children from Napari village to appear. The Napari kids finally came marching in, dressed in coconut frond skirts and sashes. All the children commenced to sing, their song followed by a long prayer from the minister and a short speech by the new administrator.

The islanders insisted that we cruisers were the VIPs, and so we stood next to the flagpole along with the few officials. The unfurling of the colorful Kiribati flag by the policeman — our friend Tabia who looked very formal and official — was perfectly timed with a torrential downpour. The younger kids took refuge under their mother's ample skirts, but everyone else stood still and got soaked. After the rain, the different villages took turns singing songs until the celebration ended.

Sarah and Stacey from *Vamanos* came over to *Mahina Tiare* to fetch me for a foraging expedition ashore. Sarah had a technique for garnering the large claws of the coconut crabs: step on their shell, then reach from behind and snap off the claw at the first joint. The first one she nailed seemed off balance, holding up stump and phantom claw as it backed into the lagoon. Sarah assured me the remaining claw would grow larger, that a new claw would replace the old one. But I felt barbaric as I half-heartedly helped create a colony of amputees.

Next, with the permission of the islanders, Sarah and I ineptly cut down a young coconut tree to make hearts of palm salad. What we ended up with was about two cups of celery-like heart and a massacred tree. It is painfully obvious why heart of palm is called "millionaires salad" — or what a way to waste a tree. I would probably starve if left on a deserted island to forage for myself.

July 14: When we said goodbye, Perry invited us to visit his house if ever we made it to Christmas Island. He spoke animatedly about his traditional style Kirabati house. "Some Kiribati native priests go into trance and call dolphins up on the beach. But my house was blessed by a Catholic priest and, without being called, dolphins came and offered themselves on the beach at my house. A very lucky omen."

When we left Fanning the sun had set, only a faint beige patch left in the western sky. We eased out of the pass, the southeast wind blowing spume from breakers toward us and bringing the smoky smell from the glowing cooking fires ashore.

We sailed close-hauled to Penrhyn Island in the Northern Cooks, a seven day, 792-mile passage. Last year we had thrown our flower leis overboard off Penrhyn with a wish to return. A Polynesian belief is that if your lei drifts back toward the island you will return. The superstition survives; we returned to Penrhyn exactly one year later. From Penrhyn we sailed two days WSW to Manihiki Island, 194 miles. The anchorage is an open roadstead so we went ashore briefly to visit the Williams family, old friends of John's, to see their black pearl farm, then headed on towards Suwarrow, a two-day sail covering 203 miles.

Suwarrow is one of the Cook Islands, a group of 15 small islands scattered over 750,000 square miles in the South Pacific. The Cooks are 1,600 miles from New Zealand and Suwarrow lies 450 miles east of Pago Pago American Samoa, the nearest main port.

Despite its remoteness, we knew we would not have the island or the anchorage to ourselves. The Cook Island government has, for the last four years, appointed caretakers to the island and the number of visiting yachts increases yearly averaging 30-40 a year. One of the few islands in the South Pacific where no fees are extracted, visitors are left alone to explore the motus and lagoon.

Suwarrow Island has captured the imagination of yachtsmen, sea captains, and hermits for the last century. Perhaps it is the fantasy of living on a deserted island, or the wide and safe passage into a lagoon teeming with fish and pearl shell. Or perhaps the lure of buried treasure brings a steady stream of adventurers and writers to Suwarrow.

At least eight ships have wrecked on Suwarrow's outer reef. American and Mexican gold and silver coins have been found buried beneath Suwarrow's sands along with artifacts that suggest Spaniards visited centuries before the island was officially discovered by Europeans and named after the Russian trading vessel Suvarov in 1814.

Aug 6: We approached Suwarrow cautiously from the northeast. Once we had located Anchorage Island, the largest of the atoll's motus, we entered the wide unobstructed pass. Suwarrow's reputation as a ship-wrecker does not come from the difficulty of the pass, but rather the lack of land mass to distinguish its barely awash reef from the surrounding ocean.

Only one hundred acres of land, divided between five islets and a dozen or so brush-covered sandbanks, make up the total land mass. These islets are mostly strung along the northeast side of the nearly circular reef, making an approach from the south or southeast danger-ous in all but the best visibility.

We anchored in the lee of Anchorage Island where three small Swedish yachts and one 42-foot communal Danish yacht, *Suleima*, swung at anchor. We had last seen *Suleima* in the Marquesas. She had a new crew on board, but we were happy to see her again.

Stepping ashore on Anchorage Island, a crude sign immediately warns: "*Suwarrow Atoll National Park. Please don't take the birds, eggs, or turtles.*" Two platforms covered with thatch roofs flank the shore end of a crumbling coral jetty. Nearby three crushed coral pathways converge at a stone memorial. The memorial is inscribed: *1959-1977 TOM NEALE LIVED HIS DREAM ON THIS ISLAND,* and above the stone, a plaster bust that bears a striking resemblance to Fred Munster. Tom Neale was a New Zealander who fulfilled a lifelong fantasy by living alone as a hermit/caretaker on Suwarrow on and off during the '50s and '60s. He became a world-wide celebrity with the publication of his book, *An Island to Myself.*

Tom's two-room clapboard house, built by the New Zealand coast watchers during World War II, still stands. Itako, the relaxed Cook Island administrator, and Suwarrow, one of the island's two resident cats, greeted us at Tom's former residence. The cat, a dark tabby, insisted on our attention by lying on the one form we were required to fill out, then followed us the rest of the day.

We asked Itako to see the famous Suwarrow Yacht Logs that Tom Neale began decades ago. Itako handed us the log begun in 1984. "The rest have been stolen." he said. "I'm sure it was an islander; yachties wouldn't steal the logs." Still, the present log chronicled fascinating material. For example, a couple and their two-year-old son who came by yacht and without permission stayed six months, planted a veg-etable garden, and were ready to move ashore when the government sent a representative to the then-deserted island to tell them to move on. Before they left they wrote in the Yacht Log:

> To us all — Children lost in the universe
> Playing all the games they dare
> Millionaires of the moment
> Rich in what isn't there — from us all
> Rori, Yacht Fleur d'Ecosse

Aug. 8: Itako came aboard for dinner and we asked him about aggressive sharks around Suwarrow. During our daily swims we hadn't spotted any sharks. "Well," he remarked, "you shouldn't have any problems unless you spear fish. A friend of mine lost his thumb to a shark when he wouldn't give up a fish he had speared. I always fish from a dinghy." From talking to other spear fishermen on yachts, the average loss was one fish to the sharks for every two that made it into the dinghy.

Aug. 9: A severe chop developed at our anchorage when the wind suddenly clocked from NW to ESE, forcing us to reanchor across the lagoon in the limited protection of the Seven Islands. Seven Sandbanks would have been a more appropriate name. Even at the most easterly part of the lagoon, the 20-knot breeze made for a rough anchorage. A wind shift here would either push us onto the sandbank or grind us on the coral heads less than a boat-length astern of us. A writer once likened Suwarrow to a venus fly trap, very alluring and easy to get into but, once inside, difficult to escape. Since the anchorages are studded with coral heads and squall systems pass with frightening force, it is only a matter of time before a wind shift swings your boat and wraps your anchor chain around a coral head. The width of the lagoon supplies plenty of fetch to produce waves that will cause your boat to pitch violently enough to snap an anchor chain wrapped on a coral head. During the day you can dive to unwrap a chain, or let it go and leave the island. At night your options diminish. One night in 1983 seven boats went aground inside the lagoon. Only five of these sailed out of the Suwarrow fly trap.

Aug. 10: I joined John for a swim but, fearful of sharks, was reluctant to leave the immediate area around *Mahina Tiare*. Then John took my hand and, imagining him as my shark shield, we swam off in the direction of some mammoth, sun dappled coral heads.

The coral was heaped in rough piles up to 40 feet high. Most of the blooms were tan or cream colored, but an occasional purple or yellow patch dotted their surface. Bright blue and purple wavy-lipped tridacna clams wedged deep into the coral, their mouths clamping shut as we approached.

A stingray slowly scudding back and forth on the bottom kicked up a cloud of sand; it resembled a living vacuum cleaner. Fish surrounding the ray sucked up what ever the ray stirred up.

The water clarity allowed us to spot a green sea turtle tucked into a coral grotto 20 feet below. His speckled head was as big as my own, and one large lidded eye opened when we approached, closed as we swam past. Swimming back to *Mahina Tiare*, a few small black-tipped sharks sulked about 20 feet from us. But then a large blunt-headed grey reef shark cruised along the bottom about 40 feet below. With a few strong lateral strokes he quickly approached.

The entire incident seemed to happen in slow motion, stretching seconds into an eternity. I let out a high-pitched scream when he was about six feet away. My scream was absurdly weak in the face of the shark which grew huge as he closed in on us. Surely John would chase him away as he has done in the past with black or white-tipped sharks. Instead he maneuvered himself between me and the big grey.

I saw clearly the shark's bold steely eye and the four gill slits as he turned in profile to check us out. John eased his flippers toward the shark's mouth to keep him away from me. "Get out of the water," John commanded. Somehow I managed to clamber up the rung of our wind vane, my flippers still on. John quickly followed.

The shark wasn't displaying the waving motions of pre-attack

Ian McNair, shipwrecked sailor, aboard Mahina Tiare

behavior, but its fearlessness and damned impudence, combined with our total vulnerability, terrified me. Grey reef sharks are territorial and do not like to be challenged. Our mere presence constituted a challenge. The 6-foot shark put into perspective how small and vulnerable I am in the face of nature's complexity, just one bit of flesh easily part of the food chain.

Aug. 12: While on Penrhyn, we had heard by radio that an English singlehander, Ian McNair, had shipwrecked his 28-foot bilge-keel cutter *Arion* on the eastern tip of Suwarrow's outer reef. He was now camped on one of the Seven Sandbanks. We hadn't originally planned on visiting Suwarrow, a weather change indicated a smoother route to Samoa via Suwarrow than by way of Puka-Puka, and while McNair was reportedly in no imminent danger, we wanted to help him get his boat off the reef. We felt safe in leaving *Mahina Tiare* for awhile, so we dinghied over to McNair's islet.

I had imagined a plump, middle-aged Englishman hopelessly devastated by the loss of his boat. I felt a little like an ambulance chaser, and wondered whether he would be offended by questions or taking pictures of his boat. As we waded through the knee-deep coral shallows, Ian McNair, a tall erect man, strode out from the beach to help us with our inflatable. The afternoon sun made his hair glow orange and the only sign of his recent ordeal was an angry sunburn on his fair freckled skin. Extremely fit at 51, he spoke in subdued tones with a British accent. He wore a soiled, long-sleeved tailored shirt which flapped in the wind, and he held onto a long pole, a rusty fish hook lashed to its top. The staff made him look like a nautical shepherd or Robinson Crusoe reincarnate.

Ian's manner was forthright as he led us into the low-growing brush on the sand bank where he had rigged his green boat awning into a very satisfactory tent. We sat inside as a rain squall burst around us, and his various pails and sails rigged for water catchment quickly filled. V-berth cushions, yellowed paperbacks, Zip-locks full of oats, and jars of popcorn cluttered the tent.

Ian told us that he had lived on his boat for the past 20 years. "When I need money, I go to Jamaica," he said. "My training is engineering, but I've worked on newspapers and skippered boats from time to time."

Ian has no family, "They've all died off," he remarked, "...it's a bit of a relief, actually." Camped out on a deserted sand speck in the middle of a vast ocean seemed perfectly natural to him...as if he had no past and lived only in the moment. He shared his motu with several red-tailed tropic birds. At high tide water flooded through the middle of his islet, so he had tied his shoes, sunglasses, mirror and other possessions into the bushes like so many ornaments on an odd Christmas tree. He had built his human nest close to those of the tropic birds. He had figured the birds knew enough to build above the tidal range. We wondered what might happen to his unprotected lair in a storm, but Ian was more worried about getting too much cholesterol from the coconuts he was eating. The sun was fading when John plucked up enough courage to ask to see the wreck.

We waded a quarter-mile through the shallows to where *Arion* lay on her side, mast still intact, and bow facing the breakers. She looked like a forlorn whale hopelessly out of her element.

"I was on a nonstop passage from the Marquesas," he said. "The weather had been bad for days, 15-foot swells with a nasty wind chop on top. I spent a lot of time changing sails and was tired. I hit [the reef] about first light. I had forgotten to set my alarm... pure stupidity on my part. After 30 years of sailing and many narrow escapes, I thought it could never happen to me. But I'd become careless. If I had done what I should have... gotten up about four hours before when *Arion* was 20 miles off and hove-to, everything would have been all right.

"Suddenly I was aware of a loud crunch. We had struck the reef. I said to no one at all, 'it appears we've arrived.' When it all hits the fan it's amazing how British humor comes out. I wasn't aware of going through the breakers. Apparently I came over on the back of a wave. I guess I was lucky the surf was running, putting the boat where it is, about one hundred yards from the edge of the reef.

"I wasn't really scared, even though I thought the boat was going to break up. Dying is one thing, but being slowly rolled around and ground up on a reef is quite another. Once I was out of the really heavy surf I was afraid *Arion* would be pushed into the deep lagoon. We were taking on water and were abeam the seas so I put out a bow anchor and swung us around. I must have held onto something very tightly because my fingernails have turned black and are falling off.

"I didn't think *Arion* would make it through the day so I tried to take off as much as I could. The first dinghy load of gear included medical supplies, my kerosene stove, food, and five gallons of water. A large swell caught me and the dinghy capsized. I lost everything.

"The rest of my gear made it to the islet okay and that's where I set up camp. After three days a big yacht passed outside the reef, saw the wreck and motioned for me to swim out through the breakers towards them. But I didn't want any part of that nonsense. The yacht must have radioed to the administrator who lives on the other side of the lagoon. I had no idea anyone else lived on the island so you can imagine my surprise when the administrator came motoring up in his aluminum skiff."

In fact, there were several yachts on Suwarrow when *Arion* hit the reef. Ian decided to strip his boat and sell the parts to the other yachts. His tiny islet was piled with line, spare hardware and miscellaneous boat bits; it looked like a nautical yard sale in the middle of the Pacific. After a few weeks on the motu Ian realized the frequent squalls meant plenty of freshwater and that there were no mosquitoes, rats, or cockroaches. He began to settle down and enjoy the adventure. He said: "I would be quite content to live a Tom Neale existence.

However, these small countries are hopelessly bureaucratic and they want me to leave. There is a 31-day visa limit."

We were amazed by the condition of *Arion* after an entire month on the reef. One bilge keel was broken off and a small hole was punched in the hull, but it looked possible, on repairing the hole and bilge keel, to get the boat over the reef and into the lagoon.

It was obvious Ian was ready to abandon *Arion*. "I've put her up for sale several times in the past," Ian commented, "but when someone showed interest in buying her, I'd leave port straight away. She'd been my security for so long I couldn't bring myself to sell her. So I left Jamaica to come down here. This makes my third trip. I had no reason to come here again, but *Arion* had become my cross to bear and now I am free.

"People worry that I'm not terribly upset about losing my boat, but only on land can I find the kind of complete solitude, the state of consciousness where I can still the inner dialog. The boat requires too much attention to achieve that. I view this as a beginning, not an end."

As we walked away from *Arion* a harsh wind blew out of an angry, grey streaked sky and the breakers hissed on the reef. John asked him, "Where will you go from here?"

"Well, that's the adventure isn't it? Not knowing what is next..."

Postscript: The last we heard of Ian was that he had patched *Arion* and, helped by the crew of *Batwing*, a Seattle boat, managed to get her off the reef. Then we heard that *Arion* was found adrift off Fiji without Ian aboard. The assumption was that he had fallen overboard and drowned. A subsequent radio report conveyed the full story. Ian had hit a reef at night, was thrown from *Arion*'s deck into the water. He managed to clamber back aboard but couldn't budge her from the reef. Spotting a light in the distance, he decided to row toward it in his dinghy. He managed to reach land and help. When he returned to where he'd left *Arion* the night before, she was gone. Shortly thereafter *Arion* was spotted adrift and brought into Tambarua Harbor on Viti Levu, the main island of Fiji. Ian was reunited with *Arion*, his cross to bear.

Chapter 12

PRINGLES IN PARADISE

Barbara: Everyone had warned me about Pago Pago. One morning, crossing the 450 miles from Suwarrow atoll in the Cook Islands to Tutuila Island in American Samoa, we heard this description of the harbor read over the single sideband radio, an excerpt from Scott Kuhner's newsletter, The Great Escape. I quote:

"...As we sailed into this protected hurricane anchorage, our eyes scanned the ridge of mountains that ring the harbor, two thousand feet high. Puffy clouds scudded above the tops of lush green peaks, occasionally bumping into the mountain ridge knocking loose a quick torrent of rain.

"As our vision descended from the heavens, it took in the steep green sides of the mountains, luscious in a savage, unspoiled beauty. It finally alighted on the white houses, roads, buses, cars and, finally, the two large tuna factories that line the harbor at water's edge.

"From the beauty of the heavens above us through the purgatory of man's construction at the shoreline, my eyes now fixed on the harbor water which, to my horror, I realized was the personification of hell itself. I was reminded of the New York subway system when I would stand on the platform waiting for my train and absently gaze at the pungent, slimy water stagnating between the tracks. I was convinced that Mayor Koch must have found someone to build a giant system that drained all that ooze via a huge pipe straight through the center of the earth, draining right here in Pago Harbor.

"Just as this scene was shattering my image of the American Paradise in the Pacific, one of the large tuna fish processing factories that was accepting the catch from the three or four Japanese fishing

171

boats tied alongside it, ...expelled the most pungent, noxious gas imaginable. I gagged and grabbed for a towel to cover my nose. Never will I be able to relish tuna fish with the same enthusiasm as prior to our stay in Pago Pago."

After hearing Scott Kuhner read that excerpt from his newsletter, I wasn't sure I wanted to see Pago Harbor. But I did want to meet Scott Kuhner.

John: My previous visit to Pago Pago in 1975 had been at an intense time in my young life. My 27-foot sloop *Mahina's* rudder had broken in a fierce tropical storm, and I had spent two-and-a-half days awake, continuously trying to beat to Aitutaki, steering only with sails and drogues. After nearly losing the boat on the reef, then being towed in the pass at nine knots, my falling in love with a beautiful and elegant Polynesian girl named Nana came easily.

I sailed from Aitutaki to Pago Pago with the intention of selling *Mahina* and marrying Nana. She planned on flying to meet me here. But her positive response to my cable asking if she still wanted to join me was misplaced in the Pago Post Office. I spent a month waiting and wondering. Had she changed her mind? I decided to sail back from Samoa to Hawaii, instead of selling *Mahina*.

As we ghosted into the harbor on our present trip, those memories flooded back. I wondered where I'd be now if Nana's telegram had reached me when I expected it instead of a few days before my departure from Samoa.

Aug. 15, Barbara: We sailed into the harbor at midnight with the help of Dave Cohen on the 35-foot cutter *Synergy* from San Francisco. He filled us in on what lights were working and what colors they were, something the port control was unable to do. We don't normally enter port in the dark, but since the seas were calm and John had entered the harbor before, we sailed in cautiously at three knots and dropped our anchor among 30 silent, dark yachts.

This would be our first time among the pack of cruisers known as the "Class of" whatever year they were moving across the South Pacific from East to West. Most came from Mexico or through the Panama Canal via French Polynesia on their way to Tonga, Fiji then New Zealand or Australia to spend the hurricane season. Many of these cruisers had known each other for months, sometimes years.

172

Pago Pago is one of the major ports in the Pacific where cruisers stop en mass to reprovision, get things repaired, parts shipped, and to find work. The average number of yachts stopping at Pago is three hundred per year.

The trend toward bigger yachts loaded with temperamental electronics means more equipment to break down. Inadequately prepared with spare parts or the knowledge to accomplish repairs, some of these boats limp from major port to major port where they sit for months while their refrigeration, engines, and watermakers are worked on. Later returned to the docks of their home countries, their owners think the Pacific is Papeete or Pago Pago Harbor. They tell the cruisers getting ready to make the trip into the big Pacific pond, "It's not worth it... it's nothing like I expected... the water is dirty, the people unfriendly... it's expensive and impossible to get work done."

These cruisers often miss the best part of cruising. They become frustrated without the comforts of home, are afraid to risk being alone in an anchorage or going ashore to meet the "natives." It's much easier to share cocktails with people who speak the same language and who don't muddy their decks with bare feet.

Aug. 16: Morning found us alongside the rustic cement quay waiting and waiting for Customs to arrive while the only available hose dripped water into our water tank.

Like Papeete, Tahiti, once warned that one isn't entering a pristine vacation land but a dirty commercial harbor, Pago Pago isn't as bad as its reputation. After all, as Dave Cohen on Synergy put it, "One has to pay a price for being able to buy 'Pringles in Paradise,' not to mention new deep-cycle batteries, engine parts, cheap meals out, ice cream, domestic rates on mail to the United States, self-service laundromat, inexpensive fabric and clothing."

Dave and his wife Sharon Jacobs, both high-powered executives in their mid-thirties, were on a two-year sabbatical from their management and computer firms in the San Francisco Bay Area. Untamed thick black hair, bare chest and a beard that covered most of his face, made it difficult to imagine Dave in an office environment. And soft-spoken Sharon, now scantily wrapped in a pareu and often sporting a knapsack, was hard to picture in high heels and pin-striped suit supervising thousands of people at Hewlett-Packard.

Dave and Sharon are go-getters with more money than time to cover all the places they want to cruise. They admit that their ambitious objective of circumnavigating the Pacific in less than two years has meant moving faster than they would have preferred. And they will not have a hurricane season lay-over in New Zealand or Australia to do maintenance.

On the other hand they expect to see a greater variety of places and cultures — the Solomons, Yap, Pohnpei, Truk, Japan and Alaska — than cruisers with less ambitious itineraries. Two years seemed the most time they could realistically take off from their careers. Limiting themselves to this time frame, they have been able to cruise now rather than wait another ten years. Every three months they have business and technical reading forwarded from California and enjoy this intellectual stimulation.

Dave and Sharon had Pago wired; they knew where to get the foods most cruisers covet: hard salamis, cheese and nuts. Dave called it 'shopping wars', spending endless time and money to locate all the items on a shopping list before other cruisers beat you to it. Having Dave and Sharon as allies saved us days of battle. It was easier to provision in Pago without a car than any place we've been, including the U.S. The major grocery stores delivered large orders to the dock and gave a ten percent discount on large purchases. Prices were slightly higher than in the States on canned goods, but overall, after Hawaii, they were the best prices in the Pacific. One boat slogged 2,000 miles to windward from New Zealand just to reprovision in Pago.

The open-air market has a small variety of locally grown produce — lettuce, tomatoes, papaya, coconut, taro — but the grocery stores carry sacks of imported onions, potatoes, carrots, cabbages. Cruisers often go in together to get case prices on things like tuna and tomato sauce.

Liquor, especially the no-name brands, is cheap. In fact, stove alcohol unavailable, we found it much cheaper to use locally purchased vodka rather than rubbing alcohol to prime our kerosene stove.

Colorful buses run regularly around the island. They start at the marketplace, a short walk from the dinghy landing, and move in either direction along the shoreline. It costs a quarter to get most of the way around the island. The trucks are homemade, with shag carpeting on the dashboard, shelf paper on the walls, and hard seats. Everything from Bob Marley's reggae to religious hymns blare over the huge speakers.

A short drive out of town, the spectacular beauty of the island unfolds as the bus winds around the curving coast, a white beach and aqua water on one side and steep mountains on the other. The villages are small and, unlike Pago, immaculate. Western-style houses mingle with traditional Samoan fales, upright wooden poles arranged in an oval to support a thatch roof. Pandanus mats, which can be pulled down in sections, form the walls of the fales.

Aug. 17: Anchored in this harbor with lots of boats reminds me of shopping for shoes. Through various social contacts we and other cruisers try each other out to see if we fit. When personalities really click, long evenings are spent in cockpits discussing our new lifestyles. Friendships deepen and itineraries are altered so that cruising routes will coincide. Dave and Sharon, Scott and Kitty Kuhner were people that fit. Tall, wiry, red hair, impish grin and an intensity that either endeared or annoyed, Scott had the personality to succeed in the competitive New York stock market and yet retain the gullibility of a child. Kitty, six feet tall, radiated warmth with her ready smile. Fifteen years ago Scott and Kitty circumnavigated the globe in a 31-foot Allied Seawind ketch which earned them the Cruising Club of America's circumnavigator's award. This time around they were exploring the world with their two sons, Alex, 11, and Spencer who was nine, on *Tamure*, a Valiant 40 cutter.

When nothing clicked with new acquaintances, we shared short encounters. Many cruisers, like many people, are poor conversationalists; they listen only long enough to enable themselves to one-up you. This is a whole different kind of snobbery than on shore. It doesn't revolve around the size or design of your boat. It's not what you drive, but where you've been and what you've been given. Most points are scored on how remote and difficult an anchorage. If no other boats were in the area at the time you visited, the score doubles. And if no other boats were there this year, you receive a hefty bonus.

The value of the gifts you received vary. Lobsters, wood carvings, tapa cloth and baskets score high. Shell necklaces and coconuts hardly count. It's difficult not to get caught in this cruiser's game of one-upmanship.

"Yeah, well, I was given five lobsters ... invited to five pig roasts ... they haven't seen a yacht there in years," someone bragged over the radio. So everyone flocked to the same place and wondered why no one offered lobsters or invited them to private homes. Suddenly twenty boats had anchored off a tiny village discovered overnight.

Aug. 28: Long before the big blow hit, John and I were below working on projects. Suddenly he shot up saying: "I think we are dragging!" Sure enough, we were beam-to in 20 to 30 knots of wind. In 20 feet of water, we thought that our 60 feet of 5/16-inch chain was sufficient. Obviously it wasn't, so we let out 110 feet. We were in the back half of the harbor which, it was later explained, is fine river silt on rock covered with layers of plastic bags that wash down into the harbor. I've heard anchor manufacturers make all sorts of claims, but never any one of them claim, "Holds well in mud, sand and plastic bags."

The wind steadily increased, and we took down our large sun awning and put out a second bow anchor. Soon the show began: first, *Homer's Odyssey* dragged down on *Wind Woman*. Lynn and her young children were alone on *Homer's Odyssey*, a 39-foot cutter; her husband was in Canada attending a funeral. John and several men from other boats hopped in their inflatables and went over to help reset her anchors. Next *Loana*, a 47-foot ketch, dragged towards the beach, and John helped reset their anchors as well. By this time I had our engine on in slow forward to take some of the strain off the anchors. I sensed we were dragging again, and called John on the radio. I told him that if he didn't get back quickly, we'd be the next boat to hit the beach!

Homer's Odyssey's anchor slipped again, and in the 40-knot gusts the boat seemed to lash out like a wounded animal. Drifting sideways down the anchorage, it pulled up *Wind Woman's* anchor and crashed into her bow pulpit. Momentarily the boats locked, dragging toward shore together. But Peter on *Wind Woman* untangled them.

Darkness fell, but the wind continued to funnel into the bay. That evening more than at any other time — more than at potlucks on the beach, much more than at any cruiser's club — I felt part of the cruising community. Everyone was up standing watch, worrying about their boat, every boat. *Wind Woman* was lying abeam us, I knew that Peter was watching us, ready to lend a hand if we needed help. We called him

John scrubbing off 18 days growth of tube coral, (inset coral close -up)

on VHF, "Tell us if we are dragging and we will call you if you drag." It was much easier to detect another boat's slipping than one's own.

The air felt charged with the noise of wind in the rigging, and the radio chatter was constant as we pitched up and down through the night. I felt a strength that night, a solidarity, that's hard to describe. Perhaps it was knowing we were all together, the same thoughts going through our heads: did we put out enough chain; should we have put out another anchor? These are the times I remember cruising, not the ones when we were rocked gently to sleep. But cruising has to involve some risks, or else it seems tame, pointless.

Aug. 24: Morning dawned gray-purple. Except for those on moorings and a couple of other noteworthy boats, everyone in the back half of Pago harbor dragged yesterday or today. Many moved to the head of the bay to anchor in over 50-feet of water; everyone else unloaded all of their chain. Few people were able to go ashore because it was impossible to row against the wind, and anything less than a five hp outboard was useless.

We had 200 feet of chain out in the 20-foot depth on our primary anchor, and 250 feet of line and chain on our secondary anchor. Wind howled again in the evening and again everyone stood watch.

Aug. 31: The wind passed but today's sky remained sullen. Grey Wicker on *Vamanos*, was doing a good diving business, scrubbing off the tube coral which covered everyone's propellers and bottoms. Nobody wanted to get in the murky water to do it themselves. Cruisers in the harbor for two weeks found themselves without power to leave, their props inches thick with the fishy-smelling stuff. Dinghy bottoms and anchor chains were also thick with tube coral.

In the afternoon all the cruisers got together at the Pago Pago Yacht Club to hear Harry Mitchell, from the yacht *Whalesong* give an informal talk on weather systems between Samoa and New Zealand and Australia. The room was noisy and crowded, too much energy for such a small space. I left on a quest for walnuts.

John had learned that there was a window in the weather. We would need to leave tomorrow, he told me, or get hit with more squalls in the anchorage.

I had become used to the comforts of being in port, and a certain sluggishness had taken over — too many meals out, trips to Amy's Bakery and no exercise. (It's easy to put on pounds in port; could this be the origin of the word 'portly'?)

Sept. 2: Today I was more or less ready to leave. It seems we only achieve this feeling after we set a departure date, rush around, then discover that we can't possibly leave as scheduled. So we get a good night's sleep, a bonus not counted on, kind of like a snow day off from school. The next day, everything almost done (it's never all quite done), we can leave in good daylight. Certainly, I was happy to have met this year's "class" of cruisers and been in one place long enough to make new friends. Yet as we sailed away from American Samoa, I realized that all I had seen was American. The Samoan side of life, somewhere out in the villages, had slipped past.

Chapter 13
NIUATOPUTAPU & WALLIS:
FEASTS AND PRIESTS

John: The Kingdom of Tonga is the only Pacific Island nation never brought under foreign domination. King Taufa'ahau Tupou IV can trace his heritage back through hundreds of years of rulers.

Under Tonga's constitutional monarchy, all lands are owned by the crown but administered by the 33 Nobles of the Realm. The system of land tenure is complicated. The ever-increasing population and limited amount of arable cropland has resulted in an exodus of young people to Auckland, Pago Pago, Honolulu and California.

Three distinct island groups make up the Kingdom, and a few scattered offshore islands. The southernmost, Tongatapu is the site of the capital and has the largest population: over 65,000. The central group of Ha'apai has 20,000 people living on 20 low coral atolls. Va'vau, the northernmost group, consists of 34 islands with a population of only 16,000. Niuatoputapu is a day's sail north of Va'vau and is a legal Port of Entry for Tonga.

Sept. 4: Our 170-mile passage from Samoa went fast, so fast that we arrived several hours before sunrise and had to slow the boat down to wait for good visibility in the pass entrance. We really didn't know what to expect. We hadn't met anyone who had visited Niuatoputapu, a relatively isolated island, but we were excited at the prospect of a new anchorage.

When we dropped anchor in the island's tiny lagoon, five other cruising yachts surrounded us. Scott, on *Tamure,* was on the SSB radio broadcasting to 50 or so yachts scattered throughout Polynesia. He was telling them what a special place Niuatoputapu is.

Falehau, the smallest of Niuatoputapu's three villages, was a short

179

walk from the cement pier near the anchorage. Ashore, sleek horses grazed the lawns or pulled ancient wooden carts brimming with children. The village, more pastoral than exotic, could have been a bucolic scene from an 18th century French painting except for the coconut trees. The houses were thatched fales or crude clapboard, and storage sheds of rough-hewn branches fastened vertically looked like a picket fence with a roof. Pigs, dogs, cats wandered freely; black and white goats tugged at their tethers.

I attributed the manicured lawns to grazing animals, but was disillusioned to find out it was the work of a lawn mower. Still, Falehau came closest to my idea of a traditional Polynesian village, something I had pictured in my mind, but never seen. This is the first place we've visited in Polynesia where fales are lived in predominantly by the islanders instead of tourists wanting to go native.

Children followed us as if we were a pair of pied-pipers. In one breath, they asked: "Where are you going, what is your name, where is my popcorn?" They repeated the question constantly until we asked them, "Where are you going, what is your name, and where is my popcorn?" When one little girl pointed at my hat and said, "Give me my hat," I pointed at her dress and said, "Give me my dress." She looked indignant: "NO!"

Obviously previous cruisers had roamed the village indiscriminately giving out popcorn, candy, hats. This turned the kids into little beggars. But how could they know any better? They were reacting to our behavior, not the other way around.

We met a teenage boy on a bicycle who stopped and shook our hands and said, "I want to have friend John and Barbara." Three lovely young girls, the Lolohea sisters, stopped us as we headed back toward *Mahina Tiare*. "Come back to our house for a dancing party tonight," they implored. It was difficult to say no, but we hadn't had a full night's sleep since leaving Pago Pago.

Sept. 5: Scott and Kitty invited us and a young Tongan man named Tui to come aboard *Tamure* for dinner. Tui was in his mid-twenties and had the compact, muscular build and slightly frizzy hair common among the people of the western Polynesian islands.

Tui, lively and entertaining, read people like a book. He had studied for the priesthood at the Marist Mission School in Fiji, but had then decided against becoming a priest. Returning to Niuatoputapu, he eloped with the chief of Falehau's youngest daughter. He admitted he missed playing Scrabble with the priests whom he could beat, and was anxious to prove his prowess with the yachties.

The islanders were good farmers, Tui said, and their usual meal was root crops and greens. Fish, pig, dog or horse were added to the menu on occasion. While answering our questions about Tongan culture, he broke into a wide grin and thrust his arms out with a magnanimous sweep: "If you are open with the people on shore they will be open with you."

Sept. 6: We toured the island on our folding bicycles, stopping at the crushed coral airstrip which accommodates one flight per month from Va'Vau. On the windward southeast shore, the rusting hulk of a recently wrecked Korean fishing boat still shuddered when the waves crashed against it. On a back road through Hihifo village we heard much laughter within a house. We shyly poked our heads in the door. Four large women were at work on Tongan wedding mats, the marriage to take place the next day. They seemed delighted to pose with their mats, but decided it would be fun to dress the skinny papalangi girl (me) in the mats. They couldn't speak English but roared with laughter as they wrapped layer upon layer of matting around me until I looked like a cross between a Tongan bride and a tamale.

Back on *Mahina Tiare* we were still coping with the marine growth from Pago Pago harbor. Tiny barnacles which had cemented themselves to the hull and dinghy bottom needed to be scrubbed off. The anchor chain still smelled of fishy tube coral as John end-for-ended it. Months of anchoring in coral had knocked the galvanizing off the first 100 feet of chain and it had begun to rust and flake off onto the deck.

Sept. 8: Dogs lapped up water from our laundry bucket as John filled it from a tap outside the Lolohea's thatched fale. John Love, a mischievous young member of the Lolohea clan, dragged something through the mud. Then everyone began to laugh as this 'something' was pulled from under a pig. And I had to claim the muddy pair of underpants as mine.

When we went to retrieve our dinghy from the wharf we found a young, blond papalangi woman speaking Tongan to a group of island girls. She responded in English to our hello. She wasn't off a yacht and no tourists were on Niuatoputapu.

Over dinner on *Mahina Tiare* Laurie, a Peace Corps volunteer on Niuatoputapu, explained her work. She was helping people build rainwater collection systems and cement cisterns to supplement the well water, something in short supply and contaminated from pesticides. She was also organizing a crafts store in Hihifo where the women could take in some cash by selling their intricately woven mats. A few months earlier a dozen or more yachts had paid the women for mats to protect their cabin and cockpit soles. The women were still laughing about all of the crazy shaped papalangi mats. Laurie had postponed her accepted entrance to Harvard Law School for one year to finish up her projects on Niuatoputapu.

Sept. 10: Tila, a cousin of the Lolohea's, invited us to a feast in honor of the yacht people. It was dark and pouring rain when we arrived at her small wooden frame house where we removed our shoes before stepping inside. Except for a screen hutch for food and dish storage, the rest of the room was bare of furniture. Finely woven pandanus mats covered the floor, and the walls were plastered with color photos from papalangi magazines: Glamour, Vogue, Life. Pale-skinned beauties covered with make-up and jewels watched disdainfully from the walls while guests sat on the floor and ate, with fingers, a meal of roast pig, marinated raw fish and root crops. Flashes went off as plumeria-draped yachties took pictures of the feast.

Then amateur hour began. An acappella chorus accompanied Tila as she danced the tamure by kerosene and candle light. Whisperings and rustlings suggested that a crowd watched from outside. Presently a huge woman danced in, using gentle, alluring motions with her hands and arms. Then she danced out again, swallowed into the gathering crowd. Someone else came from outside to sing.

Next, Thomas, a singlehanding Swede, stood and went into his version of a Polynesian men's tamure dance. Thunderous applause for Thomas came from inside and outside the house. Instruments appeared and more people crowded inside to sing and play. John sang. I got up and danced, a man from outside entering the room to dance with me.

The openness of the people enchanted all the guests. On the way back to the boats, Scott and Kitty's 11-year-old son commented, "These people don't have much but they sure aren't poor."

Sept. 12, John: A half-dozen more cruising boats arrived in the anchorage. Tavake, the customs officer, asked one of the yachts he was clearing to radio Pago Pago. Perhaps the next yacht coming could bring him six litres of rum, six litres of vodka. Laurie, the Peace Corps volunteer, declared that if Tavake got that amount of liquor he and his friends would drink it all in one sitting, then abuse their wives and children. Polynesian people, especially on the outer islands, consider it rude to leave an open bottle unfinished. Learning of Tavake's request, other islanders explained that the island was "dry" and requested that cruisers not bring liquor ashore. We radioed the yacht bringing the liquor and explained the situation, and none of it ended up ashore.

Sept. 13, Barbara: We had a terrific squall today with 50-knot winds and diagonal sheets of torrential rain. We couldn't see boats anchored 100 feet away. The gusts blew the hoses off our rain catcher, and the sounds of thunder and rain on our awning kept me awake most of the night.

John, too, was up and down all night. He let out chain, hooked on the chain snubber, and checked the anchor. He would return to bed damp and cold as stone.

Sept. 14: The evidence of last night's storm was everywhere on the island. Ancient breadfruit trees uprooted, branches fallen, a couple of collapsed thatch houses. During the height of the storm the Loloheas were awakened with cold rain pelting them, the roof blown off their house. But this evening the roof was back on and they were laughing about the storm. We sat around on the floor of their house and listened to the nine members of the family sing and play guitar and recorder. It seemed as though the storm had never happened, that their small home had never stood in danger of total destruction the prior night.

Sept. 15: Time to leave. Seeing more than a dozen yachts at anchor and knowing another dozen were enroute, we realized that we were beginning to spend more time talking *about* the Tongans than talking *with* the Tongans. Our focus had been divided between the yachts surrounding us and our friends ashore. We had started speaking in terms of "us" (the yachts) and "them" (the locals). When a group of yachts congregate, the pure interaction and experience of the local culture gets diluted. A party-type atmosphere develops and an underlying attitude implies that the place is a vacation spot whose function is to entertain visiting yachts. An immediate VHF net is established among the yachts and there is the distraction of wondering, no matter how hard I try not to, whether I am missing out on some cruiser's get-together. The feel of a place eludes me when I am involved with the subculture of other cruisers.

Ham and single sideband radio have created a tendency for cruisers to travel in packs. When 15 to 20 boats that have been cruising together for six months suddenly arrive at a small island, the dynamics are quickly changed. Almost every American and Canadian boat we met this year carried a ham radio. Many used them primarily to keep in touch with cruising friends. Niuatoputapu was the place to come, according to everyone on the radio. Some were calling the island "New Potatoes," an indication they were not interested enough in the island to pronounce its name properly. For many cruisers the experience of a place comes down to numbers: port fees, the price of ice cream or liquor, what they can buy or take away to prove they visited the place. Anchorages are less threatening if one can find out about them on the radio before arriving, know a dozen of their friends are already there, and can put a familiar name to a strange place — like "New Potatoes." Yet there is no emotional connection to the people ashore.

We stopped by the Lolohea's to say goodbye. The house was filled with women making mats, but the atmosphere was not right. Nisie, the middle daughter wouldn't look at us. Molokeine, the oldest, handed me a beautiful pandanus fan she had woven, then turned away wiping tears from her face. Then I was crying. The sobs got louder as I hugged them goodbye until everyone in the hut was crying, even women who didn't know us. The whole clan followed mournfully down to the wharf to wave goodbye. I felt we had communicated with these girls on a level where words were unnecessary. From the beginning they had watched our expressions and movements and had understood us. "It is easy to say hello, Molokeine said now, "but hard to say goodbye."

Certainly we enjoy our cruising friends, but this experience of "cruising with the pack" wasn't our style. We slipped quietly out the pass, wanting to go somewhere we knew little about, wanting to be alone to make our own assessments and discoveries. Frankly, we wanted to be "out of touch." So, when we left Niuatoputapu it was to sail to Wallis Island, a place where we could be alone, where we could explore and relax without being one of the crowd.

Our two day passage to Wallis was fast and easy. Wallis and its neighbor island of Futuna lie 400 miles NE of Fiji, 170 miles west of Samoa, 214 miles NNW of Niuatoputapu. Together they form France's smallest South Pacific territory.

Wallis is a volcanic island surrounded by a barrier reef. A tricky but well bouyed pass led into the 16 mile length of lagoon. It took four hours to sail our way buoy by buoy to anchor off Matu Uta, the main village.

Ashore was a commercial wharf with a few wooden fishing boats tied up. Beyond, a massive gray volcanic block cathedral rose from a flat treeless field. On top of the cathedral, a 12-foot statue of the Virgin Mary draped in a lei and grass skirt looked down from between square steeples. Next door, an old two-story colonial-style building made out of the same grim-looking stones served as the King of Wallis' palace. These two buildings represented the two strongest influences on the island: the traditional Polynesian monarch and the church.

We located the Gendarmarie, a very modest building in comparison to church and state. The gendarme, in khaki shorts and knee socks, was curt but when we began speaking French, he relaxed and became helpful. No fees and no agriculture, health or customs inspectors to deal with on Wallis. Unlike the Society Islands, where the Gendarmes insist on knowing the exact position of all yachts at all times, these police had no idea we had even arrived until we showed up on their doorstep. Their authority is limited, most decision-making resting with traditional island chiefs and the king. For example, there is no car insurance (unheard of in other French territories) and, in the case of an accident the chief decides who is liable and how many pigs the injured party will receive.

A few small French cars whizzed past on the narrow streets as we headed up a slight hill to the town center, located at a crossroads. A half-dozen shops made up the center of town, but we saw no customers. These pricey shops cater to the French population of 300 or so who live in the small subdivision of Afala on a hillside north of Mata Uta.

The Wallisians, including the King, rise early and spend the day tending their taro, manioc and banana plantations. They show little interest in fancy European food.

The village was deceiving. On the surface, it appeared traditional. But, in addition to the expected sights, — women doing laundry by hand and pigs wandering about, — we saw new cars parked outside the thatched fales, and at night the blue light of TV screens glowed through open doors.

The French government pumps ten million dollars into the annual budget for the 8,000 people on Wallis. The islanders are financially comfortable, but an exodus continues from the island to New Caledonia where at least 18,000 Wallisians and Fatunans live.

Sept. 19: We stopped at the Post Office to buy the colorful first-day covers and butterfly stamps issued exclusively for Wallis and Fatuna. No other customers were around and the woman at the counter wanted to chat. We seemed a curiosity; island people are just not used to American visitors. But everyone, French and Polynesian, seemed pleased that we had made the effort to visit their small island. We were treated like honored guests.

Wallis and Futuna not only have their own stamps but also their own Bishop, or Eveque. We hitchhiked out to see him, arriving unannounced. We felt awkward interrupting him at home, but followed the young woman who led us into the Bishop's manse.

The Bishop, a thin, serious Wallisian man in his late sixties, was not at all pleased when he saw two casually clad visitors blunder into his personal chambers. He looked sternly at our shoes which we had neglected to remove before entering. I reacted as always when I experience shame, —a burning low in the abdomen, the same feeling I'd get as a kid when a nun singled me out for committing some innocuous offense in school.

The Bishop immediately led us out of his house to a sterile sitting room and gravely waited to counsel us on whatever problem we had brought along with which to burden him. But we'd come to convey the greetings of a special Hawaiian priest we'd met in Hilo. Father George had asked that "If you ever get to Wallis Island, please say hello to my friend the Bishop." So in halting French, made worse by the unsmiling Bishop and my childhood remembrances, I conveyed Father George's greeting. It was then the Bishop softened. He mumbled for a long time in what we assumed was French. He then led us to his kitchen/dining room where a large pale French priest sat with a bottle of wine and a delicious-looking meal in front of him.

"Would you like whiskey, gin, vodka?" They seemed incredulous when we declined. Then, apparently recalling that Americans like beer they seemed surprised by our negative response. We did accept the three-course lunch: pork, chicken, fei, taro root and kumera, served to us on glass plates by the Bishop himself. Never as a young school girl, terrified by the Sisters of Charity nuns in their voluminous black robes and bonnets, could I imagine myself served lunch by a bishop.

When we were finished, he scraped the leftovers outside for the waiting cats, then continued a conversation in his mumbled French. We trusted he wasn't asking any questions as we kept smiling and nodding. Suddenly a torrential rain squall burst, producing a staccato beat on the tin roof and ending our chance of escape. We were on foot without rain gear.

When the rain eased up, I peeked into the hundred-year-old Lano church nearby. There were stained glass saints on the leaded windows. The face of one saint was missing, taken out cleanly so the shape remained but instead of seeing a saintly visage, you saw sky. The Lano Church was smaller than the Mata Uta cathedral, but made from the same hand-cut gray volcanic stone. The stone gave the interior an oppressive old-world feel found in many old churches in Europe but out of place in Polynesia.

Meanwhile, the Bishop and a gang of boys from the church school were trying to push start his car so that he could give us a ride back to town. Unsuccessful, he arranged for a teacher's car. Father George was right — the Bishop was a kind man. We only wish that we had been able to understand his French.

John: After dinner I bicycled down to the southern tip of the island, to Cale d'Halalo. During the war the Navy Seabees had dredged a half-mile long channel through the coral, then used the dredge spoils to build a wharf. They built a fuel tank farm on the end of the wharf, the water here deep enough for tankers to moor alongside. This same system is used today, and when the guards learned that I was an American and that we'd sailed to Wallis, they opened the gates and showed me around. They asked if we'd like to bring *Mahina Tiare* inside the small, well-protected channel alongside the wharf. They explained that a few years ago an American catamaran had gone on the reef when attempting to enter the pass. They had pulled her off the reef and the crew had spent an entire year in this tiny harbor rebuilding her.

Sept. 20, Barbara: We left Wallis feeling an urgency to continue on to Fiji before the weather — the approaching hurricane season — caught us off guard. Visiting Wallis had been like going to Never-Never Land — beautiful, but with an empty feeling, like a bit of its soul had departed with the constant migration of people.

The steady southeasterly trades had created quite a swell outside the southerly facing Passe Honikulu. Ahead we were faced with a 12-foot wall of water. It looked like some mysterious force had raised the entire level of the ocean 12 feet while we anchored, unaware, in the lagoon. The sea wasn't breaking in the pass, but on either side the same wall of water was smashing against the reef.

For miles we struggled in the throes of battling currents and wave refraction from the island, close-reaching into a stiff 25-knot breeze. Some waves were square on the nose and would fly up over the entire boat as we crashed through, others would pick us up under our port beam and drop us over 45 degrees on the starboard side with a frightening thud. The unpredictability of the waves — no recognizable pattern to them — was more upsetting than their height. We sat stunned in the cockpit, staring, not moving for hours, not even logging our position. Finally, John made our standard desperation dinner — freeze-dried chicken stew, which stayed down only a few hours.

It was fun to be off the beaten track, but I had to admit, I was looking forward to seeing our cruising friends in Fiji and New Zealand.

Chapter 14

FIJI TO NEW ZEALAND:

CROSSING
THE TEMPESTUOUS TASMAN

Sept. 24: After four days and 400 miles sailing south we approached Levuka, our port of entry. We recalled stories we'd heard over the ham radio during the past year. Patrol boats not showing any running lights had mysteriously followed one yacht during the night, intermittently turning on huge spotlights. Another boat reported seeing white and green flares fired repeatedly on the horizon. A third reported that their boat was thoroughly searched when they cleared into port, forepeak to engine room, for guns. The military, in a coup, had seized power from the elected government a year earlier. Since then several container loads of guns had been seized on their way into the country. Reportedly, the military was edgy.

When a big black boot on a fatigue-covered leg landed heavily on our cockpit seat, I cringed. The boot was followed by a muscular Fijian soldier with close-cropped curly hair. He bent down to enter the cockpit. We were face-to-face when he broke into a most incredibly gentle and reassuring smile. The soldier, Emi, was unknown to me, but previously had spoken to John ashore. He had invited us to dinner and a kava welcoming ceremony at his house that evening. Emi was accompanied by Allen, a customs officer. The two men appeared impressed and curious about *Mahina Tiare*. They wanted to know how deep our depth sounder could go, and how our SatNav worked. And they asked about life in America.

Emi told us later that the customs officer had asked him to search our boat for guns, the standard procedure in Fiji since the coup. Emi had refused saying, "I have looked at these people's faces; they are not carrying guns." Emi explained that Fijians pride themselves on their ability to judge a person's character by his face. A few weeks later this same phenomenon manifested itself in a strange way. We were in a Suva movie theater watching *Twins*, a comedy starring Danny DeVito. Each time DeVito opened his mouth to say something, the Fijians in the audience roared with laughter, the rest of us sat stunned, unable to hear the punch line. The Fijians didn't have to hear the punch line; DeVito's facial expressions were enough.

Ashore, a peeling sign welcomed us to "Levuka, the Old Capitol," where an average building is more than one hundred years old. A strict rule disallows these buildings be altered or torn down. Many date from the time Levuka was the capitol of Fiji, before the move to Suva in 1881. Levuka began as a sleepy whaling settlement in 1830 and attracted cotton growers, traders and escaped convicts from Australia. Later it was said that you could find the pass into Levuka by following the empty liquor bottles floating out with the current.

Britain annexed Fiji in 1874 and things calmed down, but the beautiful slopes behind the village prevented Levuka'a expansion and the capitol moved. Today the town's economy is based on low-key budget tourism and a Japanese-owned tuna cannery.

The main street's wild west style false-front buildings follow the curve of beach across the street. The old post office has fans and bare light bulbs dangling from 20-foot ceilings. All public buildings have antique tables, armoires and faded photos of British royalty. The police station where we cleared immigration was built in 1874. Century-old sepia-toned police academy photos hang above an ancient filigreed safe.

The Ovalau Club across the street retains its British Colonial flavor. A sign on the door reads "PRIVATE MEMBERS ONLY," but the bartender was happy to sign us in and serve cold drinks. A snooker table and a 1917 letter from Count Felix von Luckner, captain of the German WWI raiding vessel *Seeadler*, are among the memorabilia on the painted tongue-and-groove walls. Like the town, the Club has a very civilized but slightly run-down atmosphere.

Emi met us at the base of a hillside to lead us up a long line of cement steps which followed the edge of a steep, boulder-strewn river valley. We lingered by a waterfall, watching a three-inch white-bellied spider swing in her web between power poles.

Emi's wife, Maria, welcomed us in very proper English. She was part Solomon Islander. Emi was reserved, but she was vibrant, her quick sense of humor and graciousness making us feel instantly at home. Fijians and Solomon islanders are Melanesian, generally shorter and darker with more negroid features than Polynesians.

Maria and Emi explained the traditional kava welcoming ceremony, something in which we would be expected to participate each time we visited a small village in Fiji. We should present the chief of the village with a quarter-kilo bundle of kava roots, dried roots of the pepper plant. A short speech stating the purpose of our visit should accompany the presentation. The chief would then formally accept the bundle, give a blessing and grant permission to walk the village, swim, fish or do whatever we proposed. The kava roots, meanwhile, would be cleaned, mashed and mixed with water in a big wooden bowl called a tanoa. The resulting brew would be mildly tranquilizing — numbing the tongue and lips. The chief and men of the village would share the kava with us and, as the tanoa emptied, a relaxed state would prevail

Mixing kava in the tanoa, an ancient tradition

and friendships would grow.

But kava is drunk on many occasions. It is a form of entertainment, or, as Emi said, a good excuse for friends to get together and talk for hours. Since Levuka was too big a town for visitors to be welcomed by a chief, Emi had appointed himself our welcomer and provided the kava instead of the other way around. But even if you just sit drinking kava with friends, Emi explained, there is a ritual.

Somehow the mixing of the muddy-looking kava by hand and the communal coconut husk cup put me off drinking more than one cup of the medicinal-tasting mixture. John was more adventurous, and as the tanoa slowly drained, we learned a bit about Fiji.

A poster of Rambo hung opposite a larger-than-life portrait of a Fijian man in a suit. "That is Ratu Sir Joseph, a Fijian chief who, along with a Fijian-born Indian, went to Oxford University together. The two returned to Fiji and served in the government together," Emi explained. "The Indian man told his people, 'Fiji is good to you. You have your business, your freedom to make lots of money; stay quiet and enjoy it. Never try to take over the government because at that point the Fijian people will stop you.'" The Indian statesman's prophesy had been recently fulfilled — during Fiji's coup.

The priorities of the Indians are at odds with the Fijian way which does not emphasize personal wealth or achievement. Yet the two divergent cultures coexisted peacefully until the Fijians feared that an Indian-dominated government would lift laws that restrict Indians from owning land, and the Fijians might lose their native property.

Previously we had met a young Indian woman, a shopkeeper at a store in Levuka (most shops in Fiji are run by Indians). She had told us, "The coup had to happen. We were moving too fast and leaving the Fijians behind." She was unbiased, even though most of her family had left Fiji. Some had been government ministers, harassed into leaving their posts. She would be leaving, too. "The education simply is not good enough for my children. They will not be able to get well-paying jobs if they stay in Fiji. We'll have no problem leaving. We are business people and we have enough money to be welcome in New Zealand, Australia, Canada or the United States."

I wondered, as I sat with Emi's family, which way was best? Emi's soldier's pay and Maria's salary as a full-time cannery worker added up to about $60 per week. Their four children will receive an education based on their ability to pay for it. Our friends on Niuatoputapu Island in Tonga were not as well educated, had little use for money, yet they seemed the happiest of all. But it was obvious that the cultures of all the countries we visited were undergoing rapid change as the people replaced the bartering system with cash.

Many children, curious about the world they have seen in videos, leave their small islands. But to partake of that different world they need a formal education. The Indians' industriousness had advanced Fiji far past her South Pacific neighbors. The recent mass exodus of the educated and professional class of Indian has hurt Fiji's education, health care, agricultural and business sectors.

Sept. 27: We joined a group from New Zealand, Australia and a Fijian Indian woman, Surita, for a bus trip around the island of Ovalau. We rode all day in an open-sided bus on bumpy dirt roads. Most bus trips are not worth the time; stumbling off the bus at the end of the day, nothing exciting, dangerous or exotic clings to the experience. Like watching TV, one never actually meets the people the bus whizzes past, rarely tastes the fruit growing on the trees or savors their scents. I would rather go a short distance, free to poke my nose into whatever seems interesting.

This bus tour had one saving grace: we stopped at the small village of Lovoni to swim in a deliciously cool river. As we walked along the river in humid afternoon air, I asked Surita, the Indian woman, if her sari felt hot or difficult to walk in. She replied, "Not at all. Come by my hotel room when we get back into town and I'll let you try one on." Surita was in her early twenties, friendly and open, but had led the sheltered life of a Hindu Indian in the predominantly Indian town of Lautoka, Fiji. She had never tasted meat, seen a live pig until today, or swum in a stream. She had been house-bound in her father's home, taking care of her sister's children. Her new freedom lightened her heart and her child-like exclamations over the world around her endeared Surita to everyone on the bus.

An Australian man, in his fifties with the creased and puffy look of someone who has spent much of his life in a smoky pub, was also on the tour. Surita said that he was her sister's husband and that her sister was due in that day. Oddly, she and the Aussie never exchanged a word or sat near each other.

Back at Surita's hotel, she wrapped eight meters of diaphanous peach-colored fabric around my waist and then fitted me with a midriff blouse. The sari was light, cool and comfortable, and was folded so that it kicked out in front as I walked. Madge, a Kiwi (New Zealander) tourist, snapped a photo of Surita and me together in our saris, then I took it off so Madge could try it on, too. But Surita said, "No, you must keep the sari you tried on."

It was too generous a gift, but she insisted. So I went back to the boat with a sari and the hope that I could remember the way she had wrapped me in it. Later Madge said that she, too, had received a sari. And that the Aussie bloke was actually Surita's husband, not her sister's. He had been bragging in the bar the night before that he had just married Surita, a pen pal for years but someone he had never met.

I figured Surita might enjoy a Moroccan-made dress, now that she was parting with her saris to start what I assumed was a new life in Australia. John dropped a dress of mine by her room. She was asleep but the Aussie accepted it for her. Since then I have received several letters from Surita, who is still living in Fiji. She never mentions the Aussie, nor being married.

The Indians of Fiji are often portrayed as grasping merchants or penny pinching tradespeople but Surita, the one close contact I've had with an Indian person, could not have been more generous.

Sept. 28, John: At 6:30 a.m. we departed Levuka to sail 65 miles to Suva. We left at first light to make sure we would enter Suva's pass in daylight. We entered the Suva pass wing-and-wing, with the genoa to starboard and the main to port, making 6 to 7 knots. Under a beautiful sky, we sailed through the break in the reef toward the lush, tropical hills.

Aware that in the week we had remaining in Fiji we couldn't see everything in Suva, we didn't try. We would use Suva as a place to get things crossed off our lists — provision for our trip to New Zealand, repair electronics, and get our life raft repacked. What we didn't anticipate was the fun we would have in this bustling multi-cultural town of 120,000 people.

Barbara: Fifty yachts surrounded us as we anchored off the Royal Suva Yacht Club. I had thought that the further west we travelled from

Surita and Barbara in their saris

North America, the fewer yachts. On the contrary, Fiji is the meeting place for yachts coming from several directions. The mix of nationalities we were used to in the Eastern Pacific, mostly American, Canadian and European, was suddenly changed by a whole raft of Kiwis and

Royal Suva Yacht Club, Fiji

Aussies. Nestled among the yachts in front of the RSYC was the familiar silhouette of *Tamure,* Scott and Kitty's Valiant 40. Looking from the water, it would be hard to imagine a more picturesque club than the Royal Suva Yacht Club. The dinghy dock is out front, next to a floating dock which can accommodate 20 or so yachts tied stern-to. The club's lawn borders the bay and is dotted with white picnic tables shaded by palms. Children, stir-crazy from too much time aboard, work out their energy on swings or chase each other around the lawn laughing in a universal language. Their parents watch from the cool of the club, sipping sodas or gin and tonic, enjoying this bit of civilization after the primitive, far-flung islands of the Pacific.

The club has a relaxed gentility. It was built in the '40s with multi-paned windows and board and batten construction. Hundreds of burgees hang above the U-shaped polished wood bar. Fijian bartenders wear white shirts and dark Sulus (wrap-around knee-length skirts). Courteous and helpful, they add to the friendly, clubby atmosphere. Guest membership at the club is a bargain. For about $15 U.S. a week, a yacht and its crew may use the facilities of the club. This includes mail delivery, cold showers or hot depending on the sun (the water is solar heated), and use of the dinghy dock. A fuel dock and clean drinking water are available.

Large cement wash basins for laundry are available, but timing is the key. It's difficult to dry laundry when it rains every day for a week — Suva is pelted with 120 inches of rain a year, — so most cruisers opt for the laundry service the club offers. It takes a day, but the clothes come back dry. We saw no coin-operated laundromats in Suva.

The cafe inside the yacht club serves snacks, breakfasts, great Chinese food and Indian curries for around $3.00 U.S. There were so many "bargains" in Fiji that it was easy to end up spending a month's budget in a few days. Many cruisers have duplicates made of their favorite clothes. Indian tailors are excellent and prices are reasonable. I had earrings made from pearls I had traded for on Penrhyn Island. Excellent wood carvings and woven handicrafts, rare and expensive in many Pacific Island countries, are a bargain here.

Sept. 29: We were up at sunrise to join Scott and a few other cruisers for a run on shore before the heat of the day sapped our energy, but by 7 a.m. on this overcast day the humidity was enervating. A platoon of Fijian army men, running in a sloppy formation, passed us with grim faces — a reminder of the prominent place the military has taken since Fiji's coup.

We ran past the Suva graveyard, a peaceful green expanse spread over several rolling hillsides. On these hills we saw a mixture of shiny granite stones, moss-covered monuments and the tapa cloth-covered mounds of recently buried Fijians. Prisoners from the nearby jail who tend the graveyard appeared from a distance as a cluster of gray dots against the green. I wondered what they were thinking as they buried one of their countrymen and watched a band of carefree cruisers jog by. Their jail, a crumbling colonial structure with high walls topped with coils of barbed wire, is opposite the yacht club.

After fixing our SatNav and getting our life raft repacked, 40 cents bought us a wild left-hand drive taxi ride from the yacht club to the public market. The market was a feast for the senses, a celebration of life. A tangle of ropes tied to trees held up colorful tarps, protection against brief but torrential rains. Beneath, Fiji's diverse peoples mingled among tables and stalls. The tables were piled with color — red, vine-ripened tomatoes, purple eggplants, day-glow orange carrots. Fruits and vegetables were sold in heaps for 50 cents or $1. Inside the market building little shops sell everything from twist tobacco by the inch off an amber colored roll, to kava, the national drink. Spices were set out in square wooden bins: curry, fiery red paprika, little stars of anise seed and dozens of other spices I did not recognize. The scents of spice mingled with the smell of diesel fumes from the bus and taxi station next door.

English, Fijian, Hindustani and Chinese-speaking people tried to talk above the roar of worn-out diesel engines. A little Chinese girl sat on the counter of her father's stall. She grabbed a pack of brightly-wrapped saimen noodles; her father put it back. She grabbed it again, crunching the noodles. Her father, serving an Indian woman dressed in a sari, appeared not to notice.

Sept. 30: The Fiji Museum, downtown Suva, displays artifacts and eating implements from Fiji's cannibalistic past and one can vicariously examine the details of that practice. Human shin bones were made into sailmaking needles; thigh bones laid in trees were eventually encapsulated. We saw the remnants of a food tray belonging to a chief who purportedly laid out a stone for every person he ate. One Rev. Lynch, a Methodist minister, counted 872 stones set out by the chief. This occurred in 1849, before the nation converted to Christianity.

Suva Market

Sorcerer's wands made of white cowrie shells and intricately carved wooden head-bashers, were displayed against burlap. The chiefs had their own traveling hair stylists. A mural depicts several outlandish hairdos. One chief grew his hair into an "Afro" five feet across.

Suva is a crossroads of the Pacific where Melanesian, Polynesian, Indian and European cultures are reflected in a helter-skelter blend of architectural styles. British influence, for example, at the elegant Edwardian-style Grand Pacific Hotel where the Queen of England gave speeches from the balcony. Crowded Cumming Street, an Indian neighborhood, is lined with small shops that sell everything from saris to curries. There is an Art Deco style movie theater and several two-story wooden buildings with restaurants that offer open air dining on porches built above the sidewalk. Duty free shops abound, but the only truly duty free items we saw were binoculars, cameras, outboard motors and charts.

Downtown Suva is intense — crowded, noisy and hot. Coming back to the yacht club for the Friday night BBQ was a good antidote to a day in town.

Oct. 8: A crowd of adults and children from the yachts *Chewink*, *Tamure*, *Wind Women* and *Mahina Tiare* piled into one of Fiji's colorful buses at the marketplace bound for Tholo-I-Suva Forest Park, a twenty minute ride on the Sawani bus. We followed the "Falls Trail" which winds down into a tropical stream bed, past waterfalls cascading over walls of stone. We walked in the stream as it flowed over smooth stones, then beside it as it splashed along mossy rocks and collected in pools. Vines with spiders hanging in intricate webs dropped in vertical lines from the grove of pandanus trees. We continued down the path to another waterfall and the mythical rope swing the children described. Attached to a sturdy branch, the rope trails to a rock with two platforms — one 30 feet above the pool, another 10 feet. The six children took turns splashing into the opaque water.

At John's urging I grabbed the rope at the higher platform. Swinging out into the airy void, I panicked. My mind said let go of the rope, but my fear caused me to hesitate. I let go as the rope swung back toward the rock. I seemed to drop through the air forever, but I hit the cold water, not the surrounding rocks. I climbed out of the pool, feeling exhilarated and ready to go again. But this time I took off from the lower platform.

For me the rope swing becomes an analogy for this sailing trip. Like letting go of the rope, my departure meant, more than anything else, letting go — of my business, my friends, my home and the safety and security of the familiar. I let go to throw myself into a temporary void, believing it would be worth the risk. I've never felt more alive than during this time of cruising. It is like the feeling of exhilaration on the rope swing, the rush when I dropped through the air and the feeling of being really alive when I hit the water. What I viewed as a void has been filled with unexpected pleasure, discovery and friendship.

Oct. 9, John: With the hurricane (and our work) season approaching, we turned our thoughts and our bow toward New Zealand. The hurricane season for Fiji, Tonga and Samoa is November through March, with up to five tropical storms annually.

We were among the first cruisers to leave for New Zealand, but I had made the same passage at this time of year, and had had excellent conditions. The passage to and from New Zealand is often very rough, and several yachts have been lost at sea attempting it. So, we planned to stop at Kadavu — a day's sail from Suva — to replace one of the control lines for the Monitor wind vane and go aloft to check the rigging. Stopping at Kadavu shortened our distance between landfalls, effectively cutting the non-stop portion of our passage by one day. The minus side was that it increased our total time en route and we were anxious to make it to New Zealand while the weather held stable.

Oct. 11, Barbara: The anxieties of preparing for a long passage come out in subtle ways, which don't seem related to the upcoming passage, but are. John and I had been getting on each other's nerves in port, but at sea we are at ease again. With all of the pressure of leaving, once we actually sail, the tensions seem to fade.

Oct. 12: It is squally, with variable winds from all directions. We had our drifter up, with the motor running to charge our batteries and help keep our speed up to 5 knots. As John came on watch, a snow-white tropical bird alighted on our deck, and rested its head on the cabin side above our chart table port. He seemed quite content and unintimidated as John worked on the deck taking down our drifter. It was pleasing to have this uninvited hitch-hiker.

Oct. 14, John: One of the high points of each day comes just after dark when I check in with John and Maureen Cullen at Kerikeri Radio. I give them our position and current weather conditions and they tell us what weather to expect for the next 24 to 36 hours. It helps us shorten the passage. I am excited about returning to New Zealand and introducing Barbara to my friends there.

Oct. 15: HALFWAY THERE! We had sailed 583 miles from Fiji and had only 579 to go to Auckland.

Oct. 17: We altered course when I spotted the light of a ship on the horizon last night. The yacht *Helena Christina* called on the VHF this morning — they were less than eight miles away, but not visible to us in the dawn light. We both altered course and, using our SatNavs for positioning, were able to meet mid-ocean and take pictures of each other under sail. We introduced ourselves over the radio. Art and Helena Twight and their daughters, Aknita, 11, and Alise, nine, were on their way around the world. They'd sail *Helena Christina* for several months, then fly home to Holland. Art was a relief skipper on ocean-going freighters. There was always work waiting when he returned home, and the family traveled with him. His daughters had grown up on the ocean, receiving their education from Helena as they traveled.

Oct. 19: I had just reefed the mainsail this morning when I looked aft over my shoulder at a very black cloud : "I don't like the look of that squall. Maybe I should take down the whisker pole," I told Barbara. Five minutes later it was too late to remember the rule: "The time to reduce sail is when it *first* occurs to you." The force of the wind in the jib made it too dangerous to remove the pole. Rounding up into the wind with the pole between the shrouds might dismast us. I turned and ran straight downwind to let the main blanket the jib. I took the tiller and unhooked the self-steering vane to better handle the gusts. Tremendous strain on the mast and rudder worried me. Steep breakers towered above our stern one minute, then submerged us so that our cockpit combing was the same height as the body of the wave. I shouted above the wind, "We're being buried."

"Whooa," Barbara yelled back from the companionway as we took a long slide down the front of a wave. *Mahina Tiare* broached drunkenly to port, then submerged again. I sensed that we had lost our buoyancy, a terrifying thought. The seas became angrier — gray waves mottled with froth, the wind whipped their tops off and drove horizontal spume through the air. I had no chance to put on foul weather gear. Soaked through and freezing cold, the adrenaline kept me going. *Mahina Tiare* charged along like a freight train, throwing a bow wake like a speedboat, pegging the knot meter at 10 knots.

The squall lasted a couple of hours. Art, on *Helena Christina*, later told us, "With that much spray in the air and the wave tops being blown off, there had to be 60 to 70 knots of wind." Sea conditions were about the same as during the hurricane, but today we were overpowered. During the hurricane the self-steering vane handled us under deeply reefed main and a minuscule spitfire storm jib.

Barbara: The passage nearly over, we turn to parallel New Zealand's North Island. The night is damp and dark. We sense the island by the difference in the swell patterns and the smell of earth. We wear turtlenecks and wool sweaters. The water from the tap is cold, but kerosene lamps keep the cabin toasty.

We pass close to Poor Knights Island, a high black and sinister shape to starboard with a single flashing white light on its north end. Our starboard bow light reflects off frothy, curling waves and approaching white birds, giving both a ghostly green glow.

Dawn light bathes the Hen and Chickens Islets and we clearly see their emerald cliffs. I am amazed that we have sailed here. Reflecting

Nesting gannet colony, Tasman Sea, New Zealand

back four years, before I knew John or anything about sailing, New Zealand seemed a place so far away, too remote to visit, let alone sail to. Yet, here we are, making landfall. I marvel at what unexpected joy and accomplishment life offers when we least expect it.

New Zealand is really two islands — the North Island and the more rugged South. There is a smallness about the North Island country reminiscent of England, as though, when the houses and roads were built, people stayed mindful that the horizons were not limitless and that one never gets further from the angry ocean than 90 miles.

Some say this smallness is part of the national psyche, that the whole country suffers from an inferiority complex. On the other hand, Kiwis display strong national pride and want to make sure visitors leave with a good impression of their country. Kiwi hospitality is legendary. So is their own love of travel.

There is a tameness and greenness about the acres of gently rolling hills of the North Island, which has earned New Zealand the title, "The Land of Milk and Honey." The only threatening animals on the island — all imported — are found in zoos. With the exception of bats, all the mammals — including the millions of sheep and cattle — are introduced species.

Auckland is a city of one million people, mostly neighborhoods strung together. Downtown has a few skyscrapers and an imposing cupola-topped Customs House, posh shops and fancy-dressed folks. The air here is clean and crisp, the surrounding hillsides very green. It is like sailing in a 'Southern Hemisphere Seattle,' except for the water. Auckland Harbor's water is a tropical aqua color but it is also opaque, as if mixed with millions of gallons of milk. Its vibrant color seemed out of place surrounding this rather staid city.

Clearing into Auckland involved tying up to some rough cement steps pretentiously called the Admiralty Steps. Here we were boarded by polite customs and agricultural officials in knee socks, shorts and shiny black shoes. Agriculture held out a huge brown paper bag to receive all of our fresh fruits, vegetables, canned meats, honey, popcorn and any seeds or nuts capable of growing if planted. New Zealand does not have many agricultural pests or livestock diseases and they want to keep it that way.

Cruisers with pets must keep them on board during their entire stay, and are required to always anchor out. They must also pay a $1,000 bond per animal. Should a foreign pet find its way ashore the animal faces certain death by incineration and its owner must forfeit the bond. Some cruisers with pets choose to skip New Zealand.

Although your animals are not allowed, Customs has a whole pack of black Labs to greet you. These are sniffer dogs, not pets. Anyone bringing drugs into the country runs the risk of being sniffed out and having their boat confiscated. New Zealand has practiced zero tolerance of drugs for years.

After clearing customs downtown, we motored two miles south to Westhaven Marina. Although there is a waiting list for permanent slips, the marina office manager always seems to find space for visiting foreign yachts.

John O'Leary, a jovial, rosy-cheeked friend of John's, picked us up for dinner. Brenda, John's wife, had a great meal waiting at their log home in the country. She had prepared a special treat for dessert, a New Zealand pavlova. Pavlova is a meringue shell topped with fresh whipped cream and sliced fresh fruit, perhaps the only truly New Zealand gustatory creation. New Zealanders are so intent on sharing this tidbit of kiwiness that we came to expect pavlova, even though the Kiwis didn't seem especially fond of the concoction. When it comes to New Zealand, we think of pavlova, not sheep.

Mother of three lively little boys, Brenda showed a wonderful sense of calmness. Like many younger New Zealanders, John and Brenda had traveled extensively and were big fans of the U.S.A.

Returning us to *Mahina Tiare* the next day, Brenda stopped at a few of the fruit and vegetable stands which line the roads west of Auckland. Free wine tasting is offered at a dozen small wineries also in the area. The wine and wineries vary from prize-winning Kumeu River Wine to Hugo's, a raucous Yugoslavian winery. What Hugo lacks in quality he makes up in quantity, encouraging wine tasters to continue tasting as long as they wish. Patrons have such a good time they forget the inferior quality and buy a few bottles to take home.

Oct. 21: Ivor Wilkens is a yachtie gone straight. We found him clean-shaven, in tweeds and hornrims at his desk as foreign editor of the *Auckland Star* newspaper. When we met them in Bora Bora a year ago, he and his wife Elspeth, South African expatriates, were tanned, carefree cruisers. Over an exquisite breaded lamb dinner in their Victorian home in the suburb of Ponsonby, we caught up on cruising stories — theirs, ours and mutual friends'.

Ivor related the most compelling tale which involved Tom and Nancy, cruisers we had met in Hawaii on a 47-foot Swan. Ivor said that these two had owned a smaller new boat several years ago. A flock of vultures had blackened the sky above their yacht on their maiden voyage to the Caribbean. The vultures, apparently exhausted, had landed en mass on their deck and nothing would chase them away. Tom, a truly gentle person, tried dousing them with water, uttering loud noises and even kicking. In desperation he started shooting and tossing them overboard. Nancy took pictures of this Alfred Hitchcock event, but when the pictures were developed — no vultures. On their return sail from the Caribbean, in the exact same spot where they'd been inundated by the vultures, their new boat sprang a leak. A passing ship answered their mayday, but the yacht sank soon after they were rescued. I couldn't help wondering whether the vultures really had existed or were a premonition about the sinking of their yacht. However, the manufacturer of the doomed yacht refunded their money, and they were not put off sailing.

Oct. 22: We heard a yell topsides. Mark and Bev Insley, on their Niagara 35, *Saturna*, were passing our slip and recognized *Mahina Tiare*. When we met them three years ago on our honeymoon cruising in Canada, they had had no plans for cruising the world. The idea had occurred to them in the interim, and their families had encouraged them by saying "Stop talking about it and GO. You are young and healthy; having children can wait." I wonder whether they realize how radical it is to have parents who actually encourage a cruise.

Now working in New Zealand they were taking advantage of a three-day weekend to go sailing; they tossed us their car keys. Like many of the other 150 or so other yachts spending the hurricane season in New Zealand, we had anticipated — indeed welcomed — the chance to explore on land, navigating with maps instead of charts and a gasoline engine instead of sails.

The main highway out of Auckland is two lanes each direction. Yes, they have traffic jams and rush hour traffic even though the population of the entire country is only three million. British-style roundabouts, left-hand drive, standard shift automobiles, confusing signs and very aggressive drivers make driving an emotional experience for those foreigners brave enough to take the wheel. We got lost continuously, although we'd had no problems navigating 18,000 sea miles to get here.

We traveled north in their old Ford station wagon, and visited Leon and Brendda Salt and their four children whom we had met on Pitcairn. Leon, who had taught school for three years in Pitcairn's one-room schoolhouse, was now a resident teacher at a three-room schoolhouse in the tiny farming community of Tomarata.

They had turned the school district house into a mini-farm where black and white Holstein calves fed on bottles of milk, lambs poked their noses through fences, and the lovely song of a Tui bird burst forth from a blossoming tree.

We shared the latest news from Pitcairn Island. England had sent an aluminum sail/motor launch to Pitcairn as a gift to commemorate the bicentennial of the Mutiny on the *Bounty* and the settlement of Pitcairn. In typical irreverent Pitcairn fashion, the islanders had named the boat *Tub*. Two hundred years ago England had hung the mutineers they captured; today Pitcairn is a tiny, but cherished, British colony. This must be one of the great role reversals in history.

Oct. 30: It was time for us to leave New Zealand for our winter work season. We left *Mahina Tiare* tied to a mooring buoy in the Waitemata River, west of Auckland. Several friends on cruising boats anchored nearby and a family ashore were watching out for her. We would have preferred to leave her "on the hard" where the hull could dry out and there was less chance of damage. But yard space was unavailable or very "dear," as they say in New Zealand. We had the mooring lifted and checked for chafe, left a small Arco Genesis solar panel charging the batteries, flushed the engine with fresh water, drained it, put two coats of varnish on and headed back to the States.

VOYAGE THREE

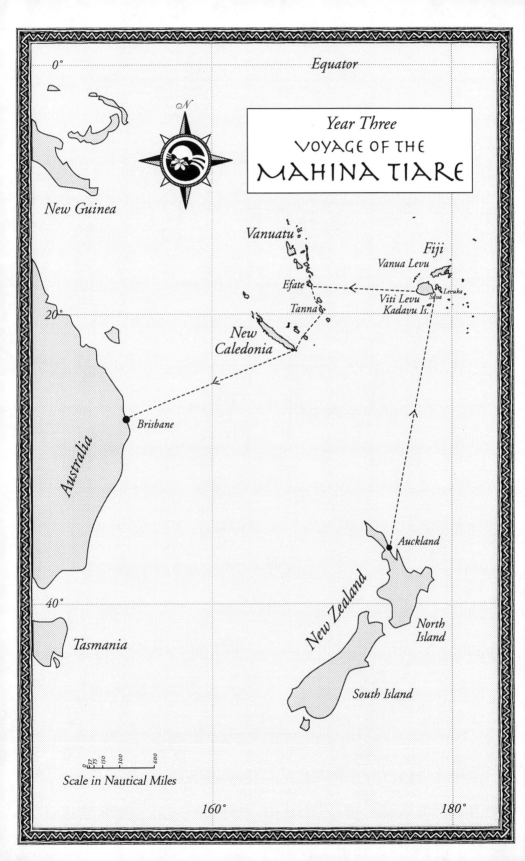

0°   Equator

N

Year Three
VOYAGE OF THE
MAHINA TIARE

New Guinea

Vanuatu

Fiji
Vanua Levu

Efate   *Viti Levu* *Levuka*
                           Suva
Tanna   *Kadavu Is.*

20°
                 *New
                 Caledonia*

Brisbane

Australia

Auckland

40°

Tasmania
                                    New Zealand

                                    *North
                                    Island*

                                    South Island

          0 37 150   300   600
          75
Scale in Nautical Miles

                    160°   180°

Chapter 15

LOW BRIDGE, TALL MAST

Five months later, Barbara: After living out of our van and friends' and families' houses for months while on the road lecturing and conducting offshore cruising seminars, it was a relief to be back aboard *Mahina Tiare*. She felt snug and homey. I felt relaxed, and what work I had to do could flow without tension.

April 21, 1989 : We were in a hurry to catch the high tide down the shallow Waitemata River to Westpark Marina, where we were scheduled to haul out in the morning. John plunged into the icy, murky river water, fighting a 2 knot current, to clear five and a half months of barnacles off the prop. Looking over the charts together, we decided to aim for a jetty where the water was deepest. That would be on the right side of the river just past the Greenhithe Bridge.

As John dried off below, I piloted us down the river. Concentrating on the jetty, I stayed to the right as we headed under the solid cement bridge which sloped— getting closer to the water on the right side. We were clipping along, motoring at 6 knots and picking up 2 knots of ebbing current.

Suddenly, I heard a crash, followed by a metallic, scraping sound. *Mahina Tiare* slowed down to 1 knot (even though the engine was charging away), and heeled drunkenly to starboard. Had I hit a metal buoy? Gone aground? Ahead, I could see nothing in the water. Still there was that horrible noise as we inched forward tipped at a crazy angle. Finally I looked UP! The mast was scraping across the bridge like fingernails across a chalk board. *Mahina Tiare* seemed a toy with a bent tin mast and loose bailing wire rigging. Seconds earlier she was solid, now she was twisted and askew. The friction of the top of the mast on the underside of the bridge heeled the boat, reducing our vertical clearance sufficiently to slide under the bridge.

John surfaced from the cabin: "Put it in neutral."

I did, and suddenly we were clear of the bridge. Something — it looked like a tin can — plopped into the water out of the sky. John said, "That was our tri-color light from the top of the mast. Don't worry about it. Are you all right?"

Still panicked, I blurted out, "I'm sorry."

All John said as he walked forward, grasping our dangling forestay, was "It's really my fault." He pushed on the twisted bow pulpit and wobbled one of our starboard shrouds. I stole a furtive glance around the river to make sure no one had witnessed my folly. It had not occurred to me that we could hit the bridge — I hadn't even glanced up. Perhaps this sounds naive, but no one warned me that it is impossible to judge a bridge's height relative to one's mast. In our offshore seminars bridges were never even mentioned. The only other bridge *Mahina Tiare* and I had been under together was the Golden Gate.

John: I had assumed that Barbara would go under the bridge at the tallest part, then change course to head for the deeper water near the jetty. When we had come under the bridge five months earlier on our way up to the mooring, she had not been on deck.

Down below, cleaning the knotmeter paddle when we hit, I was thrown flat on my face from the sudden impact. I thought we'd run aground and instinctively lifted the floorboards to check for water in the bilge.

We motored to Westpark Marina Shipyard, owned by the Lidgard family, famous Kiwi racers, boat builders and sailmakers. Kevin Lidgard was running the Travelift, had the slings down and was ready to haul us out. An amused expression on his face, he said, "I see you have already removed the forestay for the Travelift."

"Well, the Greenhithe Bridge took care of that." I replied sheepishly. Kevin laughed, "You're not the only one... I've hit that same bridge."

As soon as *Mahina Tiare* was in the cradle, I called a mobile crane company. It took only a few minutes to lift the mast and set it down on sawhorses alongside the boat. The forestay was sheared a foot from the masthead, one cast aluminum spreader fitting was broken, the VHF antenna and wind indicator were gone. But aside from some abrasion on the masthead fitting, I saw no sign of damage to the mast. The spare rope halyard that had supported the mast after the forestay broke was nearly chafed through. We were lucky the mast stayed up.

Barbara: Being hauled out at Westpark was frustrating. Living ten feet above the ground meant going up or down a ladder to get on and off the boat. There were no showers, marine stores, laundromat, grocery store or post office within walking distance and no public transportation. Simple things took forever to accomplish. Besides, there were small irritations. John went to put on his shoes and the laces had rotted. I wanted to start painting but getting masking tape meant borrowing someone's car. I would walk to the only public phone within miles, but it would be out of order.

The first night back in the water after the hellish haulout, I watched storm clouds race across the full moon. It reminded me that one of the reasons we chose this lifestyle is to be thrilled by the elements. Preoccupied with projects while living on land, I wouldn't have noticed the night sky or felt remotely moved by it.

Scott and Kitty, on *Tamure,* were also at Westpark Marina. Together again, welcomed as if only a day had passed instead of six months, reinforced my feeling that *Mahina Tiare* was indeed our home, that we were part of the cruising community. The memories of our shared anchorages and adventures came rushing back, and I felt a twinge of sadness on realizing they would be heading west, and we heading east. We would be sailing toward Chile, away from the warmth and security of their friendship. For once I wanted to join the cruising pack. Leaving my land-based friends in the States this time had been particularly painful. Now the departure from cruising friends made me feel in limbo.

Tamure had spent the hurricane season tied up in Westpark Marina along with *Chewink* so that the children off the two boats could attend school. These kids, taught by their parents aboard for the last two years, loved going to a real school (except for 15-year-old Alex, embarrassed by a uniform of shorts and knee socks). Their parents were enjoying the break from teaching. The hurricane season over, *Chewink* was ready to sail west to complete their circumnavigation.

211

They had sold their VW van and needed it delivered to the new owners who lived near Wellington, on the southern tip of the North Island. The trip would be a great opportunity for us to see a bit of New Zealand's West Coast.

The towns we passed through seemed alike, most had elaborate war memorials for World War I and II casualties, also rose gardens, little walks through manicured parks, longer walks called bush walks, and scenic overlooks.

And then it happened — the quintessence of the New Zealand travel experience. We were stopped by a herd of sheep chased by dogs across a wooden bridge. They were slipping on the mud, tripping over one another. The road became a sea of moving cream-colored wool. Then a ruddy-cheeked farmer in shorts waved to us as he hopped on his little Honda ATV. Two dogs jumped up on the seat behind him. Off they went, following the herd into the next paddock.

New Zealand is also a country of trails — they call them "tracks"– which are longer and more rugged than a bush walk. We detoured from the main highway to the White Cliff track, one that begins near the town of Tongaporutu. Seven hours by car south of Auckland, this track is perched on the top of spectacular white bluffs overlooking the Tasman Sea, sheep and cattle fenced on either side.

At Porirua, a suburb north of Wellington, we stayed with Daphne and Ken Warren, both originally from Pitcairn Island. Ken resembled many of the men we had met on Pitcairn — medium stature, sturdy, dark hair. Daphne's powerful frame and olive skin reflected Pitcairn Polynesian ancestry. Her recent visit to Pitcairn had coincided with ours. They showed us faded photos from Pitcairn taken in the early '60s before motorized launches or the landing had been changed. Ken said he'd like to go back. Salt-of-the-earth types, they fed us rich Pitcairn-style food and took the day off to act as guides. Porirua, a working-class suburb, consists of Cook Islanders, Maoris, Samoans, Tongans. Many houses were government subsidized, and we saw an ethnic side of New Zealand visitors rarely see.

Daphne and her family drove us into Wellington, the capitol of New Zealand. A monument to Admiral Richard Byrd, the first man to fly over the South Pole, sits atop Victoria Hill and overlooks Wellington Harbor, a major shipping port. Byrd had stopped at

Pitcairn on his way to New Zealand and given Daphne, four years old at the time, a good luck charm: a solid gold ring.

We took the official tour of the New Zealand Parliament Building, called "Beehive" for its conical shape. Daphne, who works as a

John goes aloft before every passage to check the mast and rigging

213

custodian in the judges' chambers, filled us in with facts the tour guide failed to mention. "Listen here," she told us, "them Judges is just a bunch of dirty old men, 'working' overtime with them young secretaries so I can't get in to clean the offices at night. You should see the kinds of magazines they leave open right up on them benches, looking at magazines instead of listening in court... and the things I find in them dust bins..." Daphne and Ken put us on the ferry, handing us food and gifts while saying, "You're always welcome in our home."

The ferry from the North Island to the South Island across Cook Strait can be a rough three-hour ride. But our trip was calm, the mountains like pastel cardboard cut-outs, the sun setting behind and the sea, a rippled blue, encircling.

I was cranky on the ferry, faced again with all the decisions of traveling. Where should we go next? Where is the best place to stay? What's the most efficient transportation? Will we meet anyone interesting? Trying to sort out from guidebooks what is really worth seeing. Traveling often seems a selfish luxury. While people around us struggle with the necessities of day-to-day living, we decide what museum or garden to visit. Sometimes the miles and miles we cover seem pointless.

New Zealand Maori (Polynesian) house post carving

If we looked and enjoyed the small things — the petals of a flower, the fragrance of a meadow, the changing patterns of light and clouds in a patch of sky — we would be infinitely entertained and content to stay in one place. But we were in such a hurry to see everything that we were in danger of seeing nothing. It all blurred while we burned lots of gasoline. Yesterday's special moments were forgotten in today's frenzy.

The ferry to the South Island docked in Picton, a fishing and vacation spot. We walked to the Marineland Hotel, passing old British-style pubs with filigreed Victorian facades. Our room upstairs with its sloped ceiling, mauveish wallpaper and chenille bedspread, smelled like my grandmother's house. The shared bath was down the hall; our only heat, an electric blanket on our bed. The ubiquitous electric kettle, tea bags and little pitcher of milk stood nearby; all New Zealand hotels furnish these civilities.

May 11: Morning fog shrouded the mountains, then evaporated off the tops of the hills to float above the water, then retreat white into crevasses between green hills. At last the day sparkled clear. We hiked high up a ridge where we could watch the arriving ferry and appreciate the rugged beauty of the South Island.

The ferry disgorged passengers until the Picton bus depot was crowded and the bus to Nelson, our destination, was full. Rather than hassle with this public transportation bus, we rented a car and solicited passengers. In this manner we met Diana, a young Canadian woman who had been hired to teach nursing in Nelson. She rode with us in exchange for a contribution toward gas. Besides practicing traditional medicine, she also healed through "Therapeutic Touch," adjusting the body's energy flows. "I don't actually touch the person," she said, "but run my hands instead along the energy fields outside the body. This readjusts the flows where they are blocked, so the body can better heal itself. I am just a beginner, but I've been able to lessen pain for many people for whom nothing else has worked. When I was learning therapeutic touch at a workshop on Orcas Island (Washington State) deer, rabbits and eagles congregated around our outdoor workshop. To realign my own energy, I think of a waterfall, the water flowing through me."

That night in bed I visualized a waterfall and it worked, relaxing my sore back and giving me a wonderful surge of energy before falling asleep.

As we headed south, there were many options of places to stay — hostels, campgrounds with stark cabins or self-contained trailers, bed and breakfasts and hotels. We stayed at Pavlova House, a hostel in Nelson recommended by Diana. Most of the people staying at the hostel were on their way to hike Abel Tasman Track, a trail along the beach of Tasman Bay and one of the easiest and most scenic tracks in New Zealand. The hostel, filled with foreigners of all ages, was presided over by Gudrun, an earthy German woman who alternated her work as a physical therapist for six months in Europe, with a year of traveling. She had just finished picking kiwi fruit for extra cash, and related how she had seen the United States by delivering a car from California to Florida.

There is a whole network of backpacking hostels in New Zealand and Australia which cater to a community of backpackers traveling around the world. It reminded me of the cruising community in that you trade information, then meet the same people as you follow the summer from country to country. The hostels charged about the same as a modest hotel but were much more spartan. The people staying at hostels didn't seem to be having much fun. Some talked as if the world owed them a free ride and resented the hostel's modest fee for renting camping gear. I am not partial to hostels. I would choose not to travel rather than have someone snoring in my face and coveting my food.

Why do people travel? For Bruce Chatwin, writer and wanderer, the nature of human restlessness was the question of questions, a major theme in his books. In *The Songlines*, he writes:

"Could it be, I wondered, that our need for distraction, our mania for the new, was, in essence, an instinctive migratory urge, akin to that of birds

in autumn?

"*All of the great teachers have preached that Man, originally, was a 'wanderer in the scorching and barren wilderness of this world,' ...and that to rediscover his humanity, he must slough off attachments and take to the road.*"

Chatwin goes on to say, based on his research in Africa on the origin of our species and his knowledge of Australian Aborigine walkabouts, "*... that Natural Selection has designed us — from the structure of our brain-cells to the structure of our big toe — for a career of seasonal journeys on foot through a blistering land of thorn-scrub or desert.*

"*If this were so; if the desert were 'home'; if our instincts were forged in the desert; to survive the rigors of the desert — then it is easier to understand why greener pastures pall on us; why possessions exhaust us, and why Pascal's imaginary man found his comfortable lodgings a prison.*"

His writing made sense to me. The ocean is like the desert, and to cruise it requires sloughing attachments, exposing oneself to the elements, and being open to them. I feel restless on land unless there is a vast expanse of water or desert in view to carry my mind and spirit away from the confinement of my surroundings and the burden of possessions.

16 May: We flew back from the South Island to *Mahina Tiare*, eager to see a bit of the country under sail before leaving for Chile.

25 May: On leaving Auckland, we noted a dark gray cloud mass gathered to the south but the rising sun lit up the Harbor Bridge and like a forest of limbless white trees, reflected off the thousands of masts in the marina. Five hours later we were anchored in Bon Accord Harbor at Kawau Island.

John: In the early days, manganese and copper were mined, smelted and loaded onto sailing ships here. Later, in 1862, Kawau became the home of Sir George Grey while he was governor and then premier of the Colony of New Zealand. He willed his extensive estate to New Zealand, and his former lands on Kawau are now part of the Hauraki Gulf Maritime Park. Today, the rest of the island is sprinkled with summer cottages and the homes of a few permanent residents. There is one small store, open in summertime, and a schoolhouse. Bon Accord Harbor, on the west side of Kawau, offers good protection and holding (except in west and northwest winds) in a number of small bays and coves. The most famous of these is the Mansion House Cove on the south side of the bay near the entrance. Mansion House, former residence of the Governor, is now immaculately maintained as part of the park.

The governor liked exotic plants, birds and animals and at dusk and dawn their descendants are seen flying and bouncing around. You can also see small blue penguins, albatross, giant petrels, shearwaters, gannets, shags, and the occasional skua.

Barbara: It poured as we toured the grounds of Mansion House. Out of the corner of my eye I would see things moving in the bush — but when I looked, they were gone. Finally I saw a wallaby, frozen in its tracks and blending perfectly with the underbrush. It bounded silently away, its tiny limp-wristed paws primly in front while its powerful back legs lifted it high in the air until all I saw was a long, fat, rat-like tail in retreat.

Wallabies are marsupials, pouched creatures from Australia but they look like small rodents grown way out of proportion. They made me feel like Alice in Wonderland when she has shrunken and everything else has grown very large.

Wintertime was coming to the Southern Ocean. Every few days another storm accompanied by lots of wind and rain would sweep through. If we didn't leave New Zealand soon, we'd have to spend the winter. We decided to sail back down to Auckland and start provisioning for the passage to Chile, Patagonia, Cape Horn and Antarctica.

Luckily, before we did major provisioning, we met with Bob and Beth Lux on *Rhodera.* They had recently rounded Cape Horn on their Hinkley Bermuda 40 and had spent several months cruising the 2,200-mile length of Chile. While John and Bob went over charts in the drizzly cockpit, Beth and I talked below about amoebas, parasites, water quality and food availability in Chile. She described living aboard in the cold, damp channels which crisscross southern Chile, the stark primeval beauty of the landscape, the shades of crystal blue glaciers, waters teeming with fish, seabirds, seals and penguins.

Listening closely, I was thinking no warm water to swim in, few people ashore, and almost no other people on cruising boats to befriend. Chile sounded lonely and difficult to reach, 5,000 miles across the stormy southern Pacific from New Zealand. Fiji, however, was just over 1,000 miles away and we had only spent a few weeks there last season. It wasn't too difficult to convince John to postpone his dream of Chile and Cape Horn in favor of taking a closer look at Fiji.

June 4: As we sailed away from New Zealand, "the land of the long white cloud," for the bright sun of Fiji, the clouds skirting the eastern horizon looked like tropical isles silhouetted in the glow of the rising sun. To the north and west all was gray and still.

June 12: The passage to and from New Zealand is a treacherous one because of the frequency and intensity of the lows that tear across the Tasman Sea. Although we escaped Neptune's wrath this trip, we had listened on the SSB radio to the plight of a trimaran which had capsized on this same passage. Missing for 90 days, it was washed ashore upside down on one of New Zealand's offshore islands. The three people aboard survived nicely. They'd been able to catch water in their upside-down state and hadn't run out of food. *Fantasy*, a Valiant 40 with an American family aboard, had also had a rough go of it. They decided to abandon their battered yacht after it had rolled, damaging the mast and causing the batteries to break loose and leak acid. They were picked up two days after the rollover by a passing freighter and brought to New Caledonia. The French Navy had retrieved the yacht and towed it into New Caledonia where the owners sold it.

We are just a day and a half from anchoring peacefully in Suva Harbor. I haven't written anything about this passage. It was uncomfortable — what passage isn't? But, I'd been like a spoiled child, not wanting to participate in this passage at all. We'd had our canvas doors zipped into the back of the dodger; the Monitor wind vane steered the whole time; *Mahina Tiare* sailed herself. We'd pop our heads out every ten minutes to check for ships or squalls. I rarely ventured into the fresh air; instead I divorced myself from the elements, even sunrises and sunsets, color of water, clouds, moon. I was totally absorbed in books with desert settings. My reading world became filled with cactus, snakes and storms over vast expanses of sand. Outside I was being transported through a watery desert. I had to be careful not to get so absorbed in the tales of others' journeys that I forgot my own.

Reading from the book *Tracks*, by Robyn Davidson, a 27-year-old Australian woman who, alone, decided to take four camels across

Australia's desert outback, I came across this quote: *"I had also been vaguely bored with my life and its repetitions — the half-finished, half-hearted attempts at different jobs and various studies; had been sick of carrying around the self-indulgent negativity which was so much the malaise of my generation, my sex, and my class.*

"So I had made a decision (to ride the camels) which carried with it things that I could not articulate at the time. I had made the choice instinctively, and only later had given it meaning. The trip had never been billed in my mind as an adventure in the sense of something to be proved. And it struck me then that the most difficult thing had been the decision to act, the rest had been merely tenacity — and the fears were paper tigers. One really could do anything one had decided to do whether it were changing a job, moving to a new place, divorcing a husband or whatever, one really could act to change and control one's life and the procedure, the process, was its own reward."

I found wisdom in her words which echoed some of the reasons I had chosen to go cruising. I'd had a feeling that if I wasn't careful I would fritter my life away attending to the myriad details of creating a successful business and a life in our society's terms, doing the same thing over and over until it seemed pointless. The hardest part had been the decision to act, to make the change — something I may not have had the courage to do without John's support. Like her camel journey, sailing has been frightening at times, challenging both physically and emotionally, full of surprises, and rewarding in the sense of feeling more in control of my life, able to shape it in a positive way.

For most of my life I dreamed about exciting situations or occupations, but always believed that the fun was in the pretending. If I actually did these things, they would become ordinary. Then it dawned on me that by changing my point of view I could make what I was doing special. Just because it was happening to me, it didn't have to be taken for granted.

Any moment can be savored — small things are large and large things often lose us. One's focus can only be in one place, the rest is extraneous. Look, smell, listen — the moment is all we have. We come into this world with nothing and leave with nothing. We owe it to ourselves to enjoy the journey, the small space between two unknowns. Getting to this viewpoint had required radically changing my lifestyle.

Chapter 16

FIJI:

SORCERERS AND CHIEFS

June 13, John: A call came on the VHF out of nowhere. A Royal New Zealand Air Force C-130 plane on its way to Fiji said they were 24,000 feet above and had seen *Mahina Tiare* on their radar.

This morning we talked with friends Sid and Stephanie Morrel on *Rainshadow*, anchored on the windward side of Kadavu Island. They urged that we get away from Suva as quickly as possible and join them in exploring Kadavu.

June 15, Barbara: After our arrival in Suva, health inspectors came on board. They inspected our passports and clearance papers from New Zealand before issuing us a Certificate of Pratique (Health Clearance). The fun part of the ancient form we had to fill out was the question: Do you have any *sick* rats aboard?

At King's Wharf in downtown Suva we were boarded by Port Security for a routine clearance check. Sigtoka, the tall Fijian soldier in camouflaged fatigues, filled out a few forms but did not bother searching for guns. In no hurry, he was honored to relate his family history on request.

"My great, great grandmother was Tongan," he said. "She came to the Lau group which is in the eastern part of Fiji between here and Tonga. She came with missionaries who converted the people to Christianity, and from there Christianity spread to all of Fiji. But even before the missionaries came, the sorcerers to the island's chiefs said, 'a very powerful God, more powerful than our gods, will be coming.' When the missionaries came, the chiefs as well as the sorcerers were ready to adopt the new God."

John: "There are still hereditary chiefs in Fiji, so are there also sorcerers?"

Sigtoka: "Yes, it is passed down in a line so the old ones visit their relatives today."

John: "You mean the spirits of the sorcerers who have died visit their relatives?"

Sigtoka: "Yes, each family gets visited by their relatives. My family are warriors, I am a personal warrior or guardian to the Prime Minister. My family has a big hairy bull dog, the size of a small calf. He comes to tell us things. He sometimes comes in dreams... if I dream he has bitten me, someone in my family will die. Sometimes if I'm day dreaming I will see him or if we are sitting around drinking kava he comes. He will tell us about relatives who are away. He'll say, 'I'm going to get so-and-so who is in Australia and bring him back because he is a drunkard and is killing himself.' Then in a day or two this relative shows up driving a fancy rental car and we help him.

"Sometimes the dog will speak through someone else. A child will wake up and speak with a deep voice like an old man, then we know it is the dog."

John: "Does everyone in your family see the dog?"

Sigtoka: "Yes, he belongs to our family. My daughter who is nine got very upset when she saw a huge dog outside her window. I told her that it was OK, that it is our family dog.

"Many of the hereditary sorcerers became ministers or priests in the church when Christianity came, but there is a different kind of sorcerer, the ones who put evil on others."

John: "Voodoo?"

Sigtoka: "Yes, voodoo. When this happens our family dog will tell who is doing this and will protect us."

John: "Many native groups have family spirits who appear as animals or totems, American Indians for example..."

Sigtoka: "Yes, all native people do. There are sorcerers on some of the yachts too. The villagers can point to those yachts as they come into the pass. Those yachts will end up on the reefs in Fiji."

Sigtoka had whetted our curiosity toward a side of Fijian culture we had no idea existed. We were anxious to leave Suva for the rural island of Kadavu where people lived a more traditional life, without electricity or running water. Here we would find how much the older beliefs merge into a strong Christian faith and how the tribal system is very much intact.

John: The morning we left Suva for Kadavu we had the sailing conditions *Mahina Tiare* loves: 20 to 25 knots of wind just forward of the beam. For hours the knotmeter never dropped below 7 knots, occasionally hitting 8 1/2. It was exhilarating sailing. Admittedly, we were a bit over-canvassed but, since we knew we'd soon be in the lee of the Astrolabe Reef, we decided not to reduce sail.

The Astrolabe Reef north of Kadavu is one of the most colorful barrier reefs in the world and since it is so far from shore, is relatively untouched by man. The reef surrounds ten islands and several yachts were anchored at Ono Island, the largest.

We had the latest chart of the area, but found that large patches of coral would just pop up without warning. It was really exciting to jibe at 7 1/2 knots with coral heads dead ahead, but we managed to miss the scattered patches. We didn't have a destination and just wanted to see how far the great sailing wind and daylight would allow us to go. We saw a small unnamed bay on the south side of the island on the chart that looked like a possible anchorage, marked only with a five fathom number.

Surprise! Our friends Mark and Bev's Niagra 35, *Saturna*, as well as *Vivant*, a Cal 34 from Hawaii with Dave and Mary aboard, and our dream boat, a Hallberg Rassy 38 from Germany named *Sandra II*, belonging to Harry and Denise, were all tucked into the bay.

The night was beautiful. After dinner we sat in the cockpit on *Saturna* looking at the stars and the outline of the island while Mark played his guitar and sang. I felt transported to another time and place, I'm not sure when or where; but the moment was powerful.

The next day we all went diving together, Mark, Dave and Harry to spear fish and Bev, Barbara and I to photograph men and fish. That night we had a barbecue on the beach I'll never forget: a bonfire of coconut husks and branches, coral trout grilled over the coals, lobster, cassava and yams wrapped in foil and baked over the hot rocks. Then sunset, going down behind Kadavu's rugged hills. Mark on guitar and Mary with her flute played jazz and folk tunes for hours. The theme of the evening was "cruising — the best of times and the worst of times, but certainly worth it!"

We allowed ourselves two months to circumnavigate Kadavu, Fiji's fourth largest island approximately 30 by eight miles. The island has little development — three small resorts catering to Australian divers and backpackers, and a grass airstrip with occasional flights from Suva and Nandi. In our two months we only explored part of the northern side. One reason for our slow progress was 'sevusevu,' the kava ceremony. In every bay we visited — indeed every village we walked through — we were expected to present a bundle of kava roots, the traditional gift one brings to ask permission and the blessing of a village to pass through or visit. Kava, once we grew accustomed to its slightly bitter taste, was a wonderful drink.

July 7, Barbara: The best places seem the hardest to get to. Our chart of Daku Bay, Kadavu Island, Fiji, showed many coral heads in the bay in front of the village. We had no information about the bay or the village, but decided to stop at Daku anyway. Threading our way through the coral maze, John slowed the engine to avoid a coral patch, but the tide and wind pushed us port-beam onto a coral head. By gunning the engine with the tiller hard to port we motored free, then dropped anchor in a small area of sand 20 feet below.

Ashore, we met Epironi Ravone, a Bill Cosby look-alike. Slim-hipped, athletic, Epi moved with catlike grace. Relaxed and at ease with himself, his laugh was infectious and his innate charisma drew the whole village to his house: the men for kava and teenagers for singing and Bible study. Even the village cats and dogs congregated at Epi's. His five-year-old twin daughters and three-year-old son obviously adored him and hung off him like extra limbs.

John and I were drawn to Epi and his wife, Kata. Kata was part Tongan, her features were smaller –more Polynesian than Melanesian. She had a strong, generous build and a straightforward manner. Both spoke English and were enthusiastic teachers of the Fijian way. The villagers, once they knew of our interest in their customs, would invite us to watch the making of tapa and weaving of mats. One day they dressed me in traditional tapa cloth wedding attire. Flattered by our constant picture-taking they said, "Thank you," every time the camera's shutter clicked.

Originally we were planning to stop in Daku only for a night or two, but Epi had other plans for us. "You must stay at least two weeks to get to know our village," he said. It seemed a long time to spend in a village of 100 people, but Epi wanted us to join him for a day on his plantation on the mountain above the village so we could see how Fijian crops are grown. And we must stay until Sunday, go to church together and watch them prepare the lovo, an earthen oven. We swung at anchor off of Daku for a month.

July 9: A woman, dressed in white, beat a hollow rhythm on ancient wooden slit drums, calling Daku's Methodist congregation to church. These same drums signaled war before Christianity came to Fiji, a time when the villagers still practiced cannibalism.

The church was new, built by the village men from mortar and local stones. I sat with the women on mats in the center of the floor. The kids in front of me threw spit balls and poked each other while the men and women sang in angelic harmony. Epi, distinguished-looking in dress shirt and sulu, walked to the front of the church. He gave a speech first in Fijian, then translated into English. He choked up, then began again, addressing John and me. "On behalf of the village and this congregation we welcome you to our village and to our spiritual community." Fighting tears, he continued now to the congregation, "We owe a lot to the United States which is like a fatherland to us... to Australia and New Zealand... to people who have given so much aid and increased our standard of living. We thank these American people because their country has been so good to ours. In 1979, when Hurricane Mele took our houses, the Americans sent big tents — like little houses — to live in. While we lived in the tents, the Americans sent us materials to build new houses. Our houses are strong now and will not blow away in the wind."

Epi continued his heartfelt welcome until I, too, had to fight back tears. John was expected to give a speech so he stood up, like a kid pushed out on stage. He looked pale and out of place in that sea of brown faces, but his simple reply satisfied the congregation.

Before dawn Kata and Epi had begun preparing food to be served after church. Epi had heated rocks, then dug a lovo (earth oven). He had buried taro root and yams, then placed the white hot rocks over all. The food would bake slowly while we attended church. Kata sweated over a wood fire in her thatched cookhouse, frying tuna wrapped in taro leaves.

Epi later made lolo (coconut cream sauce), grating the white meat of the coconut, then squeezing and pressing it through a plastic strainer. When he saw that I was filming his work, he put down the plastic strainer. He used coconut husks instead, "This is the old way," he said. "Your people back home would rather see this done the way of my ancestors."

On a tablecloth spread on the floor they laid out pork from a wild boar Epi and his dog had hunted. Smoked travallie fish, limes, Chinese cabbage, bananas and papaya in lolo, along with the taro root and yams completed the feast. Epi picked up one of the limes: "We talk to the trees. There's this lime tree in the back of our house. It would produce only a few limes certain times of the year so I told it 'you better start producing or I'll chop you down.' The tree now has plenty of limes all year. We do that — talk to the trees — that's our way."

July 10: The evening village had a summer camp atmosphere and the smell of wood smoke mingled with frying fish. We ate with Kata and Epi in their cooking shed. Epi talked: "We live happily without much money here. Our clothes are sometimes old, but we grow our own food, laugh and have a lot of fun. I was educated in Suva and had a good job at a lumber company, but I wasn't suited to that fast lifestyle. I left one day without even collecting my paycheck, and came back to my village. It's good that even with a little education I can help my village."

Epi was up on current events and could talk about a variety of esoteric subjects, from drug smuggling to coelacanths. A former village Peace Corps volunteer had sent him a year's subscription to *National Geographic* magazine. He knew all the articles by heart. Later we saw the magazines when both children and adults came to Epi's house to look at them. They were a village treasure, worn and tattered after a year but confirming the hours of pleasure they had provided the entire village.

Just south of our anchorage, a shallow river led through mangroves to the small village of Vunisea where the district elementary school was situated. The head master had asked that we come and give a talk to the children about America. The children, dressed in uniforms, sat on the floor of the classroom. When we walked in, they stood at attention.

I was not prepared for this kind of regimentation and was thrust back in time to my Catholic elementary school. We had been forced to stand at attention and shout like robots, "Good Mor-ning Sis-ter Ther-e-sa Car-mel" every time the principal would enter the class-

Epi and little Epi Daku, Fiji

room. Secretly, I was terrified of this woman who wielded so much power.

We showed the children pictures of volcanoes, snow, and skyscrapers and told them that America was not just one big city, that America had small towns and islands like theirs. The boys answered some of our questions with "Yes, madam" and "No, sir." They are taught in English and understand it, but are shy about speaking it. The eyes of the school children were bright, but I focused on their mouths, huge and filled with beautiful, white, even teeth. When they smiled, which was often, it seemed most of their face was mouth, all other features secondary.

After the assembly, the principal arranged a meke, singing and dancing by all the children. We were charmed by the children's sense of rhythm and grace, and honored by the effort the school had exerted. Elijah Stoltz, the principal, was a small, fine featured man whose excellent command of English provided fascinating insights into Fiji's culture. I asked him about ancestral spirits.

"Yes," he said and shifted his weight. "Some families still believe in family spirits. Our county's president's family totem is the shark. When he travels to his hereditary district of islands, huge sharks swim alongside his boat. The prime minister is a descendant of powerful chiefs. His district is the Lau group of islands."

The longer we stayed in Fiji the more we realized that, although Fiji considers itself a democracy, much of its politics are based on an ancient hereditary hierarchy.

We walked from Elijah's mountain top house down the steep trail through the village, crickets singing and laughter rising from groups of men who were drinking grog (kava). Kerosene lights cast a soft shine on dusky faces as women fed their children. Through half-open doors, we glimpsed colorful bits of fabric and woven mats. The life force was everywhere, chickens scratching, dogs wandering, flowers blooming, people moving. The village was open, not like neighborhoods in America where leash laws, high fences and locked doors are the order. A child waded out to retrieve our dinghy. Later, as we paddled down the river, a big bright moon jumped from behind a hill to cast John's shadow on the still water. I never tired of that anchorage at Daku. Changing hourly, the light played off surrounding hills, one moment emerald, the next chartreuse. The sky varied from purple to pink, then to blue or orange. Parrots squawked, owls hooted, fish jumped.

July 15: I sometimes find it hard to focus on one project. Part of each day is a boat project, part is writing articles, then swimming, cooking, cleaning, letter writing. Still, I have choices of what to do. The women ashore do not have my choices. They stay busy all day cooking, cleaning, mending, washing clothes by hand for large families, catching fish or doing handicrafts for extra money. They can't open cans for dinner or go to a restaurant. Kata said, "Always busy... I am a busy girl." I asked her if they ever swam. "Well, sometimes. But mostly we are too busy working, not like you people laying out on white sand beaches."

Kata was impressed when she visited *Mahina Tiare*. She understood that I didn't have to carry water into the galley or build a hot

wood fire to cook. Kata said, "I like the life you lead."

July 25: Epi met us at a bend in the dirt trail about a half-mile from his house. A headband of leaves wound around his forehead transformed him into a Bushman, a role in which he delighted. Barefoot, bush knife slung over his shoulder, he sauntered toward the rocky hillside he and his brother cultivated. Crossing a narrow strip of land, sunken swamp on either side, he stopped. "You see," he said, "where we are standing is the only easy way into the val-

Barbara, clad in a tapa (bark) cloth Fijian wedding dress, sits on wedding mats

ley, no crossing a river, no going through mud. When my ancestors lived here they always had guards in this spot, but they diverted a stream to make all this mud around us. The enemy warriors from the next village would get stuck here and the guards would club them down straight away - then maybe cook them in the lovo, ha, ha, ha."

We left the ancient stone foundations that surrounded us and crossed the river to where Epi's brother hacked away dense brush on the slope to plant taro, yams, and kava. It was back-breaking labor, slashing and burning the entire hillside, then clearing small pockets of ground by removing the rocks and individually planting the plants. This area was Epi's family's 'close' plantation, ten minutes from the village. He had another one a half hour away, still another several hours walking distance. He spent an average of five hours a day working in his gardens. On Sunday, he rested. I appreciated his gifts of food far more when I saw how difficult it was to cultivate the land with such primitive tools. Returning to Daku, Epi negotiated the rocky cliffs balancing a pole over one shoulder with a 50-pound basket of vegetables fastened to *each* end. Kata was weaving a communal mat with the women of the village when we approached, but left her friends to come home and show me how to paint masai (tapa or bark cloth). Using stencils cut from x-ray film, we dabbed black paint (made from soot) and red paint (made from clay) onto the soft white bark cloth. Kata was quick and expert, producing three neatly painted pieces in an hour. Sitting on the cool floor, talking and working with Kata, I wished I might live in the village another month just making masai, weaving mats and listening to ghost stories.

The last meal together was a joint effort, the meal followed by stories of Fiji customs. I asked Epi, "What is your family's traditional role in the village?"

"My grandfather was a priest," he said, "but those kinds of priests don't practice anymore. During a conflict, my grandfather would sit in a little bure where my house is now and drink a lot of grog (kava). He could tell what was going on in the battle without ever being there. It sounds crazy, but grog is powerful stuff."

When I asked him if he received power from drinking grog, he said "No, it takes a lot of grog-drinking." Pointing to the sky, he continued, "I am a Christian and He takes good care of me. Pretty much all I ask for, you know, is up there in one, Satan and all." Epi and his brother, descendants of 'priests', were lay ministers with the Methodist church, so again we saw Fijian's roles linked to the past.

Explaining another custom, Epi handed me two yellowed sperm whale's teeth. "These are tambua and are very old... from the time of whaling ships. When someone from our village wants to marry a woman from another village, we will give her family these tambua." Prized cultural property, the tambuas are becoming scarce in the rural villages. Epi explained that during funerals it is common practice to hold big feasts, killing many cows or pigs and giving away hundreds of cans of food as a sign of status. The feasts cost more than a family can afford, so often the whale's tooth tambuas are sold in Suva to finance an extravagant funeral.

"There are other kinds of tambua," Epi explained. "When relatives come to visit, they bring kerosene or a packet of clothing for the children. Or they bring foods like flour or rice. The relatives are fed while they stay; when they leave we give them food from our garden."

We presented the village a guest book to record the visits of relatives and the few yachts and divers who visited Daku. Gifts of fabric and clothing for Epi's family also seemed appropriate. More importantly, what we gave, I hope, was as much pleasure in our company as we had experienced in theirs and those fond memories of laughter and conversation by kerosene lamp light.

When we asked Epi, before departing Daku, to inscribe our guest book he drew: •A Bible • A kava plant. •A bundle of dalo tied to one end of a carrying stick, a basket of yams tied to the other. •A cane knife, file, and long garden spade. Underneath his drawings he wrote: "these are some of the most important materials of life that keep our family flourish(ing) with love."

July 31: Since arriving on Kadavu, Fiji's southernmost island, we have been on a quest to find and purchase a clay cooking pot like the ones in Suva's museum. A few inhabitants of a small village on the western tip of Kadavu still make the pots in the manner of their ancestors back thousands of years.

As we made our way west toward Yawe, the pottery district, fog and rain made our passage through the reefs on the north side of Kadavu treacherous. John took bearings constantly on the different peaks of

Kadavu, and we finally found safe anchorage at Vunisea, the narrowest part of the island and Kadavu's main town.

The sun broke through as we took the dinghy to shore. *Mahina Tiare* looked tiny and alone amidst the wide bay and tall mountains.

The Vunisea shops had little goods available, but the post office

Bread-making Vunisea, Kadavu, Fiji

was bustling and we had a big packet of mail waiting. Finding the town bakery was a high point. Dark, few windows and no paint on the iron walls or high ceilings, the bakery should have felt depressing inside. But four lively men kneaded, rolled, twisted and coaxed their 190 loaves of bread into pans with movements as precise as surgeons. The aroma of baking bread and the dry warmth of the wood-fired oven made the place inviting. And the freshly baked bread was only .52 cents a loaf.

The airport was the other beehive of activity. We watched as the Air Fiji flight from Suva descended. Chickens, which peck on the grass airstrip, ran for their lives as the big bird overflew the airstrip. The Air Fiji plane carries 16 passengers and the two flights a week are usually overbooked. Among the overflow crowd were six Australian surfers who had been waiting a week for a flight out.

Aug. 2: From Vunisea we sailed west to Bay Richmondi, an uncomfortable anchorage but the closest we could get to the pottery village. A boatload of men stopped by *Mahina Tiare* on their way to Nagalotu village. En route to a funeral, they were loaded down with baskets of yams and taro root. We followed them in our Avon over a reef at high tide for miles, then anchored among six wooden skiffs and waded ashore. More skiffs arrived and from one, two men waded ashore carrying a living bristly black-haired boar. The animal was tied upside down by its small feet to a stick and appeared in pain. Not sure if we were welcome, we hung back until someone encouraged us to come into the village. Here we met up with Kalepi, father of a friend we'd met in another village.

Kalepi led us past the fresh grave of the man whose funeral everyone was attending. The earth was mounded up and covered with tapa cloth, like a freshly made bed. Red bougainvillea flowers in the form of a cross rested on top. Nearby the women peeled root crops, placing them in steel cooking pots four feet in diameter. I saw enormous baskets filled with dozens of tins of canned corn beef. Whoever had died must have been important.

We had brought cameras (carried in canvas bags) and hoped for a glimpse of the feast or some insights into the funeral rituals of Fiji. Instead we were sequestered in Kalepi's house. He reminded us that we were not permitted to walk around the village until sevu-sevu (the kava ceremony) had been performed with the elders. Kalepi's wife and daughter served tea and lunch, then some young men who spoke English entertained us while Kalepi attended the funeral ritual. John asked these young men about local anchorages; he wanted to draw a chart of the area. He tapped his shirt pocket for a pen while they all checked their hair. No one had a pen. (Fijians have wonderful Afro-style hair which they use to hold pens, combs and other essentials.) Soon the young men excused themselves and we were left sitting on the floor with the women and children.

I wondered whether the women ever question their lives, the endless hand-washing of clothes, the cultivation and preparation of food over wood fires for many hungry mouths. Do they contemplate their looks in the cloudy mirrors which top their dressers, the only furniture most of them own? Do they try to stay attractive or just pile on the weight and shrug when they lose a front tooth? Do they have some additional hormones that make them want many babies? But why question these women who seem to have no choice?

The womens' complacency made me question my motivations and attempts to assign meaning to life. They seem content just to live day by day. Because I have not given birth to a child, I feel uninitiated. I feel that I am a curiosity to the mothers and grandmothers ashore. They are busy taking care of their families; their success as women hinges on the ability to bear children. I often spend time ashore with young women who do not yet have children, who lead a freer life, or with John and the men of the village. The men make an exception for me, they understand that there is less separation between the sexes in America and that John and I have a strong bond. I am allowed to go into mens' places where their women are not permitted.

In some ways I envy the women in their clear roles, their strong attachment to family, their living in the present. I am often tortured by too many choices. But I know that many of the women, like Kata, envy my freedom, my ability to chose to participate in men's or women's activities.

We finally did perform sevu-sevu after waiting five hours at Kalepi's house. Picture-taking or asking questions about the funeral would have been inappropriate.

Mahina Tiare was rolling at her anchor when we returned. I was preoccupied with thoughts about going home for a family reunion, yet wanted to live in the moment here. Suddenly I began thinking about fashion, my figure — things I hadn't concerned myself with in all the months we'd been anchored in Fijian waters. I felt as if I was caught between two cultures, neither one appropriate for me.

Aug. 3: Kalepi began to entertain us with stories of his youth. He looked about 50, but judging by his colorful past was probably closer to 70. As a child he'd been taken by his Fijian Methodist missionary parents to the Australian outback. Growing up with the aborigines, he spoke their language and adopted their customs. He still relishes the taste of iguanas, snakes and witchity grubs roasted over a wood fire. During World War II he worked for the New Zealand Air Force as a seaplane mechanic, then skippered a Fijian tourist launch for many years. Eventually he retired back to his parents' village. We explained our quest for a clay cooking pot, and he agreed to take us to the proper village to see what could be arranged.

We met Kalepi on the narrow, root-covered path which led from our anchorage to Nalotu village. After months we were finally on our way to see the pottery being made. After the obligatory kava ceremony at Nalotu, we asked permission of the elders to take pictures of their pots and possibly purchase one.

"What size?" they asked us.

"A small one."

"There are no small pots. It takes months to make a pot. No one makes pots any more. We have clay but the sand must come from the next village."

"Why don't you make them any more?"

"The chiefs of the district wanted us to pay for every pot we made for sale in Suva. It is too much work to make them for so little money."

We had asked at eight different villages on Kadavu about the pots and were disappointed when we couldn't buy a pot or see one fashioned from island clay. But word of our quest quickly spread through the village. Outside the chief's house a big oval pot was dragged from a cooking shed, heavy and blackened from use. The frail 75-year-old woman who had made it was asked to pose alongside.

A link to the past, she had revived the art of pot-making on Kadavu. She taught the art to the younger women. These pots are in and of their tradition; similar pots have been used to steam root crops for thousands of years. And although the villagers insisted it was the best way to cook, they themselves used metal pots and pans. The new clay pots were for sale to tourists.

We photographed the old woman and her mammoth pot, and then another pot appeared, smaller and newer. One of the young women asked if we would like to buy it for $20. Once in our hands, we realized the value of the pot was not in the object itself. It weighed 20 pounds and was fragile. Where could we store it safely on the boat? Owning the pot became a burden. Finding it had been the joy. Like many quests, it is the journey to the goal that is rewarding. Our journey to the pot involved us in conversations with many colorful characters on Kadavu. When the pot was shattered during shipment back to the States, we were not surprised or even saddened. Similar to other objects we have bought during our travels, it lost meaning once taken out of the context in which it belonged. Our journey through Kadavu will stay alive in head and heart while the pieces of clay pot are back in the earth.

Aug. 4: We moved east to Tavuki Bay which offered more protection in the ocean swells. Ashore, we brought our ceremonial bundle of kava to the Tui Tavuki, the king and paramount chief of all Kadavu. The king, Ratu Peceli V Nanovo, and his wife were humble and friendly. On the wall of their one-room home was a picture of the

235

Ratu Paceli V Nanovo, King of Kadava

king's grandfather one of the 12 great chiefs of Fiji who had ceded the country to Great Britain in 1874. Tall and thin, probably in his early seventies, the king was spry enough to use the windvane when he climbed aboard *Mahina Tiare* from the dinghy. His wife, Ateca, was a retired school teacher. Ratu Peceli instructed John on how to fish from the boat while Ateca spoke with me. They asked that we let them know ahead of time before we visited their village again so that they could prepare a welcoming feast. When we left Tavuki Bay and Kadavu, Ateca kissed me, asked that I write her, then presented us with a six-foot length of beautifully painted tapa cloth as a going away present. Ratu Peceli took John aside and asked him to bring a bottle of whiskey when we came back.

Aug. 24: Even cruisers need a vacation. Taking a two-week break to fly to San Diego for time with my family was a perfect escape. On land again and around familiar people restored the sense of rootedness and belonging that can get lost while cruising.

For the first time in ten years my sister, both brothers and I were together at the same time. Popping our heads up after diving through a wave surrounded by foam and hissing, and smelling the salt air, brought back memories of playing together in the surf on dozens of different beaches. Riding waves, laughing side by side, the joy of youth came flooding back. No longer were we grown-ups separated by continents and contrasting lives.

I crave the excitement of the big waves, hoping for an easy ride but knowing that I may get tumbled. Like cruising, sometimes the ocean catches you off guard and scares you. Other times it is easy, a high like flying. With a wave, the distance is short. Cruising requires a longer commitment but much the same kind: a willingness to take chances, a knowledge and respect for the ocean and a trust that it will carry you safely where you need to go.

Aug. 30: After a respite from the tropics, Fiji looked all the more beautiful. On the day I returned, Suva was sunny, dozens of yachts at anchor against a backdrop of rugged mountains — misty in graded shades of gray. The water sparkled next to the manicured green lawn of the Royal Suva Yacht Club and friends were anchored nearby.

Sept. 1: Today I splurged and bought a locally-made silk-screened dress. Its purchase set off my inner voice: "Have you learned nothing from cruising? You don't need a new dress. You're like Leona Helmsley. What lengths will you go to feed your ego when you could be feeding the hungry? Always the dilemma of travel, the inner voice is constantly comparing, shaming, tugging like a beggar at the curtains of my mind. In an attempt to assuage my guilty conscience, I went to give some money to a legless Indian beggar who usually waits on a sheet outside the market. He wasn't there.

To balance this dilemma we try, like many cruisers, to use the skills we have to help the local people by fixing boats or engines, doing construction, donating medical supplies or medical skills to the local clinics.

Sept. 4: Before we left Suva we went for a last visit aboard *Sandra II*, a Hallberg Rassy 38 built in Sweden by the same yard that built *Mahina Tiare*. Three years ago when we started this Pacific journey I wasn't at all interested in boats. They all looked the same. Some were bigger than others but I wouldn't have noticed the difference between a cutter or a sloop or a ketch, let alone a yawl. I still have trouble with that one.

Slowly, subtly, I find myself dreaming of a larger boat, not just any boat, but this Hallberg Rassy. I appreciate its fine joinery, and Swedish simplicity of design. The thought of living in a house now seems rooted, boring. Yet before we took off I hated the whole idea of living on a boat. I equated it with living in a small, moldy, fiberglass hole which constantly moved and where chores like cooking, laundry, or fetching water took forever. Living in a house was normal. Coming over to John's point of view makes me feel that I've lost my autonomy, am too easily influenced.

Sept. 5: We passed Viti Levu's long dry coral coast and anchored off the swank Fijian Hotel. The tourists appeared restless. Everything done for them, they were not actively responsible for their vacations; they seemed to wander around in a sunburned daze. Isolated from the reality of Fiji's diverse cultures — the pungent aromas of her markets, the bitter taste of kava, the sounds of tapa being beaten out in the rural villages — these tourists were missing the heartbeat of rural life.

Sept. 11: A four-hour downwind sail north brought us to Lautoka, Fiji, where we cleared customs for Vanuatu. Lautoka is smaller and less intense than Suva, but lacking in any colonial character or semblance of charm. Where Suva has a mixture of Melanesians, Polynesians and East Indians, Lautoka and the whole western coast of Viti Levu are predominantly populated by Indians. It is dry, the sky and hills faded and brittle compared to Suva's tropical exuberance. Sugar is king and the refineries pour out a black cane soot which floats down, coating everything with greasy carbon streaks.

A trip to the Hot Bread Kitchen to buy fresh bread for the passage, ice and long-lasting fruits and vegetables — completed our provisioning errands in Fiji.

Vanuatu had captured our imaginations with tales of active volcanoes and some of the most primitive cultures in the world. We had begun taking malaria medicine prophylactically two weeks before our expected arrival in Vanuatu — "Malaria Country."

"Malaria Country" has a forbidden ring of adventure about it. Now we are really going to out-of-the-way places, it seems to say, conjuring up visions of African safaris and trips down the Amazon, of Asia and the Far East, out of familiar and friendly Polynesia and deeper into Melanesia, land of vine jumpers where masks and spears are still used, not just sold to tourists.

John: Going into malarial areas scares me. I remember my father's stories of nearly dying from malaria in Africa, of being tied because the malaria had driven him crazy. Too, cruisers had contracted malaria, even though they had been taking anti-malaria drugs.

Chapter 17

VANUATU:

COWFISH
AND CARGO CULTISTS

Sept. 12, Barbara: Our first overnight passage in four months and in my enthusiasm for getting to Vanuatu, I completely blanked out the fact that I would need to stand watch. I try not to think about how uncomfortable a passage may be before we leave, and quickly forget what happened on the passage after we arrive. It is as if my brain gets suspended in a dreamy watery world, floating thoughts, like clouds, vaporizing and disappearing on closer scrutiny. Like dreams that are not remembered in the morning.

Sept. 13: We'd been talking about selling *Mahina Tiare*. I felt like a traitor, as if we should not discuss this where she could hear us, not until we were safely in port. It seemed cold and dispassionate to be ripping things down off the bulkheads, discussing her upholstery and sails like she was some sort of mannequin we were about to display, or a cow going to the meat market.

I could imagine her saying, "Is this how you treat me after getting you safely through a hurricane, only occasionally getting stuck on coral heads, (thanks to you) but always getting myself off again; never breaking down or blowing out a sail in 40,000 miles and 11 years together? And you talk of fixing me up just to sell? Wasn't I good enough to fix up before? And just what do you plan to take off me? The Marquesan wood carvings I've worn for seven years? The baskets from Pitcairn?"

Evening came and *Mahina Tiare* motored along on glassy seas. The moon was a big lantern hung in the sky to guide our way, laying a shining band ahead like a path paved in diamonds.

I'd been cat-napping below, waking up every ten minutes to come on deck to scan the horizon for ships, check course and speed. My mind had become remarkably self-disciplined, waking me up as if an alarm went off. It used various tricks — sometimes I'd think I heard John's voice asking, "Where are we?" Other times the cabin light seemed to burn through my eyelids, or the sound of a slatting sail woke me.

In those ten minutes of slumber, my mind took me all over the world, into interesting and dangerous situations. Of late I'd been reading Paul Theroux's *The Old Patagonia Express*, so my mind jetted off to South America (where most of the book takes place) in the time I allowed it to wander.

My watch over, I replaced John in the bed. It was warm and slightly damp with an odor of sweat. Nothing is more nostalgic than smell, our most primitive sense. I was instantly transported back to my junior high locker room, where the smell of ripe socks, Right Guard spray deodorant, and sweat mixed to make a memorable scent. Lockers hung open and shut with steel combination locks swinging from them. I twisted my lock, 28-34-22, the locker opened to reveal my blue one-piece gym suit with snaps. We were told that showers were compulsory after class, but no teenage girls I knew, pictures of modesty, wanted to parade naked into the communal showers. No one took showers or washed their gym suits often enough, and thus the lingering odor. I'd enjoyed my brief 'visit' to the locker room, but as I drifted back into the present, I remembered that I must change the sheets.

At 3 a.m. I was tossing and turning and swearing to myself as John kept turning the engine on and off. When it was off, the boat rolled and my stomach muscles ached from trying to keep myself from rolling off the bed. Meanwhile, John had been emptying all extra fuel jugs into the main tank so that less suction would be needed to get the fuel up to the engine. Silently, John performed surgery on the fuel line. No screams of frustration as he cut the squeeze bulb out of the outboard fuel hose line and transplanted it into the engine fuel line. This involved expanding some arteries (I mean hoses), on the main engine. When I got up, the squeeze bulb operation was complete and helped suck fuel from the nearly-empty tank up to the fuel lift pump on the engine. John had bled the air from the fuel system and had a sore back from hanging upside down for three hours.

Sept. 16: Efate Island, our destination, lays in the center of the 82 islands which make up the Republic of Vanuatu. Formerly the New Hebrides, Vanuatu is one of the Pacific's newest and most primitive nations. Located halfway between Fiji and New Caledonia, 1,200 miles east of Australia, the island appeared strange as it came into view — olive drab in the foreground, gray-blue in the distance, a long stepped limestone plateau. We motorsailed to get into Port Vila harbor before nightfall, but rounded Pango Point at dusk and ghosted up to the quarantine buoy in the dark. The lights of town enticed us, but Port Vila, administrative and tourist center of Vanuatu remained a mystery.

Sept. 17: Sunrise revealed a sprawling waterfront town of perhaps 16,000 people. The water in the bay was clear aqua, clean enough for a swim, a rarity in most large commercial Pacific island ports. At dusk the customs official arrived by inflatable dinghy and cleared us in.

Sept. 18: Ashore, we were sternly summoned into the office of the director of Immigration. The director, Andrew Bambara, scolded John for taking pictures of me filling out the Immigration forms. When John explained that the photos were to show other cruisers what to expect when they cleared into the country, Andrew's attitude softened. Australian journalists had recently been to Vanuatu to sensationalize an incident of cannibalism. The government was touchy about journalists.

Andrew had been to New York with the prime minister when Vanuatu, after gaining independence in 1980, became a member of the United Nations. He described, in excellent English, the workings of his government. The Anglo-French New Hebrides Condominium government, established in 1906, formerly governed the ni-Vanuatu people but did not allow them either French of British citizenship.

Today, Vanuatu has a parliamentary system of government, the prime minister recognized as leader of the majority party. Regional councils elect a president — a ceremonial head of state — for a three-year term of office. Since much of the country is removed from 20th century politics, a National Council of Chiefs advises on matters relating to "custom," such as traditional villages, dances, clothing, artwork or music.

Father Walter Lini has been Prime Minister since independence. We said to Andrew, "He must be an honest man." Andrew replied,

241

"Well, I don't know what he does — but the country is stable under his leadership."

Andrew's office was absolutely functional. The town was functional, clean but without much character to the modern, flat-roofed buildings, save for a few colorful murals on them. Yet the place had a happy, prosperous feel about it, with French pastry shops and lingerie boutiques next to shops selling primitive masks, grass skirts and artifacts from Vanuatu custom villages. Along the sidewalk local women in Mother Hubbard dresses sat in the hot sun, papayas, yams, taro and shells spread on blankets at their feet. Australian tourists along with British and French expatriates frequented the expensive shops. Government and business offices opened early, around 7:30, and closed during the hottest time of day, from 11:30 to 2:00.

The Vila Cultural Center, on the waterfront, housed a library, reading room, handicraft shop and museum. On the lawn outside the Cultural Center rested a large metal pot in which ni-Vanuatu had once cooked missionaries. The small museum was alive with bold, childlike artifacts, masks, clay and gourd headdresses with fibre hair and desiccated human heads. The walls displayed photographs of rituals, some as recent as the 1970's, which are no longer practised today. The museum's main function was to document the country's primitive cultures before they disappeared completely. Hundreds of films, cassettes, reel-to-reels and video tapes lay about the storeroom in dusty piles awaiting catalogers. Dozens of volunteers in the field continuously add new footage of rituals to the museum's archives.

Sept. 19: We rented a tiny Daihatsu car to tour the island, stopping north of Vila near Mele Mat at a sign saying cascade (waterfall). Kids, clustered at the base of a river, took our hands and guided us up to the limestone terraces until we reached the sheer cliffs. Hundreds of feet above, white water sheeted down, forming parallel falls and a series of pools below. The sound was thunderous and the force of the water created a spray-filled wind. Little kids jumped off ledges from dizzying heights, splashing with abandon into the pools. Sunlight filtered through ferns and banyans — it seemed the most magical place on earth.

John: After exploring Efate Island, we dropped a bow anchor and tied stern-to amidst a dozen locally-based yachts in front of the

242

Waterfront Bar. The Waterfront, a circular bure (thatched hut) surrounded by flowering hibiscus, poinsettias and bougainvilleas, was the headquarters of the Vanuatu Cruising Yacht Club. The restaurant was open air, and skinny cats whipped in and out from under tables like hungry sharks cruising for scraps of food.

I asked the first person I met at the bar — John Hamaty, an Aussie — if he knew any members of the club interested in buying a boat. Certain members had talked about buying a larger boat, he replied, and he would put the word out. He also asked to take a look at our boat. Little did I realize that a month later in New Caledonia he would buy *Mahina Tiare.*

Sept. 27 : A week after arriving in Port Vila, we sailed out of Port Vila's pass at 5:00 p.m. and set a course to the SSE. We planned to pass Erromango Island in the night and arrive at Tanna, 146 miles away, the following morning. Tanna was on the way to New Caledonia where we anticipated a better chance to sell *Mahina Tiare.*

We expected to be close-hauled, but the prevailing easterly tradewinds were more SE. We couldn't lay a direct course, but had to tack into the confused channel seas. Normally, after two hours of beating to windward into fresh tradewinds and rough head seas, we would fall off the wind and change destination to an island we could reach on a more comfortable point of sail. Instead, we endured a day and a half — the entire passage — bracing ourselves in a seated position in the cockpit. *Mahina Tiare* arrived at Port Resolution caked with salt crystals.

Barbara: Tanna is among the Southern group of Vanuatu, a land of active volcanoes, cargo cults and cow fish. In 1774 Captain Cook explored the group, naming it New Hebrides after the Scottish Hebrides. Port Resolution was named after his ship. I sensed a sadness about the bay, the same feeling I'd experienced while *Mahina Tiare* was anchored at Kealakekua Bay on the Island of Hawaii. Cook was killed while ashore at Kealakekua, four years after anchoring at Port Resolution.

Three thatched houses showed atop the dark bluffs, the rest of the bay seemingly deserted. Sulfurous volcanic smoke hissed along the shoreline or steamed up from the dense tropical vegetation. In the distance we heard disgruntled volcanic rumblings, explosions of

Mount Yasur.

To revive our flagging spirits and celebrate a safe arrival, we swam in the 80-degree water. Twenty brightly dressed locals clustered on an outcropping of rock, laughing and calling, "King, King, King!" One of the men explained, "King is a cowfeesh (cowfish)." Suddenly, an eight-foot-long beige-colored beast with a face like a walrus and a tail like a whale, swam toward us. A boy, splashing water near us to attract King, grabbed onto him and went for a ride. King is a Dugong, a gentle plankton-eating mammal similar to a Manatee, a village pet who always comes when called.

Dugongs are killed and eaten in Vanuatu, but King arrived as an orphan pup about 16 years ago and has grown up surrounded by village children, developing a playful relationship with them.

A short path led from the beach up to a soccer-sized field where several hundred Seventh-day Adventists from the southern islands had convened in tents for a week-long conference. Missionaries from Santo Island to the north had flown down to lead the conference. Marilyn Foote, whose small features, blond curly hair and green eyes made her resemble a fairy princess, was teaching the local women and men how to fabric-paint T-shirts to sell to tourists. Previously, she had taught the women how to decorate wedding cakes — European style — complete with pale skinned plastic bride and groom on top. It seemed an absurd skill to teach these women who generally cook over wood fires or in underground ovens, but they loved new things. Vanuatu was full of surprises.

David Stanley's *South Pacific Handbook* warns, *"Tanna is divided into warring factions: the people on the east side of the island against those on the west, Protestants against Catholics, French-educated against English-educated, village against village."* Yet, everyone we met seemed respectful of their neighbors.

Adjoining the Seventh-day Adventist camp was Ireupuow village, a Jon Frum cargo cult village. A family of Presbyterians lived nearby in the opposite direction, and to the south a Catholic settlement. Anglicans were spread here and there. The Adventist missionaries failed to understand the Jon Frum cargo cult. Marilyn told me she couldn't understand how anyone could accept on faith a bizarre religion which worships manufactured goods. To me, it seems a

244

natural religion. After all, most Westerners revere cargo (material goods). The difference is we know it is manufactured by man. Cultists believe it comes *factory made* from God.

Not only a multiplicity of religions exist in Vanuatu, but the fledgling nation has more languages per capita than any country in the world: 115 local languages plus many dialects. Bislama, the national language, is an outgrowth of Pidgin English learned from 19th century Australian traders. It is the intertribal tongue.

Sept. 28: We rocked and rolled in our berth last night as an easterly swell entered the shallow bay and an offshore breeze kept our beam to the swells. This morning John rowed out a 13-pound Danforth anchor on 200 feet of line. This kept our bow into the swell and made for a much easier motion below. Later a handsome local man shyly paddled his primitive dugout up to *Mahina Tiare*. "I am Remi Usua," he told us, "the brother of the taxicab driver you met in Port Vila. Someone said you were looking for me."

Remi's name jotted on a scrap of paper obliged him to act as our island tour guide. He took us up to his family's land where four thatch houses sat in a clearing. Kids ran house to house, and chickens scratched up grubs. We met Remi's elderly father who wore only a faded sarong. During World War II he had worked in the Solomon Islands as a coastwatcher for the Americans. He thought highly of Americans and was pleased to shake our hands. Remi's wife, Nellie, joined us. She was dressed in an immaculate pink Mother Hubbard. Her large brown eyes, generous lips, and thick build — similar to an Aboriginal Australian —suggested strength and quiet beauty.

Remi led as we descended a narrow trail though a grove of banana trees, the humid air was thick with the sweet smell of overripe fruit. Giant banyans created wide circles of shade along the trail, and birds sang around us. Labyrinths of trunk and vine several stories high, Tanna's banyans are among the earth's largest living organisms. A young banyan begins by growing around another tree eventually strangling it out of existence.

We passed a tree covered with round coral-colored blossoms whose radiating stamens resembled a powder puff or pin cushion. I picked one. It was vaguely familiar. Then I remembered the blossom that had floated down when I visited the greenhouses of the New York

Botanical Gardens as a child. Thirty years ago I never expected to one day see these blossoms in the tropics. I was awed and thankful that I was able to witness the marvels of the world by sailboat.

Ours were the only footprints on a mile stretch of white sand beach. No one lived nearby, the surf pounded and an onshore breeze rustled the ribbons of Nellie's dress. Remi pointed to a narrow isthmus leading to a small point of land: "We call this place Captain Cook." Here Cook had come to observe the planets. With nothing around to remind us we're living in the 20th century, we could picture Cook carrying his scientific instruments across the isthmus surrounded by bewildered cannibals.

On the way back to *Mahina Tiare* we asked Remi about getting water to wash our clothes. "Sweet water is scarce, but I know a good place to wash clothes," Remi answered. Two hours later we were walking down the dusty red dirt road which parallels Port Resolution Bay. After a mile we turned off into a football-size field surrounded by palms. A group of women sat with their laundry drying on the grass. Remi, carrying one of our buckets, waded into a steaming pool covered with scum. The scalding water smelled slightly of sulfur but did a wonderful job cleaning our clothes.

Later in the evening I read aloud a passage from Mr. Paton's *Missionary in the New Hebrides* (two volumes 1889), about this same hot pool: "*We were afterward informed that five or six men had been shot dead; that their bodies had been carried by the conquerors from the field of battle, and cooked and eaten that very night by the savages at a boiling spring near the head of the bay, less than a mile from the spot where my house is being built.*"

Sept. 29: A small intense man, his skin as black as ebony, paddled out to *Mahina Tiare* in a dugout. Politely introducing himself as Ronnie Thomas he said, "On behalf of the chief of Ireupuow village I welcome you to Port Resolution, Tanna Island."

Ronnie talked earnestly about the Jon Frum cargo cult in which he believes. "Australians and others don't believe in Jon Frum," he said. "Jon Frum tell my grandfather only America is your friend — do not trust other nation. My grandfather and other Tannese men spend 17 years in prison for believing in Jon Frum. In prison Jon visit them. Jon still sometime appear to people at Sulfur Bay when we gather to sing and dance all night in his honor."

It's difficult to decipher 50-year-old fact from fantasy but, after talking to Ronnie and several other Tannese, it seems that Jon Frum was either a World War II American GI or the composite of several GIs "from" America. Tannese men could easily assume that they had all met the same GIs; to them, all soldiers looked similar, shook their hands and gave them cigarettes. Perhaps the sight of vast quantities of war materiel contributed to the formation of the cult. American GIs treated the Tannese much better than either French or British who at the time ran the condominium government. Frequently the troops traded military supplies — fatigues, boots, tools and food rations — for help from Ni-Vanuatu people in building two airstrips, harbors, and unloading cargo.

The New Hebrides served as the most important staging point for battles in the Solomon Islands and Coral Sea. Millions of pounds of cargo passed through these islands, wondrous cargo that the Tannese had never seen or even imagined. The villagers accepted Jon Frum as a deity coming across the sea to bestow wealth and prosperity. They would come to live like Americans, but without working.

A few years later an American Red Cross officer visited Tanna. The islanders assumed he was connected with Jon Frum and took the Red Cross insignia on his uniform as one of the symbols of their new religion. The cargo cultists' allegiance to America is so strong that they will not cooperate with their fledgling government. Ronnie even told us that the reason Jon Frum has not come back as promised relates to those cult members who voted in the Vanuatu government election at the time of independence. He went on to say that Jon Frum will bring tinned food, rice, build nice block houses and give them a war ship. I told him Americans have these things but are often unhappy. He coughed, then said he had chest pains and a hernia.

John asked what Ronnie needed. He had ten children and, yes, he would like some tinned beef, a belt for his father, and some clothes for his wife. Tinned tuna, a piece of line, a Hawaiian shirt and a small American flag were the best we could manage. He loaned us a photocopy of the book *Jon Frum He Come* by Edward Rice, Doubleday 1974, a sympathetic account of the cult.

Sept. 30: We began this unusual day with a surprise breakfast of

Remi and Nellie, Port Resolution, Tanna, Vanuatu

lobster. Remi had speared it last night and told us to eat it right away.

Remi, Nellie, and Charlie, a cargo cultist, met on the beach. Charlie told us he'd take us on a short cut to the Mt. Yasur volcano and we wouldn't have to pay the $18 per person at the gate. We didn't mind paying, but Charlie and Remi wouldn't hear of it. Remi said that once the Sulfur Bay people started charging visitors to see the volcano, their coconut trees started dying, their gardens became covered in volcanic ash and would not produce.

The trail to Sulfur Bay is windy and steep, but well worn and shaded with towering banyans and tree ferns. Descending into Sulfur Bay village, the surf crashed on a pebble beach on one side. To the other, Mt. Yasur emitted vague rumblings. The air was heavy and a thick circle of cloud surrounding the volcano hung over the village as if waiting to pour down on us. Rows of thatch houses paralleled the beach and colorful bits of flowering shrubs surrounded a commons green crisscrossed with trails.

A half dozen men gazed laconically at us from beneath a tree, its tangled roots were 12 feet tall. It was a surreal place, the most primitive

I've ever witnessed, as if I had walked into an old copy of National Geographic. Save for bits of corrugated iron and cotton fabric, everything was created from local materials — no cars, no bicycles in view. This was my image of Polynesian villages, but I had come too late to see that Polynesia. Sulfur Bay villagers are Melanesian, not Polynesian. Here, no one smiled readily, there were no flower crowns in their hair as in Tahiti, no gaiety and no prosperity. Trees and crops were dying; Jon Frum, their savior, has not come. They need a hospital and a school.

Enter one John (Neal) from America off a white boat. Is their wait for Jon Frum over?

John: When I met people in the village, their first questions were, "What is your name?" and "Where are you from?" When I said my name was John and that I had sailed from America to Tanna, they whistled softly, and repeated, "Jon from America, Jon from America." Tannese legend tells of a great white ship which will someday come and anchor offshore, then transfer the wealth of the world to their shores.

Isaac Wan, chief of the village, introduced himself through a young interpreter. More men gathered around. A tall old man whose hair and beard were yellow-white was introduced as the only man still living who had met Jon.

Isaac was agitated: " Are you Jon Frum?"

"NO! I am NOT Jon Frum."

He grew angry: "Take this message to Jon Frum. We've waited 40 years for him to come back — he didn't come — he is nine years overdue."

"I don't know Jon Frum. I can't bring you cargo. But I will take the message to the American people that you would like medical help, teachers, clothing. Have you heard of the Peace Corps? American volunteers will come to places like this to help with medical needs, water systems."

One of the most intense and frightening experiences of my life; I was totally out of my element. Many of the men surrounding me had long bush knives behind their backs.

Barbara: Isaac finally calmed down and showed us cult headquarters. I was permitted to enter the dark thatch hut and take pictures only because I am an American woman accompanied by John. Sulfur Bay women are not allowed inside.

Isaac proudly showed their weapons — bamboo poles with one end pointed and painted red. The cult's interpretation of guns? Were the khaki pants and hand-tooled leather belts World War II gifts from American GIs? One sign read "Jon Frum Headquarters, 1957," below it a picture of a red flag with the words, "All to jail." Underneath that was an American flag and a Jon Frum flag. Next to the sign, a framed picture of the Sacred Heart of Jesus, and next to that a poster saying "Dreaming."

Isaac led us inside the thatch church. In front stood a large red cross. A small statue of the Virgin Mary on a block of wood had a tin can and a roll of cotton gauze placed in front of it. Were these symbols asking for food and medicine? The front wall displayed an oil painting of the crucifixion with Christ painted as a black man, and several paintings with a floating dream-like quality — a curious mixture of Christian symbolism and Jon Frum iconography pervaded the church. Isaac told us he receives songs from Jon every week and he talks to him, but Isaac's Jon is more of a helpful spirit than a physically present Jon.

He said the Presbyterians kicked the Jon Frums out of their church. As he put it, their reason was that "we stink, we smell up their church, and Jon Frum is the devil. We start our own church. We believe in Jesus Christ and our rewards in heaven. We also believe Jon will bring heaven on earth and we will not need to work." Jon Frum, they say, has white-skin and Christ is black. I couldn't help thinking that white people are the confusing influence, the promise of an easy lifestyle and luxuries which change the culture. The Christ they believe in is like them, a simple, humble person without many worldly possessions.

Outside the church we asked some of the young men if they believed Jon Frum had an army of followers in the volcano as we had read. "No", they said, "our story is about two ladies and a man who live there..." Then they launched into a delightfully involved traditional story.

We gave Isaac a huge American flag that had been given to us. He seemed pleased, but what he really needed, he told us, was a new American Navy flag and a Marines flag for which the cultists had flag poles waiting.

When we left three American flags were flying over Sulfur Bay. The flags gave me a sad feeling. The villagers thought paradise on earth was doing no work, smoking cigarettes, eating food out of tins. I knew they were counting on us to tell America their needs. Could their story bring them, not the luxuries they wanted, but the needed basics like decent medical care and schooling?

Mount Yasur was a few miles away; her rumblings enticed us to come closer and witness her fiery cauldron. We stopped under a pandanus tree to share our raisins, nuts and crackers with our companions. The two quarts of water we had brought barely quenched the thirst among the five of us.

Coconut tree trunks flanked the dirt trail, trunks without fronds, recent victims of caustic steam from Mount Yasur. Before us lay a black undulating landscape. We started our ascent of the vast steep 1,200-foot mound that is Mount Yasur. There was no trail — just us, alone, five colorful dots strung across the moonscape of volcanic grit.

Sweat stung my eyes as I placed foot before foot, slowly climbing, leaning into the hill to keep from tumbling backward. My foot dislodged a volcanic rock and sent it rolling and tumbling down the vertical slope until it was out of sight a thousand feet below. I realized that if one of us slipped, we'd have nothing to grab on to, nothing to break our fall down the mountain.

The view below was otherworldly — where the ash plain ended, mist clung to the tops of tree ferns. Sulfur Bay Village appeared as an expanse of green bordered by the white froth of the ocean crashing on Tanna's eastern shore.

At the summit the constantly changing wind buffeted us and sulfur fumes seared our lungs. We peered over the crater's rim. A break in the billowing cloud of steam allowed us to glimpse jets of lava a mile below. The mountain shook and groaned beneath our feet.

I pulled my T-shirt up to cover my nose and mouth and crouched down on my hands and knees to escape the waves of noxious steam. Deciding it was no place to linger, we scrambled down among the boulders which the angry mountain recently jettisoned.

Remi pointed to the expansive black plateau below. "Two people shot themselves down there," he told us, "a man and a woman from Sulfur Bay. Her father, that white-haired man you met today, wouldn't

Angry cargo cultists, Sulfur Bay, Tanna

let her marry the man so they ran away to this place. Stayed two weeks, then the man went to a shop and bought bullets. He came back and killed himself and the woman he wanted to marry." A true-life version of Romeo and Juliet, I thought to myself.

Charlie and Remi discussed the best way back to Port Resolution without: (1) Going the long way through Sulfur Bay, (2) paying the landowner to use the most direct trail back to Port Resolution through his land, or (3) getting lost in the jungle. We had waited too long to make it back in daylight. But now Charlie said he thought he knew a short cut to Port Resolution.

At the jungle's edge, Charlie looked for the short cut. We followed him deeper and deeper into the dripping forest. The path became more intuition than trail.

I smelled pig. "Yes," Remi told me, "we hunt wild boar here with our dogs." I wondered whether the circuitous path might be a wild pig trail where we could be attacked at any time.

We ducked under fallen trees and caught our ankles in vines tangled like barbed wire. We waded through fields of ferns up to our waists. I had a raging thirst and fantasized finding a coconut shell that had collected water, but there were no coconut trees here. I looked longingly at a curled leaf holding a few sips of water. I envisioned spending the night in the bush, hunkered down on the damp ground in the drizzling rain, shivering, with a cloud of malarial mosquitoes whining in my ears.

Charlie and Remi frequently headed off in opposite directions, then Charlie would yell for us to follow him. Two hours later, as darkness approached, we reached an open area. The ocean was below us, but we had to travel several miles to get to it — miles of steep volcanic terrain. Reddish patches of earth emitting puffs of steam, like slowly festering wounds, dotted the landscape. It was as if someone had booby-trapped our exit, as if we were playing a survival game. To test our endurance we had to make it down this hill without falling into the bowels of the earth.

"Too dangerous!" Remi and Charlie rejected the trail, opting to go back into the jungle. I suddenly appreciated having a trail, however rudimentary. Now we were sliding down a narrow ravine, slippery on the bottom from fallen leaves and choked with pandanus trees, their sword-like fronds and limbs pimpled with barbs. Down, down we slipped, clothes tearing and blood oozing. We picked up a trail and caught a glimpse of Port Resolution — miles away and more than a thousand feet below. We submerged into the gloomy forest again, the tropical drizzle starting at dusk, slowly increasing to a torrential downpour. Red clay soil stuck to our shoes, getting thicker and thicker. Every few minutes we stopped to scrape off the goo to prevent slipping.

Nellie, six months pregnant, had kept pace but she and I were starting to tire. In the dark we could barely see the men only a few yards ahead. We whistled back and forth to make sure we stayed on the trail which seemed to disappear. Unseen insects screamed from the trees. Port Resolution was ahead. We descended to the main road in pitch dark and pouring rain. But we reached the beach and our dinghy. Remi and Charlie apologized for getting lost.

We hurried to *Mahina Tiare,* exhausted and dirty. Standing on the pitching deck we let the rain splash the sweat and dirt from our skin while we scooped up the sweet water and drank cup after cup of it. How much more alive can one feel?

Oct. 1: Isaac Wan and his son, Maliwan, paddled their tippy dugouts three miles in open ocean swells from Sulfur Bay village to

Port Resolution. Their mission, to ask us to type a reply letter to an investment banker in Redmond, Washington whom they'd written asking for cargo. Judging by the questions the banker asked, he didn't have a clue about Vanuatu or cargo. Ronnie joined Isaac and Maliwan in our cockpit. Huddled together, they spoke in the throaty tones of their own dialect. Obviously they wanted the banker to continue thinking he dealt with the official Vanuatu government, not a band of renegades from Tanna. Soon they decided to have Ronnie respond to the letter, not us.

The next day Ronnie paddled the letter out to us. Sealed in an official Vanuatu Government envelope, it was addressed in a childish sloping script. Resisting the temptation to open the letter, I mailed it a few days later from Noumea, New Caledonia. I can imagine the investment banker's consternation when he opened it.

I was somewhat uncomfortable when Isaac and Maliwan both gave me beautiful brightly-dyed grass skirts and tightly woven pandanus purses. I hadn't met their wives who made these gifts and sensed barter, not friendship, in such a presentation.

"What would your wives like in return?", I asked hesitatingly.

"Whatever you want to give."

I gave them a blouse, fabric and a few hundred vatu, the equivalent of a few dollars. I am always in turmoil about what to give the local people. Giving too much is as inappropriate as giving too little. Customs vary from island to island, even village to village. In some Vanuatu villages, if you give people too much, they are insulted. They feel you are trying to belittle them since they cannot reciprocate. In places visited by many yachts, some people ashore stop their normal subsistence routines and become traders. They supply the cruisers with fresh fish, lobster, fruits and vegetables. In return they may get exorbitantly generous gifts or trades from cruisers who are unsure what is appropriate.

"Visitors changed paradise forever," goes one quote, "when they offered to pay for that which once was freely given." If cruisers encourage the local people to seek payment for their gifts, then they no longer are truly gifts, items the locals can spare.

After trading with a dozen boats, the locals have plenty of baseball caps, cassette tapes, candy, Rambo and Madonna T-shirts. Cruisers generally dislike trading with money, but I think this sometimes works out best. The locals can then buy what they need (if it's available) rather than end up with cruisers' cast-offs.

Often the first local people out to visit an arriving yacht make their living by trading. They've seen hundreds of yachts and have cruisers pretty well pegged. Their response to "Do you need a diving mask or kerosene light?" is always "Yes". It's their business to get as much as they can from cruisers to share with relatives. Yachts are like treasure troves, crammed full of wondrous cargo they can't secure elsewhere.

In primitive areas of the Pacific the people share abundantly with each other. They don't understand the concept of personal property, or why we aren't willing to share more with them. They are, in general, willing to share what they have with us. Many aboriginal peoples believe that accumulating goods is bad karma, that possessions must be passed around to keep them from working against their possessor.

We've learned to take our time trading or gifting. Spending time ashore helps determine appropriate, healthy and needed gifts. Village teachers, health care workers, priests, ministers, are good to consult about gift giving. Fishing gear, caulk or silicon sealant, sandpaper, paint, fabric, volleyballs, sterile dressings, roller gauze, adhesive tape, topical antiseptic scrub solution, antibiotic ointments, a snapshot of someone's family — such gifts are generally appreciated in small Pacific villages.

Oct. 8: Under the shade of a banyan, roosters crowing and kids darting in and out of doorways, we said goodbye to Remi and Nellie. Our friends had not asked for anything but we gave them gifts of clothing, our thank-you for showing us around the island and bringing us food. They looked shyly at the pile of clothes, then brought out a beautiful grass skirt, and a woven purse for me, and some lap-lap (coconut cream and manioc) cooked in an underground oven. Embarrassed, Remi asked us to send some baby clothes for his soon-to-be-born baby. It was obvious Nellie had made him ask for the clothes.

"Yes, we'll gladly send some baby clothes...."

Remi broke the awkward silence: "Would you like a live rooster to take on the boat?"

"No, thank you." Remi's offer both touched us and made us smile.

In Port Resolution, more than any other place we visited in the

Pacific, people ashore acted concerned about our food supply and gave us everything from lettuce to potatoes, coconuts to lobster. Their concern stemmed from the fact that they generally only eat food they grow, and couldn't understand what we were eating since we grew nothing aboard. Remi told us that he did not like the capitol, Port Vila, where people actually charged money for food! "Here on Tanna," he said, "we don't need money to eat."

The trail sloped toward the bay where *Mahina Tiare* waited. Remi stopped amidst the lushness; he said, "It takes time to know the people... some people at White Sands steal. Jimmy steals, but Charlie is OK. You don't know our people. If I go to your country I won't know the good people from the bad ones. Charlie and Jimmy, it's their job to meet the boats. I usually don't go out to the boats, but you had my name and asked for me so I came to meet you."

Remi in a sense was saying, "You are lucky you met me. I watched out for you." A Catholic priest in Vila told us that on the most remote islands in Vanuatu, cruisers should not go ashore. It is easy to break a taboo and get into serious trouble with the locals. Granted, Tanna is not one of Vanuatu's most primitive islands, but we felt fortunate to have met Remi and had him watch out for us when we were surrounded by angry cargo cultists at Sulfur Bay. Remi is right, a cruiser doesn't know a good person from a bad person. The longer you cruise, the more you learn to sense who the "operators" are in a village. Their gifts have strings attached. However, the vast number of locals we meet are truly looking for nothing but friendship.

With *Mahina Tiare* for sale, I wondered whether I would see Remi and Nellie and Tanna Island again, or ever again visit a place so different that it forced me out of my day to day introspection, and stimulated all my senses. If we buy a larger boat, will we step over that invisible line that turns life on a boat from simplicity to complication? Will the new boat corrupt us, taking along too much of our culture, denying the new world unfolding around us? Will we sell *Mahina Tiare* in New Caledonia, or sail on to Australia?

Chapter 18

NEW CALEDONIA TO AUSTRALIA:

FAREWELL TO A FRIEND

Oct. 3, Barbara: A gentle sail under overcast skies. We passed Mare Island in the Loyalty group around sunset. As night descended we saw the lights of six yachts surrounding us, part of the fleet participating in the Port Vila to Noumea Yacht Race. They, like us, had their sails reefed to slow down to avoid reaching Havannah Passage before sunrise. Havannah Passage is the easternmost passage through the reef surrounding Grande Terre Island, the main island of New Caledonia. The sailing directions and charts show strong current along the coast of Grande Terre, and the chart shows many reefs and rocks around the entrance. This is one entrance we would never attempt at night or in poor visibility.

Oct. 4: At 1:00 a.m. our SatNav was giving inconsistent fixes, so we contacted another yacht to check our position. Their SatNav was also giving fixes hundreds of miles off.

At sunrise Grande Terre was in view and we were able to take bearings on mountain tops and islets with our hand bearing compass. Using dead reckoning, with the help of the British Admiralty Sailing Directions, we were able to pinpoint the entrance to Havannah Pass. One of the yachts we passed came on over the VHF; "We'll follow you in, *Mahina Tiare!*"

"How do you know we know where we're going? We've never been through this passage either."

When there are other boats around, a strange herding instinct takes place. One starts questioning one's own judgement. It's tempting to follow a group of boats even if you think they are going the wrong way.

257

Grande Terre is studded with steep green mountains. The green is mostly scrub, with red patches from mining. I forgive the red scars, because from a distance they catch the light in a warm glow, adding a striking beauty to the landscape. The island is huge and splinter-shaped, 250 miles long and 30 miles wide, almost equal in size to the North Island of New Zealand. Yet, to most North Americans, it's a total mystery. Who lives here?

The native people are Melanesian, related to the people of Vanuatu, the Solomons and New Guinea. When Cook arrived toward the end of the 18th century, the people had a Stone Age culture and practiced ritualized cannibalism and headhunting.

In the 19th century, French missionaries, traders and English settlers came to the islands. The Melanesians resisted this invasion, staging several bloody revolts.

Today, the Melanesians would like independence from the French who govern New Caledonia as an Overseas Territory. They are outnumbered by Europeans and immigrants from Vietnam, Tahiti, Wallis, and Indonesia who want to remain a French Territory. The tenacity of the French is due to the extreme mineral wealth, predominantly nickel, found in the mountains of Grande Terre.

According to the locals, the bloodshed of the pro-independence movement a few years ago was over-blown by the foreign press. The French seem to have taken a conciliatory attitude, finding it easier to buy the rebels' favor with cars and trips to Paris for meetings on future independence.

After seven hours of traversing Grande Terre's lagoon we entered into Baie de Moselle, where a squatty Westsail 42, *Sagittaire,* swung at anchor. In Vanuatu several cruisers mentioned that if we needed help with anything in Noumea to talk to Ron on *Sagittaire.* John suspected that Ron was Ron Paton, an old cruising friend. A burly Scotsman boomed in a deep Richard Burton Voice, "Hello, John, tie up to the main wharf and customs will be right along."

Clearing customs was a breeze. Normal formalities were cut short because so many boats were clearing in from the race. Race participants had the $25 U.S. customs fee waived and were greeted with baskets of wine, champagne, pate and fresh baguettes. We should have joined the race. Organized for cruising sailors, the race it not at all serious.

258

Visiting yachts tie up or anchor in Baie de Moselle or Baie de l'Orphelinat. The French forbid anyone to anchor in Baie de Moselle, but it is crowded with yachts. This law absolves them of responsibility should a yacht get damaged in the harbor.

We anchored in Baie de l'Orphelinat and dinghied ashore to Cercle Nautique Yacht Club which was hosting the race. The yacht club was clean and modern and much more sophisticated than any other tropical club we had visited. The French were polite but slightly aghast at how obnoxiously drunk and loud some Kiwi and Aussie racing yachties became. It *was* embarrassing.

Noumea is mostly nondescript cement buildings with flat roofs, punctuated by pockets of affluent shops surrounded by potted palms and wrought iron gates.

The centerpiece of Noumea, the Place de Cocotiers, has heroic statues, fountains and tall trees — a seedy, tropical version of a Paris park. The rues have French names and blue enamel signs with white letters. A faint smell of sewage (Ron told us the sewers dump right into the bay) mixes with French perfume. A large percentage of Melanesians live in grim cinder-block low-cost apartment houses on the outskirts of town.

Oct. 14: A few miles south of Noumea we visited the tourist area and topless beach at Anse Vata. Admiral Halsey directed the Solomon Islands campaign from this area.

Whenever yachts congregate in the Western Pacific the topic of World War II inevitably comes up. Jack on the yacht *Lilli Sohex* had been stationed here during the war. Ellis Gidons on *Gra Geal Mo Crea* had an uncle whose buddy returned here after the war to marry and settle. Joel and Sharon on *Christopher Robin* had a plaque to place on a grave on Guadalcanal.

Ron, one of the youngest members of the Royal Scots Fusiliers, told us how they loved it when the Americans entered the war. "The Americans were so gung-ho we let them go first into battle as cannon fodder. We used to raid the American camp; we had long ago run out of spare tires and engine parts. One night a bunch of us stole the V-8 engine out of the American commander's car and replaced the broken one in our own commander's car."

Ashore the older Polynesians and Melanesians we met love Americans because they feel we kept their islands from being overrun by the Japanese during the war.

Oct 15: We met John Hamaty (J. H.) again, the Australian fellow who had looked at *Mahina Tiare* in Port Vila. He was sailing with a friend on a bachelor boat, unkempt and unclean, a bit leaky, a boat that hadn't had a woman aboard in years. For this reason, I think, *Mahina Tiare* looked more beautiful to him when he came on board on Tanna, then again here. He decided to buy *Mahina Tiare* and we agreed to deliver it with him on board to Australia.

J.H. is intense, part English, part Lebanese, a handsome man with a Roman nose, the focal point of his long face.

Oct. 16: J.H. is anxious to leave for Australia but he doesn't realize how much work goes into getting ready for a passage: food, water, fuel, stowage, fixing the myriad things that need fixing on a boat.

Oct. 19: We leave at noon. The start of a passage seems a private affair — people turn inward to cope with discomforts, fears, apprehensions, not much gets said. I sit in the cockpit assuming a fetal-like position, knees bent against my chest. I rock back and forth, stare at the horizon and rest my head against something soft. My abdominal muscles are tired from tensing and untensing. My thighs throb from staying in the same position for hours.

Oct. 20: I never felt much affection for *Mahina Tiare* until now, now that we have sold her. Unlike many people's boats, we haven't personified her, nor given her equipment pet names like Wendy Windvane or Otto Autopilot. Mostly I've just gotten impatient with her inconveniences, her small, tightly packed spaces. I've cursed her many times but never spoken affectionately to her.

And now that she is almost gone, I look lovingly at her sleek lines, at the wood I worked so hard to keep varnished. I pat her cushions and rub my hand over the soft curved teak hand rails. I notice the subtle details which make her special, a cut above every other boat.

Mahina Tiare is where John and I had our first date, our honeymoon. Even I, who didn't care for boats, was impressed with her when I first stepped aboard on a cold December night. She felt warm and safe, like I felt in John's arms that first night when he hugged me.

She's taken us to magical places and I never thanked her. Hurricanes, white squalls, we've tied up in impossible harbors, impossible anchorages like Easter Island and Pitcairn, but she has never lost an anchor, blown out a sail. I ran her into the Greenhithe Bridge in New Zealand, broke her forestay but she heeled over sideways and managed to slip us through without losing her mast.

John always treated her gently and lovingly, but I just took her for granted. John earned her, but I married her along with John, competing for affection until slowly I spent as much time on her as John did. She has become home and I have learned the patience to live aboard her. She represents the happiest years of my life and with her passing, that chapter closes.

Mahina Tiare, it was I who talked of a larger boat, John who decided to sell you, and now I find myself crying at leaving you. Someone else will have to polish your lamps and dust your small surfaces. At first I thought you might want to get back at us for selling you, but you have been on your best behavior, dry and comfortable. I know you want to give us a last good ride.

It seems strange to leave you in Australia, a place you are not familiar with, a place where we won't see you again. We will not be around to baby you and you will get a new name, but will you remember us? Has our laughter somehow seeped into your bulkheads, our concern for you become part of your atmosphere? The years of treading your carpet and sitting in your settees while you took us through a hurricane and weeks of gales, all this is part of you, and yet to someone else you are just a new boat, a blank slate. Life will be easier for you now, you won't be crossing oceans. It will take John Hamaty time to learn how to handle you; you'll get bumps and bruises.

Oct. 21: Finished Nevel Chute's *The Ruined City.* At one point the protagonist, a successful but driven businessman, goes to prison. For him, prison brings memories of boy's school and a return to innocence. Prison frees him from overwhelming responsibilities and gives him time for reflection, many hours to read. He thrives. All his needs — food, clothing, shelter — are provided. His description of prison reminds me of a long passage, where life is stripped down to the bones. A person experiences, for the first time since childhood, large blocks of time to exist for oneself.

Jack London in *The Cruise of the Snark* wrote about the education one receives at sea: "— *oh, not a mere education in the things of the world*

261

outside, of lands, and peoples, and climates, but an education in the world inside, an education in one's own self, to get on speaking terms with one's soul."

I dream that we lose *Mahina Tiare*, then find her again but she is in chaos — everything pulled out of her lockers. In my dream we sail her this way in rough, rolly conditions. I see a black gaping hole into darkness through the companionway. The world seems huge and black and empty outside.

Oct. 22: I always resist picking up the log book — as if I have nothing to write. But once I start writing words flow out in an effortless stream. I am always aided by the night; the night is soothing, manageable, not much to focus on but thoughts. I have learned to trust in spontaneity, letting a description flow through my pen rather than a tortuous route through my brain. But to trust the voice that comes out naturally, that wants its thoughts shared on paper, is not easy.

Oct. 24, John: The passage from New Caledonia to Brisbane Australia is a lot like the one to New Zealand; you want to get it over with as quickly as possible, so we ended up motoring for three of the seven day passage. If we had sat and waited for the wind to come up, we would have ended up beating into 35 knot headwinds as did the boats that left two days after we did. On this last passage *Mahina Tiare* seems to be really strutting her stuff. We passed both a Valient 40 and a Tatoosh 42 on the way here from Noumea.

Barbara: I find myself resenting J.H. for saying it's *his* boat when it isn't his yet. John and I breathed our life into the wood below. We know how to open cupboards, pad about without crashing into things. The oil from our palms makes the hand rails glisten where they curve over the wood.

Perhaps I view him as an intruder on our last passage with you. He points out your faults, like pointing out a child's shortcomings to his parents: "John, I see rust on this stereo speaker. John, this chart table light doesn't work, that sail's hanks are worn." He pokes into our lazarette and cockpit lockers. I know he doesn't quite understand that you are more than a boat.

John was up on the bow this afternoon. "I am sad," he told me. "I wish this sale had been quick. It's as if we are mourning. *Mahina Tiare* has been my home and part of me for 11 years, over one third of my life! I think I'm crazy, and that we've made a big mistake. I think that we'll never find a boat as pretty, as well built and as forgiving. I think about going into debt for a larger boat, I hate being in debt. But then I think of the new opportunities and possibilities that would accompany a larger boat, the volunteer medical work and sail training we could do. I hope these thoughts will keep me going through the rough time of giving away and boxing up 11-years worth of dreams, adventures and romance."

I recall *West with the Night* in which Beryl Markham expresses this same sentiment about ending her exciting life as a bush pilot in Africa for a change of pace.

"I have learned that if you must leave a place that you have lived in and loved and where all your yesterdays are buried deep — leave it anyway except a slow way, leave it the fastest way you can. Never turn back and never believe that an hour you remember is a better hour because it is dead. Passed years seem safe ones, vanquished ones, while the future lives in a cloud, formidable from a distance. The cloud clears as you enter it. I learned this, but like everyone, I learned it late."

"... A life has to move or it stagnates. Even this life, I think. It is no good telling yourself that one day you will wish you had never made that change; it is no good anticipating regrets. Every tomorrow ought not to resemble every yesterday.

"Still, I look at my yesterdays for months past, and find them as good a lot of yesterdays as anybody might want...

"I have had responsibilities and work, dangers and pleasures, good friends and a world without walls to live in."

This trip, the events of my life, have shown me that when you decide to do something and everything works quickly in your favor, that it is the right time for the change.

Tonight the boat was rolling heavily. John and I couldn't sleep. J.H. was trying to calm *Mahina Tiare* down. John got up and coaxed him. "I'll put the pole up and turn us on a beam reach to help lessen the rolling. Sheet in the jib — gently or you'll stretch the line too much, ok, ok. Now slowly let out the jib sheet." John knows how to tweak and trim; ease and sheet, and *Mahina Tiare* responds like a lover. She has started to let me handle her too. But she twisted and jerked, luffed and flapped when J.H. handled her.

Oct. 25: Toward dusk we saw Australia in the distance. The land seemed flat, which is how I always pictured it. Terra Australis, the Great Southern Continent. As we get closer, her shape grows with the jagged edge of a mountain range. The Glass House Mountains, Cook named them. Tonight they look like glass as they reflect the sun.

Certain places call to us throughout our lives — something read or heard captivates the imagination. Australia, a continent of red earth and strange marsupials — an elemental place — has drawn me. I never had the same urge to see New Zealand, or the islands of the South Pacific, yet it was never in our plans to sail to Australia. But the trip has been like this, taking us where we need to go.

Oct. 26: Early morning, 19 miles off the smell of pine and eucalyptus is tantalizing and makes me fall in love with land again.

The blank page I created with my life at the start of this three year journey is filled. I want to cling to the page, cling to *Mahina Tiare*. But there are many more blank pages appearing before me, there is a whole book I didn't know about when I started. Because I wrote on the first page many more have been given to me.

In *One Writers Beginning* Eudora Welty describes how her stories take life as she goes, her characters never pre-set but reveal themselves to her as they interact with each other. Her writing comes down to love and human relationships. This is how my stories evolved when I turn to the log book. Pacific Islanders believe that a gift, to maintain its spirit of increase must be passed along. Sailing with John, this journey, the people we met, were gifts; writing about them has been my way of discovering the gifts and passing them on to you.

Meeting the marsupials, Brisbane, Australia

BOAT CONFIGURATION & TERMINOLOGY

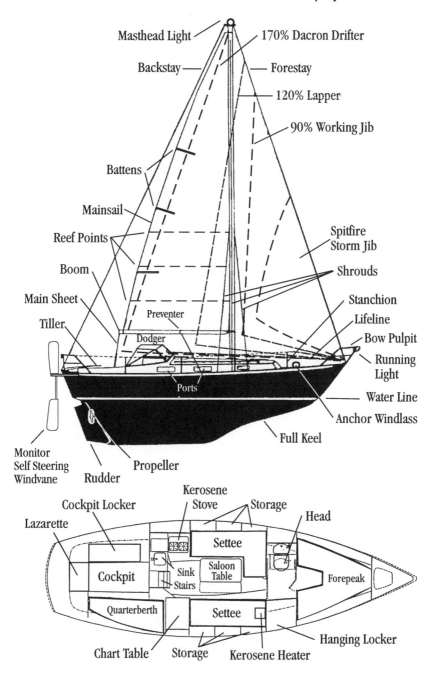

Masthead Light

170% Dacron Drifter

Backstay

Forestay

120% Lapper

90% Working Jib

Battens

Mainsail

Reef Points

Spitfire Storm Jib

Boom

Shrouds

Main Sheet

Stanchion

Tiller

Lifeline

Preventer

Dodger

Bow Pulpit

Running Light

Ports

Water Line

Anchor Windlass

Full Keel

Monitor Self Steering Windvane

Propeller

Rudder

Kerosene Stove

Storage

Head

Cockpit Locker

Lazarette

Settee

Sink

Saloon Table

Forepeak

Cockpit

Stairs

Quarterberth

Settee

Hanging Locker

Chart Table

Storage

Kerosene Heater

HOW TO DO IT

MAHINA TIARE

Monsun
Hallberg Rassey 31'
Designer: Olle Enderlein

Length over all .... 30'9" .... 9,36 m
Length waterline ....24'8" ....7,50 m
Beam ....9'5" ....2,87 m
Draft ....4'7" ....1,40 m
Displacement ....9,250 lbs ....4,0 ton
Keel weight...................4,200 lbs ......1900 kg
Sail area ....430 sq. ft. ...39 sqm

Engine, ...Volvo Penta MD2B, 25 hp
Max speed under power 7.2k
Berths 6

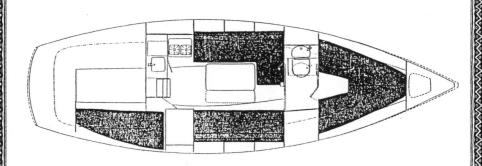

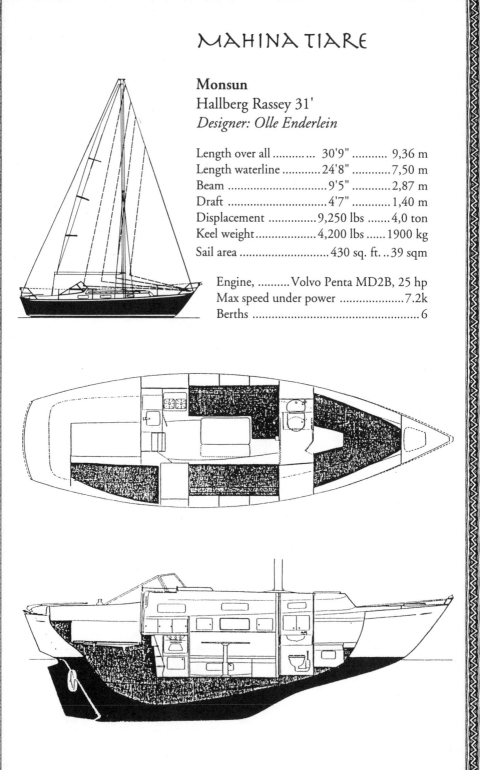

HALLBERG RASSY 31'

When I purchased *Mahina Tiare* in 1979, I was hoping to buy a larger boat, around 35'. The Hallberg Rassy Monsun caught my eye for several reasons and was within my budget of under $35,000. According to Hallberg Rassy Yacht owners, this was one of the best cruising boat yards in the world. I wouldn't have to worry about osmotic blisters, delaminating bulkheads, poor quality wiring, tankage and engine installation with a Hallberg Rassy yacht.

A hull shape that would be fast on all points of sail, could carry several thousand pounds of additional gear and tankage, would be comfortable at sea, and have a protected rudder was high on my list of priorities. The sailing performance was better than I expected, with our best 24 hour run of 173 miles, and many days of 150 to 160 mile runs. Because of the relative fine bow entry, modest beam and high ballast/displacement ratio (for a cruising boat) *Mahina Tiare* could consistently maintain 130+ miles per day, even close-hauled in tradewind conditions. Even with all of the cruising gear we added, we never had to raise the waterline. The easily-driven hull shape, large (25 h.p. Volvo) diesel engine and fixed three blade propeller translated into 1/4 gallon per hour fuel consumption and a maximum range under power of over 1200 miles at 6 knots and a top speed of 7.2 knots. Engine access was excellent through a hinged, gasketed cockpit sole.

After my first 23, 000 thousand miles through the South Pacific I had the area under the forepeak where some flexing had occurred reinforced with a transverse plywood riser, a new stronger battery box built and replaced the rigging. After 42,000 miles, the boat is still in excellent shape, and John Hamaty sailed her in the Fiji to Vanuatu race in 1992.

The gear that proved the most important and reliable over the years of cruising were the Monitor self-steering device, Avon Rover 310 sportboat with 7 1/2 hp Johnson outboard, 35 watt solar panel, Simpson-Lawrence 9555 manual 1,100 lb. anchor windlass, CQR anchors – 25 lb. and 35 lb., and ICOM fixed and handheld VHF radios and ICOM 735 ham radio. The Si-Tex A300 satellite navigator was a great help during several landfall situations in poor visibility.

Because of the quality and comfort of the Monsun 31, the boat we chose to replace her with is a 1983 Hallberg Rassy 42 ketch.

Chapter 19
CUTTING LOOSE
PREPARING YOUR BOAT AND YOURSELF

Personal Preparation: Undertaking an ocean cruise is a major lifestyle change for most of us. People tend to spend more time preparing their boats for sea than themselves.

Despite the growing number of competent woman skippers, the female partner is too often included in offshore cruising solely on the basis of being married to, or living with, a man with the dream. Unless she feels an integral part of the team, the relationship suffers on an ocean passage. It is vitally important to take each partner's fears, apprehensions, capabilities and interests into consideration when planning a cruise. Many cruises and relationships end because one of the partners doesn't feel comfortable at sea, or included in the overall planning of the cruise.

There are several ways to address these fears and concerns. One of the most important is that each person feel safe and comfortable sailing the boat, as well as being capable of retrieving an overboard partner. I have met several couples who had sailed thousands of miles, even though one of them (often the woman) doubted her ability to cope should her partner, often the only skilled navigator, fall overboard or suffer an injury.

Consider the following solutions to these very real concerns:

Choose a boat that even the smallest adult of the crew can singlehand. In most cases this is under 40 feet.

If any member of the crew lacks sailing experience, he or she should enroll in a sailing course taught by a professional. Women often find that female sailing instructors are the best teachers.

Practice man-overboard procedures using the Lifesling technique. If you sail in cold waters, for practicing purposes, the overboard person can wear a wet suit or sit in a dinghy. It is essential that every adult member of the crew be able to stop the boat and get the heaviest person back aboard using a pre-rigged block and tackle arrangement tailed to a winch. There have been several incidents in which the smaller partner was able to get their partner alongside the boat, only to watch them drown because they didn't have a method for lifting them back aboard.

Take a shakedown cruise on the ocean *before* undertaking a long voyage. This is important not only to learn what needs to be added or modified on the boat, but also so that each crewmember has a chance to see what lies ahead. Usually the first few days at sea are the hardest and scariest. Get as much blue-water experience as possible before you cast off your lines. Try to make an ocean passage with someone experienced before committing to go long distance cruising. Expect the first three days to be the most difficult. Seas are generally roughest and most confused when close to land, and your body must adjust to the motion and to new routines of eating, sleeping and standing watch. After the first three days, queasiness and anxiety usually fade.

Outfitting an Older Boat: *Mahina Tiare* was 11 years old and had served me well for 23,000 miles of sailing. It was clearly time to upgrade and replace some of the original equipment. I replaced the stove with a new stainless-steel, Optimus two-burner kerosene model and the heater with a new stainless Shipmate bulkhead kerosene heater. Most cruisers favor propane these days, but I've found that it takes a lot less space and weight to store a six-to-eight-month supply of kerosene. Kerosene is now more difficult to find in low-cost, pump-your-own outlets in the United States, but often is cheaper and easier to find in isolated cruising areas where it is widely used for cooking.

Other projects included sewing up a new dodger, backdrop and awning; anti-fouling the bottom with Petit Trinidad 75, which is great for the tropics; fiberglassing the V-berth where it came unbonded from the hull; installing new rings in the engine so it would start more easily; and rebuilding the head.

Rigging: We replaced the original standing rigging, which was ten years old. If the rigging on your boat is over five years old, particularly if it was made in the Orient, plan on replacing it before sailing offshore. You'll also want to have a spare length of stainless wire, as long as your longest stay, with an eye fitting in one end and tools to cut the wire and make an eye in the other end in the event of a rigging failure at sea. Also carry the appropriate size Norseman or Sta-Lok terminals or wire rope clips for 1 x 19 wire.

We replaced the halyards and topping lift with all-rope pre-stretched Dacron. Dacron is much easier on hands and masts than wire halyards. New England Rope's Sta-Set is top-rated and has performed well for us. We also replaced our sheets with prestretched braided Dacron.

We wanted to upgraded the Lewmar 40 two-speed sheet winches with larger, self-tailing winches. These winches are easier for one crew member to use and provide more power for winching the boat off in a grounding situation.

Sails: After rigging, sails are probably the most important gear on a cruising boat. Amazingly, they often seem to be one of the last priorities in the cruising outfitting budget. Having financially supported myself for three years of cruising by repairing sails, I strongly recommend having a sailmaker personally measure your boat, note peculiarities of your tracks and rig, and then build your sails with sufficient reinforcing and handwork to make them last for perhaps 15 years or 30,000 miles. Only a handful of sail lofts remain in the United States that do the handwork that protects sails from stress and chafe, and makes them hold up longer for offshore cruising. These lofts include; Hasse and Petrich, Port Townsend, WA and Schattauer Sails, Seattle, WA. Some of the differences in their sails compared with normal production sails include: external boltropes tapering to rat tails on mainsails; multi-layered, multi-tongue reinforcing patches in the corners of sails; hand-sewn jib hanks and sail slides; and hand-sewn grommets and clew rings.

Our inventory on *Mahina Tiare* included a new mainsail, a 120-percent lapper (this is the jib that is used 75-percent of the time), a 90-percent working jib, a 170-percent drifter made of 2.2 ounce Dacron, storm jib and storm trysail.

Ground Tackle: Another area that deserves attention is that of anchors, chain, windlasses and bow rollers. If you plan on sailing offshore, four working anchors, each with its own chain and nylon rope are a minimum. *Mahina Tiare* displaced 9,600 pounds; I kept a 35-pound CQR permanently mounted on the bow roller. I replaced the well-worn 135 feet of 5/16 inch proof coil chain with 200 feet of 5/16 inch BBB chain, followed by 150 feet of 5/8 inch nylon. Additional bow anchors were a 25-pound CQR and a 27-pound Danforth Hi-tensile light-weight type. I replaced my 13-pound Standard Danforth stern anchor that had bent into several interesting shapes when it became caught on coral heads.

I replaced the well-used, but reliable, Simpson-Lawrence Hyspeed windlass with a more powerful version (SL9555) to handle an additional amount of chain. An electric windlass would have been advantageous, but for simplicity's sake I stuck with a manual, two-speed windlass. For boats over 35 feet, or for those without sufficient strength, I would certainly go with a power windlass. Many cruisers install too small a windlass, then complain when it wears out quickly.

Tankage: *Mahina Tiare* came with one 45-gallon plastic water tank in the bow. To supplement this, we carried three five-gallon jerry jugs in the lazarette, plus one to three additional collapsible five-gallon jugs, depending on the length of the passage. This has proved sufficient for two people on passages up to 20 days, including a daily freshwater rinse-off. Many places where offshore cruisers sail do not have docks to accommodate sailboats alongside to fill tanks. With the 30-gallon capacity of our jerry-jugs, we were able to fill our tanks without too many trips back and forth in the dinghy.

Here are some tips on water storage while cruising in the tropics:

•Incorporate a water catchment system into your awning, using plastic thru-hull fittings with hose running to your water tank fill, or to a jerry jug.

•Don't fill tanks from shore water after a big rain. Even in some major cities like Honolulu, Hawaii, the drinking water becomes cloudy after a heavy downpour.

•Before filling your tanks with water from shore, ask other cruising boats in the harbor if there is a history of dysentery or hepatitis from the water. If there is, and there is no other source of water, boiling it vigorously will destroy the toxins.

•Another method of treatment is to add iodine tablets (available at pharmacies or sporting good stores) or five to ten drops (depending on clear or cloudy water) of two percent tincture of iodine from your first aid kit per liter of water. Clorox chlorine bleach can be added to water tanks to cut down algae growth, but it is not effective destroying giardia.

•Every four to six months, or when you have access to a hose, drain your tanks completely. Then add a few gallons of water and chlorine and scrub the tanks as best you can, using a long-handled scrub brush if necessary. Afterward, rinse the tank out twice to remove the chlorine taste. My water tank is under the V-berth in the bow. To drain it, I just remove the hose and allow the water to run the length of the boat back to the bilge sump, and give the bilges a scrub out at the same time. Don't use chlorine if you have aluminum tanks, as it reacts to the welds in the tanks.

•Install a water filter close to your galley tap.

•Replace clear PVC waterlines every five years to reduce "tank taste".

A way to reduce the amount of sediment that gets into your system is to pre-filter it. Before filling your tanks, fill a clear glass jar, hold it up to the sun and see if there are sediment particles suspended in it. If there are, pour the water into your tank through a funnel fitted with a sterile gauze pad suspended on a screen, or use a charcoal pre-filter (*these require adequate pressure from a hose*).

Fuel Tankage: In many cruising destinations, fuel is scarce and facilities primitive, so it may be necessary to bring jugs ashore by dinghy to fill them. It is a good idea to carry three or four five-gallon jerry jugs, but fill them with only 4-1/2 gallons and tie them securely so they can't tip over. If possible, stow them in a cockpit locker so they won't be degraded by the sunlight and so you won't be tripping over them in heavy weather. Otherwise, cover them with acrylic covers to protect the plastic from ultraviolet rays.

When filling your main tank, or jerry jugs that will be used to store diesel fuel, add the prescribed amount of diesel fuel bactericide-container to each tank. This will keep a jelly-like algae from growing in your fuel, which can be a real disaster to your tank and fuel system.

Self-Steering: Unless you're cruising with more than three people, a reliable self-steering vane is really a necessity. I've found that a dependable vane reduces exposure and fatigue, and makes ocean passages enjoyable, rather than an endurance contest. A comfortable, well-rested crew is able to make better and safer judgments than a crew that is fatigued.

Some vanes are better designed and use sturdier materials than others, but there isn't any one vane that will handle all types and sizes of boats.

Some points to keep in mind when shopping for a vane:

•Can the rudder be raised from the water when motoring or heaving to?

•Does the rudder have a break-away section so you won't destroy the vane if you sail over floating logs or debris?

•Is the vane constructed of non-corrosive materials (such as stainless steel or bronze, with Delrin parts), which will hold up well in a salty environment?

I had excellent service from my nine-year-old Monitor vane. I serviced it regularly and replaced the bushings and bearings as needed.

Autopilots are not a necessity for ocean cruising, but they are a great asset, particularly for motoring, for light air sailing, and for boats that won't respond to a mechanical wind vane. New devices have recently been introduced that combine both autopilot and wind vane units.

Dinghies: I feel that an inflatable dinghy with floorboards or hard bottom is unbeatable as a primary dinghy. After returning from my last cruise, I replaced my well-worn but dependable Avon Redcrest with an Avon 3.10 Sportboat that featured a wood transom and floorboards, an inflatable keel and beaching wheels that folds down. After we sold *Mahina Tiare* I bought an R.I.B. Rover 3.10 with fiberglass bottom. Contrary to what many people say, a well-designed inflatable with a keel or hard bottom rows quite well, provided that sufficiently long oars are used. However, such planing boats are at their best with a suitably large motor that takes them up to planing speeds. For the new dinghy I've chosen a 15 horsepower outboard. This is a heavy motor to lift aboard to its storage spot on the stern pulpit, but it provides enough power to plane with four people and can carry a heavy load of gear at speed. It has enabled us to be self-sufficient in getting ashore at isolated islands like Pitcairn, where many anchorages are far from the village or landing. The extra power is great for crashing through the surf and for reaching distant dive spots. I never carry gasoline below deck, nor do I carry it on board during ocean passages. In most cases, gasoline is available at the next port of entry.

Electronics: I kept the electronics to a minimum on *Mahina Tiare*, both because of reliability and cost. I continue to be amazed at the poor track record of some marine electronics when subjected to a year or more of offshore cruising, especially in the tropics. When last on Bora Bora, I rowed around the anchorage and conducted an unofficial poll. Few boats anchored at Bora Bora had functioning wind speed or direction instruments and there had been several failures of depth-sounders, knotmeters and logs. Bear in mind that the simpler the instrument, the greater the likelihood that the owner can troubleshoot and remedy problems without having to airfreight it to the manufacturer for repair. Digital read-outs offer quick readability, but if mounted in the cockpit they should be protected by a dodger or other cover to protect against long-term exposure to the elements.

The most basic instruments are a depth-sounder, knotmeter and log. A depth-sounder on a long-distance cruising boat should have a minimum range of 100 fathoms. Ideally it has a choice of scales-in feet, meters and fathoms, dual depth alarms and is completely sealed.

As for knotmeters and logs, the very simplest is the Walker-type trolling log. I personally don't care for trolling logs, as the line has a propensity for getting tangled in the propeller or the rudder can be fouled by floating seaweed and the rotator may be snapped by a shark. I prefer a thru-hull paddle-wheel-type log.

SatNavs were carried by more than half the boats actually "out there" long distance cruising a few years ago, but GPS, offering 24 hour fixes, is now the navigational aid of choice. A revealing statistic is that all of the yachts wrecked on reefs or islands in French Polynesia in 1985 carried SatNavs. GPS and SatNav are great tools for navigation, but they do not replace the sextant for celestial navigation, or the critically important task of dead reckoning. It is important to remember that few of the charts available are anywhere nearly as accurate as GPS or SatNav, so be careful!

After GPS, radar and weatherfax are next on my personal list of optional electronics. I am a real chicken when it comes to heavy weather sailing, and try to use every available piece of weather information in planning departure times of passages and in avoiding storms at sea. Since I don't own a weatherfax each time before leaving on a passage, I either visit or call the local weather office or monitor single-sideband high-seas weather broadcasts. I try to plot and follow the weather daily for a week before departure. An easy way to do this is to lay a clear sheet of plastic over a large chart of the ocean and to mark the weather systems (highs, lows, ridges, troughs and so on) with a different colored marking pen each day. I continue to do this daily while at sea. During hurricane season, I also do this while at anchor. I also receive much helpful weather information from ham radio and single side-band nets and other boats and ships at sea equipped with these radios.

Single-sideband transceivers are used on nearly all oceangoing commercial ships and are an excellent option for cruisers not able to get a ham license, or needing to be able to place business calls to the U.S., Canada and Mexico. There are now several informal nets throughout the world utilizing SSB frequencies. Unlike ham radios, marine SSB radios are built for marine use, and allow you to legally order parts, check on bills and bank balances.

Ham radio is a very useful tool for getting emergency medical advice, weather data or information about your next port of call. Many 12-volt transceivers also feature full-coverage shortwave reception, useful for picking up SSB weather broadcasts, weatherfax transmissions and WWV time signals. I have had excellent results using a small Hustler vertical-whip antenna, without a tuner, mounted on deck near the stern pulpit. This is a very simple three-to four-foot antenna designed for use on car bumpers. It requires changing screw-on tips for different bands and a good grounding system.

Radar is a great navigational tool for coastwise sailing and obstacle avoidance and is useful for spotting reefs and low islands in the tropics. The antenna is somewhat susceptible to moisture and corrosion problems in the tropics. Radar, even more than other electronic instruments, should be turned on and allowed to run at least one day per week in the tropics to allow it to "dry itself out."

Refrigeration: Refrigeration is a luxury that many cruisers opt for today and expect to work, with mixed results. The amount of insulation is critical to efficiency, but even the best designed and insulated refrigeration systems on board need one to three hours of engine running daily in the tropics. My personal preference is for either skipping refrigeration or going with a low cost thermal-electric icebox insert (like the Unifridge) or a 12-volt, compressor driven system. With these systems you aren't tied to running your engine, but can instead power them with wind, trolling or solar generators. If you opt for compressor-driven refrigeration, it is an excellent idea to learn how to bleed and refill your system, and carry the tools, gauges and spare Freon to recharge your system.

Generating Power: Carrying a lot of electrical devices places heavy demands on the ship's power plant, often necessitating running the main engine several hours per day. Besides shortening its life, running the main engine for a couple of hours at anchor generates a lot of heat, even several hours after it's turned off. This is fine in the higher altitudes, but can be pretty uncomfortable in the tropics. I personally think that adding a separate generator, whether a permanently in-stalled diesel generator or a portable gas generator, is not the best solution for small and medium-sized boats. I have had reliable service from a trolling generator that continuously provided five amps of electricity when sailing at five knots. This has proved to be enough power to run my tri-color running light, compass lights, interior cabin lights, ham radio, cassette deck and small electric refrigerator on long passages without starting the engine for weeks. A trolling water generator can be adapted to function as a wind-driven generator that is very useful at anchor particularly in the trade winds. I've also added a 30-watt movable solar panel mounted on the stern pulpit.

Instead of bringing along 110-volt power tools and a generator to power them, I purchased a 12-volt drill, soldering iron and sewing machine motor. If you have some 110-volt tools or appliances that you can't live without, consider purchasing an inverter, which changes 12-volts DC to 110-volts AC and is much smaller, lighter and less expensive than a diesel or gas generator.

Would I have preferred to have a larger boat for this voyage? Sure, it would have been great to have more storage space for provisions and for projects. But *Mahina Tiare* was paid for, proven, and a very comfortable boat at sea.

280

Chapter 20
KEEPING IN TOUCH
HANDLING MAIL, PHONE, FAX, E-MAIL

Communication. We wish we could cruise without worrying about phone calls, faxes and mail, but the reality is we are often conducting business while we cruise. Staying in touch with home is a necessity, not only a pleasure. Cruisers often end up playing tag across the ocean with their mail, waiting weeks for letters and packages waylaid in their last port. If you follow these guidelines for mail and package handling, your communications can get through.

1. Designate one person in your home country to forward mail. Have all your business and personal mail sent to this designated person. Do not give friends a projected itinerary. Weather, customs officials and whim will change your itinerary.

2. When you are sure of your next reliable address, have mail forwarded altogether in a padded mailer secured with strapping tape. If more than one package of mail is sent, have your forwarder mark the envelopes, 1 of 2, 2 of 2, etc. This way you'll know to look for more than one package.

3. Because word order varies country to country, have your forwarder avoid using your middle name, or Mr., Ms., Mrs. Have your surname appear in capital letters. When a clerk checks for mail, ask that they look under both your first and last name as well as the boat's name (if it has been included in the address). Check for mail in both the ordinary mail area and the parcel area. Be prepared to show your passport.

4. Have your mail forwarder mark the outside of the mail envelope: "Hold for arrival of yacht in transit." The forwarder will need to fill out a green customs declaration slip for anything that isn't obviously a single letter. Make sure this is filled out, "Contents: forwarded mail,

no commercial value," otherwise it may be held up in customs and mired in red tape. If you are having a package sent with spare parts, have the invoice packed outside the box in a separate envelope. The box should be marked for "Yacht in transit." Customs agents will generally allow spare parts into the country duty-free.

5. Have mail sent to a reliable place. Our choice for mail pick-up is American Express offices. You must either be a card holder or have an Am-Ex traveler's check to receive this service. They will hold mail for at least a month or until you arrive (time varies from place to place). For a $4 fee they will forward your mail up to one year. You can pick up a brochure which lists the addresses of their international offices at any branch.

In our experience, Port Captains' offices don't cut it. It's not their business to play post office. Mail often ends up in a big pile available for anyone to sort through and it doesn't get forwarded.

We've been to several yacht clubs catering to cruisers who do a conscientious job of sorting and holding mail.

Most general delivery mail at post offices (including the U.S.) is held two weeks then returned to sender, often by surface post. If you miss your mail, arrange to have a fellow cruiser re-address it and forward it airmail.

General delivery mail is picked up at the city's main post office. Mail sent this way should be addressed care of General Delivery. Outside the U.S. some English-speaking countries and all French-speaking countries call General Delivery, "Post Restante." Spanish-speaking countries call it "Lista de Correos."

If you have a ham radio or single sideband radio, talk to the cruisers in your next port of call to find out the most reliable way to handle mail.

6. Regardless of where your mail is sent, let the office know your expected arrival time and ask them to hold mail for you. We have seen post offices in major ports hold mail longer than two weeks for yachts that sent a postcard asking mail be held until a specific date.

7. Never have mail sent to a place you plan to stay for only a few days. Depending on the port, you may have to factor in several weeks for inefficient mail service.

8. Don't have mail sent until you are sure you are certain of your next destination. Beating to weather can be a very persuasive reason for

a change of itinerary. If you have a ham or single side band radio (SSB), you can call your mail forwarder en route, timing the mail arrival with your own. Air mail generally averages two weeks in major ports worldwide. Calling or writing from your last port of call is less desirable; a lot can change on a passage.

9. Postage rates for domestic and foreign mail are generally much higher worldwide than in the U.S. Sending aerograms (lightweight three-fold sheets available at post offices worldwide) will save up to half the rate for an ordinary air-mail letter. U.S. territories, such as American Samoa, U.S. Virgin Islands and Guam, charge domestic postage rates on letters sent to the U.S.

10. Courier services, such as DHL, Federal Express or U.P.S. are available in many major ports worldwide, assuring you of delivery within a few days of shipment. Surface mail is not a good option for packages, which may take from two to six months, and may never arrive.

11. Ads for professional mail and bill-paying services can be found in the classified sections of many cruising magazines. Tracy's Homebase, P.O. Box 3289, Friday Harbor, WA 98250 (360)378-4359 is recommended by many cruisers.

Fax machines can be found at many main post offices or telecommunication offices in major ports or resort hotels. Be prepared to pay an average of $12 per page.

Arrange for an AT&T International Telephone Credit Card before you leave (dial 1-800-CALL-ATT) You'll save up to half the cost of the call placed in most countries by paying with AT&T credit card, and will usually not have to use a telephone office to place the call. In Third World countries many cruisers rely on their ham or single side band radios to place calls.

If you have a ham radio aboard, give your telephone credit card number to a ham operator in your home country who is willing to do phone patches for you. Never give the card number over the radio! This is an inexpensive way to keep in touch with family and friends, but it is illegal to use amateur radio for ordering parts or conducting business.

Marine single sideband opens up worldwide communication to those who have not passed a Morse code 13 word-per-minute test and received a General Class Amateur Radio license. Prerequisites are: SSB radio and tuner ($2,000-$4,000), radiotelephone station and operator's licenses (contact: FCC, P.O. Box 1040, Gettysburg, PA 17325), and a radio station log book.

A single side band radio allows you to make calls through AT&T High Seas Radio Service. AT&T has three coast stations:
KMI, Point Reyes, California (415) 669-1055 collect
WOM, Ft. Lauderdale, Florida (305) 587-0910 or 800 538-5936
WOO, Manahawkin, New Jersey (609) 597-2201 collect

To register for the AT&T service, call 1-800-752-0279. No charge for registering. You have several billing options when placing a call from your boat with the High Seas operator including: collect, bill to a third number or your calling card. You are charged only for the amount of time that you actually talk to your party. At $5.00 a minute, charges may seem expensive. However, often costs are less than placing calls through the telecommunications office in foreign countries.

By purchasing a modem which links your SSB radio and a portable computer, servers such as Pin Oak Digital and Globe Wireless Company will allow you to send and receive e-mail through the SSB. Since this system is dependent on good radio propagation and channel availability, it is not as dependable as SAT-COM systems.

A SAT-COM C system provides direct satellite link for sending and receiving e-mail, fax or telex messages utilizing its own antenna and modem connected to your PC. The cost, approximately $4,000 for the unit and 1¢ per character, is greater than e-mail systems utilizing ham or SSB radios. However, it is the choice of those who must communicate with home or business on a regular basis. In addition, the system has a built in GPS and EPIRB giving vessel I.D. and location in an emergency.

At a cost of approximately $8,000, SAT-COM M which allows direct voice and data access at roughly $5.00 per-minute charge, is the choice of those who require reliable voice communication worldwide. The required 2 amps of power to receive calls may make it impractical for some cruisers to leave it on 24 hours a day.

Cellular phones are now in use in the Caribbean and many inland and coastal waterways. The more affordable satellite and cellular worldwide communications systems which are on the horizon will make it nearly impossible to stay out of touch, unless you want to be.

Chapter 21
THE COST OF CRUISING
FINDING WORK

It's time to share the nitty-gritty part of cruising: the cost. We wrote this chapter in New Zealand because this is where reality hits for many Pacific cruisers. They haul their boats out for the first time in a year or two and are faced with the accumulated wear and tear they've ignored up until this point. They look into their spare parts and provisions lockers only to find that the cupboards are bare. Unless they have carefully budgeted, their pocket books are empty as well.

You can't live on coconuts in New Zealand, and trading for fish and fruit doesn't cut it either. It's hard to get around without a car and it's inconvenient or difficult to anchor out in many places. Being in New Zealand means spending more money than most people have planned.

The solution: budget more carefully or GET A JOB. Many cruisers who spend the hurricane season in New Zealand and Australia, work. Some even chose to spend an entire year replenishing their cruising funds.

The best way to land a good job is to plan ahead. Write to the Department of Immigration, or stop by any consulate and request their List of Needed Job Skills brochure. If your particular skill is listed, contact perspective employers and get a formal letter of employment before you arrive. Rick Berg of *Sueno* had a job waiting for him as an economics professor at Auckland University by planning ahead.

In reality, most cruisers do not plan ahead; still, many were granted permission to work after they had arrived. They were able to get formal offers of employment. Mark Insley and Kelly O'Neill were building Michael Fay's luxurious new office building in Auckland and Scott Kuhner was having a ball making calls to former Wall Street cronies to set up appointments for brokers from Fay's banking and investment company.

It took nurses, doctors, and dentists several months to get accepted into their respective professional bodies before they could seek employment. Two nurses, a doctor, a dentist, a clinical psychologist and a lab technician from cruising boats found work in their fields after jumping through many bureaucratic hoops. Ivor Wilkens, a South African journalist, cruised to New Zealand and landed a permanent job as the foreign editor of the *Auckland Star*.

Others worked in low profile jobs under the table (without work permits) housecleaning, varnishing, and doing boat carpentry. There has been an exodus (fully 10 percent of the population) of talented, energetic, and educated New Zealanders to Australia, Canada and the U.S. This exodus, combined with their open-door policy toward unskilled islanders and welfare programs, has hurt New Zealand's economy. Skilled labor jobs go begging. Cruisers have developed a reputation as energetic, reliable workers and are taking advantage of opportunities offered to them.

So how much does it really cost to cruise? It takes as much as you have. After outfitting, we had $600 a month to spend our first year cruising. We sailed to remote anchorages, had no breakdowns or haul out charges, and stayed within this budget. Our second year we had $1,300 a month to spend, and guess how much we spent? Right, a little over $1,000 a month, including a haul-out, replacing two deep-cycle batteries, plus some touring and nights in modest hotels.

A definite correlation exists between your lifestyle on land and your lifestyle and spending habits cruising. Cruisers who tie up at fancy marinas, frequently eat out, and go touring on land spend more than the frugal cruisers who anchor out, catch their own food, or eat with the natives.

Where you choose to cruise will affect your budget as well. French Polynesia, Scandinavia, the Med and New Zealand are far more expensive to cruise than Mexico, Venezuela, or Spain. Other variables affecting the cost of cruising include the size, age, construction material, and condition of your boat. The number, age and condition of crew will also affect costs.

Preventative maintenance of the sails, engine, rigging, and boat equipment makes a difference to your cost of cruising. It obviously makes more sense to buy new rigging versus putting it off and having to replace the mast after the rig crashes at sea. Likewise, spending the money to have sails and engine overhauled before leaving the U.S. makes more sense than waiting to see what breaks once you're "out there" where repairs are difficult and expensive.

The quality of equipment and sails you install when outfitting really affects your cruising costs, more in the second and third year than at the start. Buying the least expensive equipment is the least cost effective over the long run. On a cruising boat you're using the gear all the time, not only a few weeks a year. Better to spend an extra 20 percent for the top-of-the-line radios, electronics, and sails and know that they will hold up better with fewer expensive (and often difficult to get) repairs later.

When figuring the cost of cruising, remember that the dollars you spend on provisions, spare parts, navigation books and charts, and boat supplies before you leave on your trip will affect how much you spend while cruising. Spare parts in foreign countries almost always cost more — if available. Carrying what you need prevents waiting months in expensive ports for elusive spare parts plus saving you expensive air freight costs.

Monthly expenses the first year cruising outside the U.S.A. may seem deceptively low; you are living off what you bought before you left and you will likely have no haul-out or major repairs. The reason I say outside the U.S. is that people who spend their first year cruising in Hawaii or continental states seem to blow their budgets, spending a lot more money than those who leave the country. It's easy to spend money here and it takes leaving the U.S. to shift to a more frugal lifestyle.

Don't base your budget on what you spend the first year out unless you remain in the same spot subsequent years. Cruising costs vary widely year to year, and unexpected costs replacing a lost dinghy or outboard or having to rebuild an engine do crop up.

If you buy a boat and outfit it to cruise offshore, expect to spend 30 to 50 percent (I've heard up to 100 percent) more than the purchase price for gear unless you plan to cruise without engines or electronics. Typical cruisers over-spend their budget buying the boat, then over-spend still more on outfitting, leaving only a small amount for living expenses. Keep in mind that what money you have left after outfitting plus monthly income (if any) creates your cruising kitty. Buying a less expensive boat, and saving money earmarked for some fancy cruising gadgets may mean you can enjoy a few more months cruising some fantastic area!

We've compiled a list of what we spent on *Mahina Tiare, before* we left the U.S. and then a list of what we spent *while cruising.* Our 11-year old boat was already outfitted to cruise offshore and had 23,000 miles under her keel. Had she not cruised previously we would have added a windvane, autopilot, single-sideband or ham radio, life-raft, GPS, storm sails, and more charts and pilot books to the list below. These items would have **more than doubled** our pre-departure costs.

Costs Before Cruising:

Medical and dental supplies:	$285.00
Charts and navigation books ($800+ already on board):	$125.00
One set foul weather gear, sailing clothes, deck boots:	$246.00
Safety harness and Lifesling:	$185.00
Re-rigging (includes an insulated backstay, $110):	$694.00
Anchor lines, sheets, and halyards:	$626.00
New anchor windlass:	$548.00
Sail modification:	$134.00
Misc. boat supplies:	$1,485.00
Haul-out, epoxy barrier coat bottom:	$1,319.00
Interior woodwork, cushion cleaning, new battery and chain boxes:	$800.00
Engine top-end overhaul (valves, rings, de-carboning):	$1,500.00
Spare parts (for engine, head, etc.):	$890.00
Deep cycle batteries:	$198.00
Snorkeling gear, wetsuit, used scuba tank:	$450.00
Total tab:	**$9,485.00**

Note: Most of the above prices are discount prices. Food costs are figured into the first year's budget below.

Costs for 13 Months Cruising, First Year Out:

Cruising ground: French Polynesia, Cook Islands, Galapagos, Easter Island.

Postage and office supplies (business):...............................$285.00

Postage, cards, and stationery (personal):............................$385.00

Gifts, clothes, souvenirs:..$635.00

Film and camera supplies (business and personal):.............$219.00

Eating out:..$400.00

Food, liquor, ice (includes provisioning before we left): ...$3,713.00

Moorage, exit fees, anchoring fees:...................................$328.00

Kerosene and engine oil:...$99.00

Diesel fuel and gasoline for the outboard: $482.00

Laundry:..$28.00

Bank fees, wire transfers, etc.:...$66.00

Mail forwarding and bill-paying service:.............................$75.00

Phone calls (mostly business):..$287.00

Boat purchases, misc.:...$281.00

Total tab: **$7,283.00**

$7,283 divided by 13 months =...........................**$560.00/month**

If we add in the total pre-departure costs, the average comes to $1,289.00 a month for the first 13 months of cruising.

Costs for 7.5 Months Cruising, Second Year Out:

Cruise included three months in Hawaii, three in Western Pacific, one half in New Zealand.

Medical and dental supplies: $30.00

Postage and office supplies (business):...............................$254.00

Postage, cards, and stationery (personal):............................$250.00

Freight (excess baggage and UPS charges bringing gear back with us)
....$165.00

Gifts, clothes, souvenirs:..$323.00

Film and camera supplies (business and personal):.............$208.00

Eating out:..$140.00

Food:...$2,323.00

Liquor: $100.00

Moorage, exit fees, anchoring fees:...................................$450.00

Kerosene and gasoline for outboard engine: $22.00

Diesel fuel: $123.00
Laundry: $25.00
Entertainment (movies, taxi, hotel, bus trips): $246.00
Car rentals, ferry fares: $246.00
Bank fees: $30.00
Bill paying and mail forwarding: $188.00
Phone calls (mostly business): $316.00
Electronic repairs (SatNav and two depth sounders): $338.00
Boat purchases and haul-out (bottom paint, batteries): $2,305.00
Total tab:... **$8,027.00**
$8,027.00 divided by 7.5 months = ...**$1,070.00/month**

Note:: Airfare to return to the U.S. to work: ($488 round trip from Hawaii) and ($1,966.80 round trip to New Zealand) was not figured into the above itemizing. If we added our airfare, monthly average becomes $1,397.00. Cruisers seem to return home once every year to three years so it is wise to figure in airfare when figuring your budget.

Every one of the ten Pacific countries we visited in the last few years charged an entry or exit fee for either the boat or its passengers. In addition, port fees or anchoring fees. Rarely did the fees total more than $50 per country, but the fees add up when you visit six countries in a season.

Like many cruisers, we carried no health or boat insurance while cruising. Although our cruising ground varied, we averaged $300 to $350 a month for food for two people. Writing articles, taking photos professionally, and conducting business as we cruised meant higher than average phone bills, postage, and film costs. On the other hand, we spent less for liquor, souvenirs, gear breakdowns so our costs were similar to the average couple cruising on a 30- to 40-foot boat. All of the long distance cruisers we spoke to in Fiji and New Zealand (people who had sailed over 10,000 miles and been out at least two years), were spending more than $1,000 a month per couple in 1989. Yet just about everyone we spoke to on similar sized boats cruising Mexico or Central America was spending less than $1,000 per month. We know couples cruising on $400 a month, others on $2,000, but the money they spend is not proportional to the fun they are having.

The key to a successful budget is planning one that realistically assesses outfitting costs, fits your cruising lifestyle, and takes into account where you will cruise.

One more thought — we keep a reserve in an interest-bearing account for emergencies, such as a dismasting, medical crisis, or unexpected trip home. If, like us, you are not retired, this money is essential for re-entry expenses such as buying a car and getting set up to work. Instead of working abroad to replenish our cruising funds, we choose to return to the U.S. every seven to 12 months. This allows us to visit family and friends while earning money for our next cruise.

Chapter 22

CRUISING DESTINATION TIPS

How to get to the Galapagos
Be prepared for a two-tiered pricing system on several items, ranging from airfare and park admissions to food and fuel. One price for Ecuadorians, one for visitors.

The entire island group is a military district, administered by the navy, which closely controls all matters including immigration, customs and movement of vessels. The navy's headquarters are at Puerto Baquerizo Moreno, (Wreck Bay) San Cristobal Island, one of two ports of entry. It is better to check in at Academy Bay, Santa Cruz Island where there are more amenities.

There are three modes of travel to the Galapagos, the most difficult by private yacht. The passage is about 30 days from California, 9 days from Panama, or 4 days from Cocos Island. The real difficulties are getting permission from the Ecuadorian government for permission to visit the islands longer than 72 hours. And to see any other anchorages other than the two ports of entry. To get a detailed set of instructions and application in English, contact the Ecuadorian Embassy 2535 15th Street, Washington D.C. 20009 (202) 234-7200.

We recommend you apply a year in advance, five months at the minimum. When you start getting nervous because your permission has not arrived (maybe three months before your departure) call the Embassy in D.C. The Embassy may say that there really isn't anything they can do. Have your congressman give the embassy a call; after that happens it is usually smooth sailing.

Once you arrive in the Galapagos with your permission, you must hire a guide if you want to visit the outer islands ($30 to $50 per day for an English-speaking naturalist, $20 to $30 per day for a Spanish-speaking auxiliary guide, plus meals), and give a proposed itinerary to the port captain to approve. Even without prior permission the port captain may allow you to stay a week or longer, but will charge you a moorage fee.

Several islands are not open to tourists. The ones that are, have specific landing spots and trails which the guides will show you. This is definitely the way to go if you are sailing on your own boat. You'll learn a tremendous amount from the guide who will travel with you, and you won't have to be looking over your shoulder, worrying whether the navy is going to catch and fine you or throw you in an Ecuadorian prison. An option for seeing some more of the islands — if you arrive on your own boat without a cruising permit — is leave your boat anchored in Academy Bay with crew or guard aboard and take a cruise on one of the local charter boats.

About 300 cruising yachts per year stop in the Galapagos, four days is an average stay. A very small percentage will have cleared the hurdles and received a cruising permit.

Most yachts use the Galapagos as a place to stop and break up the long ocean passage from Panama or Central American to French Polynesia. Fresh produce is available on certain days in Puerto Ayora, an excellent selection can be found at the farmer's market on Saturday morning. A large supermarket/hardware store has a good selection of canned goods, a reasonable selection of refrigerated items and a modest frozen food section.

The recent introduction of satellite telecommunications has made telephoning from Port Ayora much easier than in the recent past. Changing money is a breeze and many stores have signs in the windows stating, "We buy dollars." A good selection of boating supplies is available. Skilled mechanics and boat workers can be hired through the navy base. Even a Volvo Penta parts dealer can be found.

The second way to get to the Galapagos is by ship; three of which make the scheduled trip at least once a month. The nicest (and most expensive) ship is the cruise ship *Santa Cruz*, which is owned by the Metropolitan Touring Company. It sails once a month to Guayaquil to pick up supplies and passengers. It normally cruises the islands on a weekly schedule, starting and ending in Academy Bay.

The *Buccanero* is an old freighter converted into a cruise ship that has a similar schedule, but is not as well organized as the *Santa Cruz*.

If you are really on a budget you could take the monthly supply ship from Guayaquil, the rusty old *Pinta*.

The third, and easiest, way to reach the Galapagos is to fly to Quito and then fly to Baltra Island (near Santa Cruz Island) on TAME airline.

If you book ahead, you can go directly from the airplane to your chartered sail or power boat, complete with guide. The boats range in size from a handsome 32-foot cutter to a 108-foot classic motor yacht, and several are equipped for scuba diving. Arrange your boat charter before arrival, the boats run full.

Bond Information for French Polynesia

As of November 1997, it was possible to apply for and receive a temporary three-month visa upon arrival in the Marquesas at either Taiohae or Atuona. Expect to deposit approximately a $900 bond per person (including owner-skipper) into a trust account at the local bank, or have a return ticket to your home country on board. If you plan to arrive in Papeete, Tahiti within 30 days, the Gendarme may let you wait until you arrive there to post bond. If you are staying in the territory less than 30 days you will not need a visa, nor need to post a bond. If you would like to extend your visit over three months you must go to Papeete to apply for an extension for an additional three months. Bond money will be returned when you clear-out of the territory.

You may also obtain a three month visa in advance from the French Consulate before you leave the U.S. Authorities request visiting yachts leave the territory by mid-October, the beginning of hurricane season. Yachts may return in April, the end of official hurricane season.

Tahiti Information / Clearing Customs

When arriving in Papeete for the first time, even if coming from the Marquesas or the Tuamotus, fly a yellow quarantine flag and check in with Immigration, Customs and Harbormaster at the first opportunity. Offices are conveniently located in one building by the quay.

When checking in, bring along the yacht's registration and ownership papers, all passports, the green "Passeport du Navire Etranger" issued at your first port, receipts of deposits made with the bank for bonds or airline tickets for each person (including owner) back to

Hawaii. Also, any papers or documents that demonstrate your financial resource: credit cards, a letter from your bank stating your balances, savings passbooks, letters documenting income from house rental or retirement. The men that run these three offices are courteous if approached with the proper attitude. They take their jobs seriously. Used to dealing with professional ships' captains, they think nothing of throwing improperly dressed, rude yachties out of their office, out of their country. Attitude and appearance make a huge difference in dealing with these officials: a clean sports shirt and shorts or slacks for men, dresses for women (not shorts and T-shirt) are in order here.

These men have seen plenty "Ugly Americans" over the years. Don't even think of trying to pull something over on them. If you're polite and play by the rules, they are great guys. Twice customs officers have invited us home for lunch.

The harbor charges in Papeete are reasonable, and much less than in most West Coast cities. There is a one-time only charge to enter the harbor (about $40) and the daily rate for a 35-foot boat to drop a bow anchor and tie stern-to along the shoreline in the "low rent" district is $4. It costs more to tie stern-to the quay in the "high rent" district where 110 and 220 volt power and water is available, but this space is generally full of local boats.

A much quieter anchorage is four miles around the corner of the island, past the airport at Maeva Beach where there are some moorings available for visiting yachts. Ashore are shower, laundry, telephone, fax and garbage facilities at Tahiti Aquatique, run by Dick Johnson, an American. He also acts as agent for the Port and collects modest monthly charges for use of the moorings. The Maeva Beach Hotel offers a nightly Tahitian dance program at 10 p.m. so buy a drink at the poolside bar, sit back and enjoy the dancing and music under the stars. The buffet dinners are expensive but outrageously good!

It is possible to haul your boat in Tahiti for about the same cost as in Hawaii, but you may have to wait a few weeks for an opening at one of the two marine railways. Petit, International and Woolsey paints are available, along with parts for Perkins, Volvo, Cat, Johnson, Evinrude, Mercury, Mariner and Yamaha engines. Several small welding shops (Soudure) are located near the shipyards. Excellent stainless steel welding and fabrication at reasonable prices. The French Navy also has extensive machine shops and will help yachties if the local machine shops can't solve a problem. Two sail lofts in Papeete do good work at fair prices. An excellent new boatyard with the only Travelift in French Polynesia has recently opened near Utaroa, Raiatea, about 100 miles west of Tahiti. Raiatea Carenage is expertly run by Henri Valin, an ex-cruiser and manager of The Moorings charter operation. Marine supplies, sail, engine and refrigeration repairs are available.

About a half-mile south from Maeva Beach Hotel is the Moana Nui shopping center. Moana Nui is home to Continent, French Polynesia's equivalent to a super Safeway, K Mart and Sears all rolled into one.

Continent is clean, air-conditioned, and overwhelming. The selection of food, tools and clothes is incredible: strawberries, blueberries, mushrooms, broccoli, lamb, beef and excellent cheeses from New Zealand and Australia; wine, crackers and cookies from Chile; escargot, pates, sausages and smoked salmon from France; frozen scallops, prawns and fish from Iceland; nuts and dried fruit from Africa.

We did our first major provisioning here after seven months of cruising. An added bonus to fair prices and choices is no cockroaches or weevils in the food from Continent. The air-conditioning and quick turnover of stock probably accounts for the lack of bugs.

French Polynesia is expensive when compared to the U.S. Overall prices are probably 50 to 100 percent higher, on an item-for-item basis. But there aren't any sales or income taxes in the territory. Import duties alone raise capital for the government operations and services. Highest duty items include liquor, cigarettes, perfume, junk food, fancy food, cars. No duties (no profit at Continent) on a list of essential food items that includes rice, flour, sugar, dried beans, pasta, powdered milk. On the plus side, powdered milk, butter, cheese, lamb and beef from New Zealand are often cheaper and better quality than in the States. Good French and Chilean wines start at $6 per bottle.

If you can resist Pringles, peanuts and hard liquor, you can get by in Papeete without fatally damaging your cruising budget. If you are headed west, Pago Pago, American Samoa is only a few months away — and there you'll find the best prices in the South Pacific.

Hints for Cruising the Big Island of Hawaii

Charlie's Charts of Hawaii and, to a lesser extent, *Charlie's Charts of Polynesia* contain excellent practical information. Remember, a $25 U.S. Customs entry fee, payable once a year, will only be charged to you when you clear customs back into the U.S. after sailing from a foreign port. You can also expect to pay $8.40 a day for a boat under 40', slightly more for larger boats, to moor in a commercial harbor. The State of Hawaii issues temporary moorage permits for a maximum of 30 days at a time in each commercial harbor. However, space available, you may keep renewing the permit. Unrestricted harbors have a 72 hour stay limit and are free.

In Hilo, water is available along the wharf in **Radio Bay,** shower and bathroom facility is nearby. A 200 gallon minimum single purchase is required for the fuel truck to service Radio Bay. Most cruisers fuel up at Honokahau Harbor's fuel dock on the west side of the island, or jerry jug it from Hilo. Propane tanks can be filled at the Gas Pro store three blocks away. The Safeway in Prince Kuhio Mall or the Wal-Mart across the street are the best spots to provision on this side of the island. You can ride the county bus to the malls or use the free shuttle vans from Radio Bay on days the cruise ships are tied up.

From Hilo, two ways of sailing around the island are possible. The roughest area in the state is around Ka Lae (South Cape). For a mellower passage, sail northwest from Hilo along the Hamakua Coast and around Upolu Point. Expect to pick up at least a knot of current and have the winds behind you on this trip. The first possible overnight anchorage is Mahukona, 66 miles from Hilo.

Mahukona is near an abandoned sugar mill. The area provides interesting hikes, but the anchorage is often uncomfortably rolly.

Kawaihae, 10 miles south, is one of the best all-weather anchorages in the state. A large man-made breakwater to the north and smaller breakwater to the south provide several anchoring or mooring options to yachts and commercial boats. The harbormaster can direct you to the most appropriate spot. Puukohola Heiau, an important Hawaiian religious site, overlooks the harbor. The interpretive center offers a fascinating look at native Hawaiian culture.

The coastline between Kawaihae and Honokohau Harbor, 24 miles south, is often subject to strong gusts of wind coming down from the mountains. Hug the coast and be ready to reduce sail quickly.

Honokohau Harbor, completely man-made, is one of the newest small boat harbors in the state, blasted and dredged out of solid lava. The harbor is nearly chock-a-block with expensive sportfishing charterboats. The only fuel dock on the island is located inside the entrance, and the harbormaster's office is located behind the dock. Even if the harbor looks full, they can usually find you a spot for a few days. You may clear customs at Honokohau Harbor.

Gentry's Kona Marina is an excellent boat yard located inside the harbor, the easiest place in Hawaii to have your boat hauled. Besides a new Travelift and paved work and storage yard, several small boat-related repair businesses are located in the boat yard. The prices at the yard are lower than most on the West Coast. Gentry's stored *Mahina Tiare* when we flew back to the States to work for a few months. Dry storage space, once very limited, has been recently expanded. If you want to leave your boat or schedule a haul-out, contact them at (808) 329-7896.

Kailua Kona, four miles south of Honokohau, has little to offer the cruising sailor, other than good provisioning at the new Cost-Co store. The anchorage is rolly and tourist shops abound.

Kealakekua Bay, where Captain Cook was killed in 1779, is one of the most dramatic and historic bays in Hawaii. A monument to Cook stands near the lighthouse. The northern part of the bay is an underwater park (no anchoring), but you'll find good anchorage in the southern end of the bay, out from the beach in 40 feet with good holding, on a sand bottom. Some of the most spectacular snorkeling in Hawaii is found in Kaawaloa Cove near Cook's monument. About five miles south from Kealakekua is Pu'uhonua O Honaunau (City of Refuge). At one time a sacred sanctuary for tabu or law breakers, it is now a fascinating park with restored buildings and carvings. You may hitchhike, or possibly anchor offshore for the day, to explore the village.

Milolii 18 miles south of Kealakekua, is an exposed and rolly anchorage. When I first went ashore here in 1974, I thought I was in a time warp, whisked back 50 years. There is no electricity in the village, and outrigger canoes are pulled up on the beach with nets hung on lines to dry in the sun. When we went ashore this time, the door to the only store was wide open, and a white cat, the only occupant, slept on a dusty wooden counter. After a few minutes a Hawaiian man appeared, "Big Al", a cousin to the owner who was taking a nap. Until his relative returned he kept us company. He told about fishing from his open 14-foot boat every day and offered to show us the village church that he had restored. They had used all local hardwoods in the restoration and his pride in the craftsmanship was obvious. For us it was reassuring to find a village where Hawaiian people still lived their own lifestyle, no tourist buses or hotels interfering in their lives, not even electricity.

Okoe Bay, two miles south, is a much better anchorage with sandy patches among the coral in depths of about 30 feet. We set bow and stern anchors in these open roadstead anchorages. The wind generally reverses direction, coming from the land at night, and the stern anchor keeps the yacht headed into the swell. Big Al told us about the importance of the heiaus or temples and a holua or slide ashore at Oke Bay. Ashore, we were surrounded by reminders of an earlier civilization and, when we looked up at the hills, we saw a paved stone walkway — the "King's Highway" — extending over the top of a distant ridge. The razor-sharp lava made walking anywhere but on the King's Highway very difficult. Big Al had explained that the early Hawaiians had paved this trail with smooth lava stones from the beach. The trail circles the island, perhaps 250 miles. Fishermen once lived on the desolate lava strewn beaches, on the west side, and used the highway to trade with the Hawaiians living in the green mountains and valleys.

Suva Fiji Cruising Tips

To check in, call Suva Port Control on VHF Channel 16 once you're within their range, about 50 miles out. They will ask you to anchor in the Quarantine Area, marked on the harbor chart and about a half-mile south of the yacht club. Once anchored, call them again. During office hours they will send out the Port Doctor on the Port Health Department launch. It looks like the original African Queen. Once cleared, Port Control will request that you come alongside the main shipping wharf to check your boat for guns.

Next, you go to clear customs in the office on the wharf. The last stop is Immigration, about a ten-minute walk away. By that time you'll really be ready to head to the nearby anchorage off the yacht club to settle in.

A warning: make sure you have lots of fenders and maybe a fender board rigged before you pull up to the main dock. It is designed for large ships; the wake of a passing fishing boat can damage your toerail.

The Royal Suva Yacht Club asks that you check in with their office during business hours as soon as you arrive. You may anchor for free or pay to use their dock. Laundry facility, showers and mail service are available for about $18 U.S. per week. On the bottom of their Handbook for Visiting Yachts is printed, "All RSYC personnel — Office Staff, Barmen, Doorman, Maintenance, Boat, Grounds and Security men have been with the Club for many years and are quite willing to answer your inquiries. Courtesy wins the day."

The Fiji Hydrographic Office, in cooperation with the British Admiralty, publishes six excellent local charts. They sell for $9 U.S. each at their office four blocks from the RSYC. Carpenter's Shipping, across the street, is the British Admiralty chart agent and has a good selection of charts, enough to get you to New Zealand, Vanuatu or Australia.

Marine Safety Service Ltd. is located in the back of the Communications Pacific Building, a factory authorized repair and repack station for Avon, RFD and other brands of liferafts. They pick up and deliver your raft at the yacht club dinghy dock. While they have it inflated, they encourage yachties to come and inspect the rafts, climb in them and check out the equipment packed inside. We had them pack an EPIRB inside our raft, in addition to the EPIRB we carry in our ready bag. They left our raft inflated overnight to check for leaks and returned it to the dinghy dock at the yacht club by 9:00 the next morning. The bill came to half of what it would cost in the U.S.

Communications Pacific repaired our navigation system and one of our depth sounders. Maybe it's the humidity, or perhaps it's the fact that most of the boats have been out for at least a couple of years by the time they reach Fiji, but it seemed like nearly every boat in the anchorage had a depth sounder or a radio in need of repairs.

RSYC, General Delivery Downtown Post Office, American Express, are all options we've used for mail.

There are several supermarkets downtown. Canned and packaged foods in Fiji are similar to Australia and New Zealand prices but slightly higher than in the U.S. Foods, like tuna, processed in Fiji are generally a good buy. The best tuna we've found is Ovalau Blue and Old Capitol albacore, both canned in Levuka and sold in cases of 48 at excellent prices. If you are buying in quantity, the Indian-owned grocery stores may be willing to give you a discount and free delivery.

Carpenter's Motors is the Johnson-Evinrude dealer. Motors are assembled in Australia and are up to 20 percent less than in the States. Their Fijian outboard mechanic is fast, knowledgeable, friendly.

Marina Alternatives in Fiji

Fiji is fast becoming one of the Pacific's most desirable cruising grounds, as a result, several new marinas have opened recently. Savusavu on Vanua Levu is now a port of entry and home to the first class Copra Shed marina. Musket Cove on Malololailai Island, in the Mamanutha group, has a new marina as well as a resort hotel nearby. Rather than sail to New Zealand or Australia for hurricane season, many cruisers are choosing to store their yachts at the Vunda Point Marina near Lautoka in the northwest corner of Viti Levu.

New Zealand Passage Tips

The passage to New Zealand is much more challenging than most sailors realize. Many of the summertime tropical storms and winter-time gales cross the sailing routes to New Zealand, so the 'safe' season for sailing is very short, early October to late November. The best departure points are either Tonga or Fiji. Passages from the Cook Islands or New Caledonia may encounter stiff headwinds.

Cruisers making the passage usually get clobbered by at least one storm system, with 35-50 knot winds (usually headwinds) for 24 to 48 hours and are pretty worn out by the time they make landfall.

The low pressure cells, which continuously march eastward around the southern latitudes, dominate, the weather picture here. These low pressure cells come across the Coral Sea, or else further south from Tasmania and track eastward as fast as 40 knots. The high pressure cells, or anticyclones, are unstable and often dissipate rapidly. Different weather systems at different altitudes, mean occasionally a low, seemingly out of nowhere, will drop down to the surface. This occurred during the Queen's Birthday Storm in June 1994, resulting in the loss of three lives and the abandonment of eight boats.

The best time to leave Tonga or Fiji is when the weather is lousy in New Zealand and when a low or front has just passed where you are. There are usually two to seven days between the weather systems this time of year, so you make ready to move quickly once you get a good weather window.

If you're making this passage in November or later, keep a close eye on the lows in the vicinity of New Caledonia and the Coral Sea. They can rapidly turn into tropical storms and cyclones. These storms often form around 10S/160E, north of Fiji and New Caledonia, and move south-southwest until they hit 20S, before changing direction to southeast. The wind rotation around weather systems in the southern hemisphere is the opposite of that in the north — clockwise around lows and counterclockwise around highs, or anticyclones.

When you leave Tonga or Fiji, you'll probably have some rough going initially, plowing to windward into the often fresh southeast trades. As you get further south (to 25S and occasionally as far as 32S) you'll tend to lose the trades and enter an area of calms, squalls, and variable winds. When you do, turn your engine on and keep your speed up as long as you have fuel. Don't just sit and wait for the next weather system to plaster you.

This isn't a pleasure passage, and you'll want to minimize the time spent exposed to the volatile weather patterns of this region. After all of these warnings, I must say that my first two passages to New Zealand were fast (under nine days from Tonga and Fiji to Auckland.) We did not experience sustained winds over 25 knots, although we did experiece a 60 knot squall which lasted for half an hour. By watching and tracking the weather systems and looking at weather facsimile printouts you can learn how the systems move. Also, try to keep your boat speed above 5 knots, even if it means a lot of motoring. Using these suggestions should help you avoid most major squall systems.

Cruisers may obtain weather information from Russell Radio, at 0415GMT on 12,353 and Whangarei Radio at 0730GMT on 4,535. The ultimate is to have your own weatherfax machine on board. Lacking that, it's easy to get weather from other boats or from shore stations.

Pre-Departure Checklist

1. Find out if you enjoy long-distance cruising by completing an offshore passage with a reputable offshore school or experienced skipper before going to the expense of purchasing a cruising boat.
2. Figure out a realistic budget. Few people realize that outfitting a boat can cost 30% to 50% more than the initial purchase price. This can mean another $15,000 to $40,000 for a boat in the 35-foot range, for essential equipment including sails, ground tackle, liferaft, dinghy and safety gear. This doesn't take into consideration non-essentials such as refrigeration, electronics, outboard engines, etc. Figure out essential equipment costs, set aside money for initial provisioning and spare parts, set aside another $1,000 to $3,000 a month per couple, per month of cruising, subtract these sums from your cruising kitty. The money you have left is what you can spend on boat purchase.
3. Purchase a suitable cruising boat, preferably several years before you plan on taking off.
4. Get to know your boat. Go sailing in a wide range of conditions.
5. Take a course and practice coastal navigation: log keeping, dead reckoning, taking and plotting bearings, chart reading, tides and currents, etc.
6. Practice heavy weather sailing: reefing, sail changing, storm management tactics. Go out when gale warnings are up.
7. Complete a passage where you'll be out of sight of land for at least two consecutive nights.
8. Take a celestial navigation course and practice until you're confident.
9. Take a sail repair course and go over each of your sails with a sailmaker who specializes in cruising sails. Purchase a sewing machine, cloth, fittings and tools.
10. Take a diesel repair course and go over every inch of your engine with a qualified mechanic. Purchase engine spare parts.
11. Purchase spares for every system on the boat: pumps, motors, repair kits.
12. (Optional) Study for and pass amateur Radio (HAM) General License. Install ham radio, tuner and antenna.

13. Install and practice using a self-steering vane, and an autopilot.
14. Arrange a reaching/downwind pole and stowage system.
15. Remove mast(s), remove fittings and spreaders, check for wear. Replace all standing rigging if over six or seven years old.
16. Hire a rigger to help tune the rig and go for a test sail.
17. Haul your boat. Check and lubricate all ball valves or seacocks. Have an offshore insurance survey done, if necessary. Purchase or repack life raft. Assemble an abandon ship kit.
18. Install optional electronics: GPS, radar, ssb or ham radio, weatherfax.
19. Take a marine refrigeration course, or at least have a technician show you how to replace the drier and recharge the system, purchase spares.
20. Take an offshore medical course, practice CPR.
21. Move aboard, ideally six to 12 months prior to departure.
22. Sell or lease your home. Have a garage sale. Find a storage unit.
23. Calculate if you still have enough savings to leave on ETD or if you should work another year. Ugh!
24. Quit your job or sell your business.
25. Reassure family and close friends that you are not crazy, but you are looking forward to having them visit you.
26. Get a complete dental checkup six months before departure and a final cleaning just before you leave.
27. Get a thorough physical exam including blood tests, inoculations and vaccinations. Discuss drugs, herbal or homeopathic remedies with your physician and request written prescriptions.
28. Purchase and stow medical supplies and books.
29. Do initial dry goods and cans provisioning and stowing.
30. Sell vehicles.
31. Arrange with someone to pay bills and forward mail. Sign a limited power of attorney agreement.
32. Complete fresh food purchases and stowing.
33. Have a Bon Voyage party as a way of saying good-bye to many friends at once, and to thank those who helped you prepare.
34. Sail to a nearby quiet anchorage where you can catch your breath and finish final stowing.
35. NOW THE REAL ADVENTURE BEGINS!

Acknowledgments

Thanks to Mitzi Johnson and Tracy McClintock without whose friendship and prodding I never would have finished; Dave Poe and Kitty James at *Santana Magazine* for their enthusiasm and generosity; Bill Parks at *Bay and Delta Yachtsman* for his time and encouragement; Bruce Conway for his sense of design, humor and computer wizardry; Ruth Beebe Hill, Pamela Marrett and Mitzi Johnson for their editing insights; John Dustrude for photo printing and all the readers who encouraged us to put our adventures into a book.

Thanks to the Pacific Islanders who opened their homes and their hearts to us and the friends who have helped us on land and sea; Dick and Ann Wightman, Jim and Kathy Bybokas, Dave Cohan and Sharon Jacobs, Al Smith and Arunee, Lois and Dave Adams, Rich Everett and Sue Harris, Randy Repass and Sally Christine Rodgers-Repass, Geoff Eisenberg and Bob Brunkow.

Thanks to my healing friends: Maliki, Brad, Sylvia, Lois, Kirsten, Betsy, Kerri, Rita and Ian.

ABOUT THE AUTHORS

Barbara Marrett was raised in Katonah, New York. She is a graphic designer with a degree in Fine Art from Marymount College and a certificate from The City and Guilds of London Art School. She is West Coast Contributing Editor for *Cruising World* magazine, a lecturer and USCG licensed captain.

John Neal was born in Sudan, Africa, and grew up in Seattle, Washington. He studied psychology for two years but became enamored with boats and the sea and has been sailing ever since. John has logged over 150,000 sea miles. He conducts sail training expeditions on the ocean and offshore cruising seminars in the classroom.

John and Barbara's articles have appeared in *Cruising World, Latitude 38, Sail, The Seattle Times, Yachting, Santana, Bay and Delta Yachtsman, Northwest Yachting* and *48 North.* John's book, *Log of the Mahina,* is considered a classic on ocean cruising.

Although still good friends and business associates, John and Barbara's lives have continued on separate paths.

For information about Sail Training Expeditions or Offshore Cruising Seminars contact; John Neal, Mahina Expeditions, P.O. Box 1596, Friday Harbor, Washington 98250. Phone: (360) 378-6131, Fax: (360)378-6331, E-mail: sailing@mahina.com, Web site: www.mahina.com